Praise for

PUNK PAR

Louder, "Best Music Bo

"Greg Graffin's new memoir documents the endless trials and tribulations, as well as the colorful characters who come along with it, all taking place on the allegorical campus of Graffin U. Rather than focusing on elements like the now-iconic crossbuster logo or major moments in the band's rich musical canon, *Punk Paradox* tells a compelling—and sometimes turbulent—tale of an artist and academic's pursuit for understanding and (dare I say?) enlightenment." —*SPIN*

"There's much to commend in Graffin's thoughtful, thorough autobiography." —*Louder*

"Fascinating…Written with the nuanced detail for research of an academic, but balanced out with a punk rocker's experience, *Punk Paradox* is a rock memoir unlike most…Greg Graffin knows how to tell a compelling story." —*New Noise*

"A captivating character study of someone pursuing his passions in seemingly contradictory fields and staying true to himself and his own inner compass. Ultimately being able to experience that journey in detail as a reader may be *Punk Paradox*'s greatest gift." —*Flood*

"A well-crafted memoir and manifesto…An entertaining, memorable look at 'the most intractable paradox of all: punk as a positive force in society.'" —*Kirkus*

"The hard-driven Graffin compellingly and eloquently describes the rewards and pitfalls of a career as successful musician and academic that will fascinate general readers." —*Library Journal*

"[A] thoughtful, deeply personal memoir…[Greg Graffin's] descriptions of the natural world in relation to his emotional growth is as compelling as it is astute, and Graffin is passionate in his reminiscences of a time when punk rock was not distorted with the often-deserved stereotype of violence and anger. Readers will discover a trove of insights into the music industry and living creatively."
—*Booklist*

"Greg Graffin has been in the guts of the Punk Rock machine for literally decades. I would dare say there's not a lot you can tell him he doesn't already know. Any observation Greg makes is from the front line and worthy of consumption. In *Punk Paradox*, Greg meticulously lays out the evolution of Bad Religion not only as a band working to stay relevant but also as an entity that's had to carefully navigate great success and the myriad challenges that come with it. Good stuff."
—Henry Rollins

"Fearlessly pulling back the veil to show us the unpretentious, self-aware, deeply sensitive pacifist with a love for humanity and going against the grain, Greg Graffin shatters all expectations and assumptions of what it means to be punk rock, inviting us all to evolve."
—Aimee Allen, lead vocalist of the Interrupters

"Before Nirvana ever recorded a note, Greg Graffin's band, Bad Religion, was brilliantly fusing punk rock intensity with philosophy. Who else but Graffin would cite both Black Flag's 'Nervous Breakdown' and Charles Darwin's *Voyage of the Beagle* as major influences? With wit and brutal honesty, Graffin brings to life his unique journey: his parallel paths as an academic with a PhD in zoology and that of an internationally influential punk rocker. He offers insights into band dynamics, the creative process, the way that art and career intersect with personal lives, the Southern California punk scene of the '80s and '90s, and the currents of the music business that artists deal with along the way."
—Danny Goldberg, author of *Serving the Servant: Remembering Kurt Cobain*

PUNK PARADOX

A MEMOIR

GREG GRAFFIN

hachette
BOOKS

New York

To all who hold dear

memories

of my mother, Marcella June Carpenter Graffin,

my father, Walter Ray Graffin,

and

of the events and friendships detailed on the following pages.

Hachette Books
Hachette Book Group
1290 Avenue of the Americas
New York, NY 10104
HachetteBooks.com
Twitter.com/HachetteBooks
Instagram.com/HachetteBooks

First Paperback Edition: November 2023

Published by Hachette Books, an imprint of Perseus Books, LLC, a subsidiary of Hachette Book Group, Inc. The Hachette Books name and logo is a trademark of the Hachette Book Group.

The Hachette Speakers Bureau provides a wide range of authors for speaking events.

The Hachette Speakers Bureau provides a wide range of authors for speaking events. To find out more, go to hachettespeakersbureau.com or email HachetteSpeakers@hbgusa.com.

The publisher is not responsible for websites (or their content) that are not owned by the publisher.

Print book interior design by Amy Quinn.

Library of Congress Control Number: 2022942474

ISBNs: 9780306924583 (hardcover); 9780306924590 (trade paperback); 9780306924606 (ebook)

Printed in the United States of America

LSC-C

Printing 1, 2023

CONTENTS

SECTION ONE

1

INTRODUCTION

"**I told John go get gun. Graaaaagh, why did not John get gun?!**" George was looking at me with welts forming on his cheeks, grabbing for my lapel to bring my face closer to his as he searched for an answer, bewildered at his condition. "Twenty people to jump on me, Grag, TWENTY PEOPLE TO JUMP ON ME!" George trusted me. He and his cousin John, both Russian immigrants with buzz cuts, John, short and stocky with a massive "unibrow," George, slender, of average height, a boxer's head with chiseled cheekbones, were both punk rockers like me. They were a tandem pair. Whether cruising the streets looking for action or slam dancing at a gig, they were inseparable and spoke to each other in their mysterious foreign tongue. But they looked at me as the sensible kid from outside of Hollywood. Unimpaired by drugs or alcohol, I was, to them, the one who had an answer for everything.

"I don't know why John didn't do what you wanted, George, but he's driving the truck now, he's right next to you, why don't you ask him yourself?" But George was too pissed off, inebriated, and punch-drunk to be

3

sensible at this moment. So he continued to harangue me. "Grag, those mutherfuckers! Kick me, stump my body. Gun in glove box!" "Just keep driving, John, until you get George out of here," I said. "No shit, Grraeg. Wot dee faahck! I keep driving all the way to Okee dogck, back to home ground, yew dough?"

Even though I knew that George and John were likely packing heat somewhere in the vehicle, these guys weren't hardened criminals and they sure as shit weren't murdering types. They, like so many Los Angelinos, were first generation, blue-collar immigrants, whose families brought them there or shipped them off to work with cousins and extended families who settled in the Southland for the dream of a better life. They could be found every night outside any punk rock gig that was going on in the greater Hollywood region, looking for fun, girls, alcohol, or pills. They were just like all the other regulars of the scene at that time, in the fall of 1981. This night, however, was a slow night for punk gigs. No shows were going on in Hollywood or elsewhere, but as devotees of the punk lifestyle we had to hang out somewhere, and that meant the trusty safe haven of a hotdog stand on Santa Monica Boulevard in Hollywood called Oki-Dog. Here, punk rockers were always welcomed. While every other fast-food hangout shunned us, the Oki-Dog proprietors greeted us with their Asian-accented hospitality: "Haaaaay my freyend! What you have?" Soggy french fries and chili dogs were the norm. But even if no food was purchased, they were ever tolerant of the chaotic punk antics in their parking lot each night. We felt accepted there, and we were always up for causing a stir nearby on the streets of Tinseltown or commencing an impromptu punk parade anywhere people might take notice. "Let's head over to Westwood," said someone in the Oki-Dog's parking lot.

Westwood, with its glimmering wide sidewalks, glamorous movie houses, high-end restaurants, corner stores, donut stands, and fashionable clothing shops, was a melting pot of affluence, youth, and academic culture. Bordered by Wilshire Boulevard on the south and Hilgard on the east, its roughly twenty-four city blocks served the needs of many Los Angelinos. Across Le Conte Avenue sat UCLA. Just a few miles west down

Wilshire was the beach. In the other direction was Hollywood and central Los Angeles. All roads led to Westwood, which had neither the dark-and-dirty sleaze of Hollywood, nor the crime and violence that characterized the rougher parts of LA since it served as the college town for UCLA students as well as the preferred site of weekly world premieres for the big film studios. Westwood saw its sidewalks thronged with the pulse of students mingling about with the multifarious citizenry from other neighborhoods who had come in to grab some of the gusto of its highly active nightlife. On the wide avenues were "cruisers," guys and gals of various ethnicities that made car culture a way of life. Some of them, like the punk rockers I associated with, were out for disruption of Westwood's highfalutin, predictably upbeat evening tranquility, or worse, for violence.

I felt right at home in Westwood. UCLA was the reason the Graffin family moved to Los Angeles when I was only eleven years old. My mom had relocated from her job as an academic dean at University of Wisconsin–Milwaukee to take a deanship at UCLA in 1976. Occasionally she would take my brother, Grant, and me in to work and let us wander around on campus and into Westwood Village. This was no big deal. Even as little kids we roamed university campuses. Our dad too was a university man. He worked at the University of Wisconsin–Parkside and some of my earliest memories are going to work with Mom or Dad and being told to "get lost" for a while as they tended to a meeting or taught a class. The unique smells of classrooms, libraries, mimeograph (xerox) rooms, and professors' offices are some of my most deeply familiar, comforting associations. Nothing, however, felt comforting or familiar this night. As we piled out of cars at one of the university parking lots, it was clear that this handful of punk rockers were heading into a gauntlet of hostility in Westwood's festive environment. Tonight, we would be the entertainment.

I had been chauffeured that night by Greg Hetson, who was a notorious scenester, having played in two legendary bands—one, Redd Kross, no longer needing his services, and the other, Circle Jerks, already on top of the heap of LA bands, in the process of expanding their influence. Greg drove an El Camino and said: "Hop in, I'm heading home anyways." He lived not far from Westwood, and we hung out together at his apartment regularly, especially as a starting point for an evening of adventure. I jumped in Greg's passenger seat and stuck my head out the window as we cruised west on Santa Monica toward the intersection with Wilshire. "Maybe we'll find some chicks in Westwood," said Greg, confident that, besides punk rock music itself, that was one topic that motivated the two Gregs equally.

Hanging out with Greg Hetson was always an adventure. If you ever needed to know where the most happening parties were going on in Hollywood or any secret gigs in some warehouse in Hawthorne or any other of the myriad neighborhoods dotting the LA basin, Greg was your man. Always sweet and courteous, with an agreeable smile and intelligent wit, he nonetheless had his finger on the pulse of the sleaze and debauchery that made the punk scene legendary. Not that he partook in all the action, but being friends with him meant that we didn't have to consult some anonymous taxi driver or something to find out where the fun was. Greg Hetson was our resident expert. Hell, he even had a German taxi for a while as his daily driver, a diesel Mercedes sedan just like the ones driven in Berlin. Hearing him expound from behind the steering wheel that always seemed too big for him, on details and microgeographic particulars about the hot spots in LA that were worthy of our attention on any given evening made you feel like you had your own in-house Rick Steves as your best buddy.

Upon reaching a parking lot off Gayley Avenue in Westwood, a score of cars, including Greg Hetson's El Camino, emptied their contents of punks. Combat and engineer boots slapping on the pavement made a formidable thud as we hopped out of our vehicles and began parting the crowds outside Mann's Westwood Theater. Greg always wore the same army surplus green jacket, jeans, and tennis shoes. I always wore the same motorcycle jacket, painted with a white Bad Religion crossbuster symbol on the back. The chains dangling from my leather jacket pocket zippers rounded out my wardrobe, and I felt elated to be parading around with my friends, some of whom were in famous bands, showing off to the world some of punk rock's royalty and pageantry. In a few short minutes, however, these familiar streets of my youth would become literal stomping grounds. Our collection made a spectacle, and university jocks gathered in their own gaggle, their fraternity brothers mocking us and following us around. In addition, cruisers on the street honked their horns at us and brandished weapons. They would not be upstaged by a bunch of tatter-clothed, unwashed punks. They were there to be noticed and show off their automotive handiwork.

We were a loose conglomeration of kids from various walks of life. A lot of us didn't know each other. Most were generally good-natured but some were addicted to alcohol or pills or something worse, like heroin. They were unlikely to hurt anyone except themselves. The gang violence that was overtaking a lot of neighborhoods throughout the Southland had gripped some of the punk rock community. Beach gangs and others from Orange County were violent and starting to make up sizeable portions of the audience at Hollywood clubs. But on this night our group was made up of various smaller "independent" collections of friends and acquaintances who were from various SoCal neighborhoods diffusely distributed throughout LA County.

In Westwood, as in our own neighborhoods and at school, we looked like easy targets of ridicule and mockery, whether we were by ourselves or in a group. Formidable we were not. But something was shared among all punk rockers outside of Hollywood: we were hated. There was a seething ire among non-punks that sought to destroy and bring harm to anyone who willingly tattered their clothing, altered their hairstyle into mohawks, painted "anarchy" on their leather jackets, or promoted bands that sang about fucking shit up. The violent reaction to punks was at its apex, and parading around in an otherwise peaceful part of the city was seen as an act of aggression. And we knew it.

Cars honked and George walked into the street shouting like a lunatic, "Faaach you!" raising his arms and flipping the bird as we all watched nervously, but with good humor. Other cars were starting to slow down, hit their horns, and shout expletives as they slunk by. "Punk sucks you faggots!" Greg Hetson and I lingered behind as the mob of punks edged closer to George, egging him on and blocking traffic. Some of them were carrying beer bottles and at least one was flung in the direction of the traffic.

Within minutes a clutch of cars pulled over and a "gang" of maybe twelve bangers got out intent on brawling. Legends of "South Central," African-American gangs were well known around the Southland, and whether or not these guys were affiliated with the Crips or Bloods we didn't want to find out. As they poured out of their vehicles a few of them made a beeline for George, while the rest of us dashed in every direction. Being chased was no fun, but I quickly realized that my flight response was not necessary. I realized after about a block of sprinting that no one was chasing me. "What the hell am I running for?" I asked myself. I turned back, calmly walking to where the ruckus started and saw the action was getting hot. None of the punks were putting up much of a fight, but the ones who did were getting pummeled. High on liquid courage, George was the loudest and most brazen among us. He also was not much of a street fighter. By the time I got back to the corner, jocks and their frat brothers had joined in with the other fighters and the unlikely conjoined force geared up for another round of rooting out punk rockers and chasing them out of town. George was on the ground getting kicked by a mixed bag of punk haters as a big jock came charging toward me. He tried to grab me at full speed, but my own athletic prowess allowed me to avoid the tackle, stiff-arm him to the ground, and run off back toward the parking lot. Greg Hetson had already made it to his car, and John had parked the truck right next to him. "Get in!" John shouted. "Graaag, we have to go get Jshorge." We drove over in two cars and found poor George abandoned and bleeding, but with no life-threatening wounds. I helped him into John's truck and lay him across the bench in the cab. George grabbed my jacket lapel with two iron fists and looked into my face with wild-eyed bloodshot expression. "Did you see that, Graagh?" "Twenty people to jump on me." He just kept rambling. "Why not John get gun? Chjaaaahn, why not get gun, mutherfaachar?"

Aside from welts, bruises, and a few landed punches, none of the punks were seriously injured, and luckily no weapons were drawn in the Westwood scuffle. But it was a typical night of dodging hatred for punks in LA. I wasn't ever attracted to the gang mentality. In fact, I hated violence, and I wasn't a fighter. But I believed in the music and I felt an immediate kinship with anyone who appreciated it too. Unfortunately, at this point in time, it seemed that everyone hated punk rockers.

Police seemed to hate punkers as much as the general public did. I had witnessed evidence of this from two previous experiences. One was in East Los Angeles, October 24, 1980, around 9 p.m. Police showed up to Baces Hall in riot gear. With their shields set, jack boots cracking, they advanced on a crowd of mostly juvenile, taunting, silhouettes, darkened as much by their domestic disharmony as by the failing overhead streetlights in this part of the city. Assembled to raise hell inside, many of the punk rockers found themselves outside, prevented from entering the oversold Black Flag concert. Despite having just formed a band of my own, I wasn't well known enough to be on any guest lists, so I was outside too. Just fifteen years old, and childish in many ways, I could nonetheless conclude that riots, while good for the adrenaline rush, were bad for the aspirations of a punk musician. If venues continued to get closed down like this every time a punk show was announced, how would Bad Religion ever get to play?

Among the punks, there was no doctrine nor prescribed behavior to follow during a police raid. Punk and I were both too young for such formalities. The "norm of reaction" punk rockers adopted may have been borrowed from the still-vibrant images of protesters to the Vietnam War or the fights for civil rights barely a decade prior. Whatever they were, our reactions to the police brutality in LA were completely unorganized, and we found no precedents in the punk scenes of London, New York, Detroit, or anywhere else we read about in fanzines or music magazines. Therefore, the disunity of the scattering crowd was to be expected. The flight instinct overtook me and, unlike some of my cohorts, who had more bravado than common sense, I fled the scene as the batons started swinging.

Just a month prior, on September 19, my new friend and bass player Jay Bentley drove me to a gig near Alameda and 4th, at a "club" called the Hideaway, near downtown LA. We were excited to see Greg Hetson and Keith Morris perform with the Circle Jerks. I had seen Keith play at a Huntington Beach venue called the Fleetwood. He was my favorite singer. He was fronting Black Flag at that gig. Little did I understand that the T-shirt he donned at the Fleetwood, a homemade job that read "Circle Jerks," was a preview of his next band. That Fleetwood show was his last as the singer of Black Flag, and now Jay and I were stoked to see him in his new band at the Hideaway.

As was fashionable, we missed the opening band, the Descendents, but while the next band, Stains, was setting up, the police arrived outside the oversold venue. A guy from the Stains camp came on stage and grabbed the mic. "If everyone just takes a step backwards! The Man is outside and won't come in. If we just mellow out we can party down." At that suggestion, a crash was heard in the lobby space. The Hideaway was nothing more than an auto-repair shop whose front glass-paned garage doors were closed. When the police arrived in the hope of sending the loitering punks home, the sight of the squad cars sent everyone into a frenzy and the punks pushed an old Chevy right through the glass garage doors.

"Somehow, I don't think we're gonna get to see the Circle Jerks," Jay said. Within seconds after the crash, the police came in busting up the place, sending punks scattering. Jay and I scurried to his green Toyota truck and drove off, back to the serene monotony of our West San Fernando Valley neighborhood. He dropped me off at my mom's house. "See you for school on Monday." "Later," I said, and entered my quiet domestic place headed by my divorced mom who worked hard to support me and my older brother, Grant.

Police rioting against suburban kids at music clubs may have been unique to this time and place, but my reaction to it was predictable: aversion. Take care of thyself, turn inward, and run! Protect the head so that later that night you might be able to reflect and learn from what just happened. Understanding and human reason took precedence in my world rather than effrontery, retribution, or obsessive rabble-rousing. Intellectualizing violent or emotionally disruptive events was a method of coping. It was also a family enterprise.

Back home in the quiet, suburban Los Angeles enclave of Canoga Park, that night, as the evening's adrenaline wore off, I reflected on a tumultuous recent past. I had had enough emotional family trauma, and turning punk was supposed to help mollify it rather than add to it. I began to long for the simplicity of another lifestyle and the childhood pals I left back in Wisconsin. They were probably scraping together teams—minus me—for another epic neighborhood touch football game tomorrow. Here I was in a seemingly directionless household in the equally directionless San Fernando Valley, at home by ten o'clock, settling back into my discordant slumber, dreaming of a journey to a better future from a past, only three years distant, that brought me to this place on the edge of the continent where I felt like the last boy in America to watch the sun set and hope that the dawn would erase the trials of yesterday.

2
PROFESSORS' KIDS

We were professors' kids. They, in the other room drinking wine or spirits, playing Sheepshead, releasing sonic booms of laughter from incessant cynical quips about current affairs and the failures of humanity. We, in the TV room (den) trying our best to emulate the worldliness of our parents, watching *Monty Python*, understanding some of it, and secretly wishing for attention from the paternal gods in the other room that they might share little bits of their wisdom and provide us an edge over the philistines at our Wisconsin grade schools.

There was me, about eight years old, my brother, Grant, nine, Wryebo and his sister Katy, the same ages as us, whose parents went to college with our parents at UW-Madison, snagging PhDs in English before taking their lifelong jobs in the same department at a different campus, UW-Parkside in Kenosha. Some families, I suppose, are all about money, emphasizing its importance to the kids from the get-go. An old family saying in ours was, "You can't have any fun-yuh if you ain't got no mun-yuh." That was the extent of our dad's advice to us about money. But that came from our family friend, Dan Zielinski, also a professor, a lifelong bachelor who joined our multifamily gatherings each weekend where the grown-ups gathered in the kitchen or outside around the Weber grill to laugh about the week's headlines or other worldly happenings. They never touched the discussion of moneymaking or other vulgar concerns because they wanted us to believe that such concerns suck the life out of you. The concerns of a professor were the stuff of adventure and excitement. In fact, the university provided tenure to professors so they could focus on the important things in life like *Moby Dick*, tennis, and *Richard III*.

The world was full of important higher-order knowledge, like the difference between truth and fiction, or the mechanics of throwing a curveball, and we were encouraged to never stop searching for it.

Wryebo's dad sauntered past us on his way to the can. "You kids should watch that Peter Lorre flick on *Night Gallery* tonight." We were expected to have good taste in film and music, understand things that other kids didn't, be exceptions to the average schlubs who made up postwar, midcentury modern America. The early 1970s had no specific identity, so our parents knew that all the templates of their own upbringing could be rejected. What better gift, they thought, to give our kids than to make them worldly beyond their years? Wryebo and Katy had been to London and Paris by the time they were in third grade. They brought back card games with geographic themes, such as Mille Bornes, and they, in turn, expected that I knew its title reference was NOT some city in Australia.

Professors hadn't much money, but they had treasure troves of knowledge, and that was what they could provide in spades. Wryebo and I would have preferred material goods to knowledge, any day of our youth. Grant and Katy got the particulars of our parents' logic at a young age but had not the years to put any of it to use.

My dad, the English professor, loved music and discussed lyrics with me. *How high's the water, mama? Five feet high and risin'.* "You see, Greggo, when the water reaches the height of the levee, it's going to overflow. So Johnny Cash is singing about their house on the floodplain of that river!" I wanted to impress my dad, so I couldn't admit the truth: I didn't understand fluvial mechanics. I had no idea what a levee was nor even how rivers could over-flow their banks from time to time. Where would I ever have learned such a thing? We rode our bikes along the cement paths lining the Lake Michigan shoreline nearly every day; we lived in vast neighborhoods paved with concrete, nowhere near any floodplains. I just couldn't understand the peril inherent in the lyrics because I didn't know the words. Not knowing words was as bad as not knowing concepts. Our older siblings, my brother, Grant, and Katy, Wryebo's sister, read much more voraciously than the average kid. They read novels, they read magazine articles, they even read the un-abridged dictionary! Wryebo and I lagged behind.

Once Wryebo's dad asked if the kids would like to go see a movie at Milwaukee's art house theater, the Oriental. What a treat! To go see a movie with their dad. But there was a stipulation; they had to read a book first, because it was the original story that the movie was based on. There were still four days before the showing, so Katy and Wryebo agreed to the as-signed reading. When I heard there was an assignment, I knew it wasn't even worth trying. I had never read even a kid's book by the time I was eight. I just couldn't concentrate. The world had too much going on simul-taneously for my senses to pause and focus on paragraphs. The title of the movie was *The Stranger* (à la Albert Camus), which sounded so cool, and I was sorry that I couldn't go. Wryebo quit after chapter three, but Katy finished the book.

It turns out that the movie was subtitled and there was no way I would have been able to read that fast. Wryebo was allowed to go with Katy and he came home knowing nothing about the story except that he could verify to me that, indeed, some films have words scrolling across the bottom of every scene. What a pain in the ass!

Dad taught pop art as a part of his class on contemporary American literature. He took his students on ambitious field trips to New York City. Closer to home, he took me and Grant to exhibitions at the then recently established Museum of Contemporary Art Chicago. Peering at the huge canvases, some painted in solid colors, others with blended fields of orange, blue, whites, or yellows, Dad wouldn't even try to explain what the hell we were supposed to be seeing. "Isn't it terrific, kids?" "Wow, look at that one! Hahaha, all greens and yellows, chartreuse!" "Now boys, look at this next one, it's Dada. Terrific, right?" I wanted to go along with his enthusiasm so badly. But secretly, I was in psychic torture. I saw no subject. I saw only color, no outlines, just blended borders fading into other colors, or cutouts of mixed media that formed patches or swatches in so many endless rooms of these canvases. "Is that all there is?" I asked about one of the dichromatic paintings. "Well, that's partly the point," Dad said. If that was the point, it certainly was beyond the comprehension of this eight-year-old. I just couldn't wait to get an ice-cream cone Dad promised afterward, but I had to feign some interest first. There was so much more to see in this exhibit before that tasty reward.

"Here in this next hall, now these are really something!" "Oh, I get it, Campbell's soup cans, right?" I said. "Right-o!" said Dad. I felt I had made great progress in impressing him. "These are from Andy Warhol," he said. "Now this guy believes everyone in America will be famous for fifteen minutes. Isn't that something?" I couldn't wait to be famous! But still, I didn't understand how that had anything to do with the huge image of Campbell's Golden Mushroom Soup that was making me salivate with hunger. To me it all seemed like a big "fuck you" to the academic notion of what an artist was "supposed" to be. Artists, it has been said, are supposed to show society what is possible, to comment on human potential, even if they cannot put into words or symbols any means of achieving that potential. Artists are supposed to transcend the here and now, to reveal something beyond the utilitarian necessities of life, and depict the fundamentals of human experience. Here, among the masterworks of pop art and murals of modernism, I was starting to believe that any kind of bullshit could qualify as art. What was key to making it legitimate was how and where it was presented. If legitimate institutions, such as the Museum of Contemporary Art Chicago, deemed an artist worthy, seemingly anything, even infantile canvases with a few lazy brush marks, or collages of cutouts, like we were doing in grade school, might be seen as fine art, and could be interpreted as reactionary protest works. I thought it was cool that Dad was excited by this anti-authoritarian tradition, but I had no perspective on what any of it meant at the time.

No. To me, the concepts were all hazy, the words were elusive, the art was confusing, but from this very early age I began to understand what made the professors tick. As human beings, they wanted unfettered freedom to accompany their armchair curiosity. But as parents, they were intellectually intimidating, perhaps like all parents. In their aspirations for their offspring, they pointed us kids toward concepts that were way beyond my grasp. Art judges before we could even draw. Literary critics before we were literate. Existentialists before we even knew we existed! I have no ill will nor permanent damage from this, but my footsteps never strayed too far from the influence of my upbringing.

To please the professors was a full-time job. By the end of third grade, without any instruction, we felt it our duty to know how to properly use a bow saw, how to interpret the subtext of *Rocky and Bullwinkle*, how to finish reading an entire novel, understand the military significance of the battleship model you just built, and how to solve mathematical puzzles and win at chess, none of which I could do. I walked with a constant fear that I would be delegitimized or excommunicated by the tribal elites. My brother could do it all, and his status was secure. He was the brains, I was the brawn. If not for the shelter provided by Katy's and Grant's proclivity, both of whom always seemed in lockstep with the professors' intellectual wit and wisdom, I would have been lost. I emulated their bravado, never realizing at the time that Wryebo and I shared an equally valuable trait that never left me: adaptability.

Wryebo and I somehow adapted or coevolved in parallel with an almost irreverent disregard for doing things the right way. When Grant and Katy could produce the right answer to any question, Wryebo and I simply challenged the legitimacy of the question. When Dad would quiz us from the front seat of the car: "Okay boys, how many planets are in the solar system?" Grant, who studied *National Geographic* magazines—actually read the articles rather than looked at the pictures of naked Pygmies as Wryebo and I did—could always be counted on for the right answer. Wryebo or I would chime in quickly, "Yeah, but did you see that other article in there about the tribe of natives they found in the Amazon jungle?" The art of misdirection was a skill we learned early. It was a coping skill rather than a mastery of elite-level intellectual material.

Luckily, the professors also loved baseball, basketball, tennis, and hockey. I showed some promise in these activities, a bit more so than Grant. Even though it was a consolation prize to the quiz-show guild, athletics was an acceptable appendage of the collegiate corpus, and our parents approved. As precocial kids, we knew, after all, that the Greeks invented civilization and established our aesthetics, of which modern sports are veritable reflections, and now they can feasibly serve as archetypes of high culture in one way or another. It's not the fashion of sports that was emphasized (we had not the money to buy expensive sportswear, shoes, or equipment) but rather the unconditional love of the game: the striving to perfect a technique and strategy in the development of one's civilized refinement.

Sports weren't the only extracurricular activity approved of by university men. In addition to countless trips to arenas and ballparks to watch the pros, jaunts down to Arlington Park in Illinois to "play the ponies," and hours of fun in the front yard tossing the ball, an even earlier experience is most significant to my later education. The word *lagoons* popped into my brain and stuck decades before I ever studied ecology in college. Dad asked, "Greggo, do you want to come with me to the lagoons to look at birds?" I had no idea what he meant, but it sounded adventurous. It was associated with a ride in the car, maybe thirty minutes or more, and it entailed the repetitive consultation with a guidebook containing scientifically precise color illustrations and distribution maps of our winged little cohabitants. Who knew that there was such variety twittering in the treetops and shrubbery? Furthermore, the activity required the use of a hefty, robust technological tool, the binocular, which brought the natural world close-up and surreal once you learned to master the focus knob. This refined, academically acceptable act of outdoorsmanship piqued my early imagination.

Watching birds was a grown-up exercise, acceptable and even encouraged practice for professors, and yet, though I was drawn to its accessories and inherent adventure, I was far too fidgety and impatient to ever master something so crucial as looking through a binocular scope at the age of four. Yet, between the clenched-jaw, restrained admonitions to "quiet down or you'll scare the birds!" and "let's move down a hundred yards where we'll have a better view," something sunk into me in the wetlands near Chicago. Despite being bored, something imprinted on my young, receptive brain: the smell of the freshwater habitat, the quiet whir of wind rustling the shrubs we used as screens, and the warm vernal sunshine experienced with someone who seemed to know what he was doing, and who cared enough to bring me along. It may have established an emotional connection that one might describe as a love of quiet, outdoor places, the spirit of discovery, and the study of nature. Thematic dramas that have never left me.

It was all done out of love. But the professorial style of love is shown through a unique blend of judgment, expectation, praise, mania, concern, obligation, and compulsion. It's a strange joy when it works, but so often it devolves into a dysfunctional, disappointing failure.

Through all of this we were also administrators' kids. The Moms represented the softer arm of the university body. My mom was a dean at UW-Milwaukee. No less industrious than the professors, they were the ones we could turn to for more leniency and comforting emotional encouragement in our freshman attitudes and untethered reasoning. More important, they had spent years perfecting and advising kids on how to navigate the complex web of psychological and pragmatic friction in dealing with the professors. They were the ones in later years with whom we could enjoy the music and lyrical nuances of Elvis Costello and the Cars without justification for our tastes. But often there were unbridgeable rifts between the administrators and professors.

The Moms always preached compassion and inclusion for others. Whether it was a person of another race, creed, or body shape, prejudgment was never allowed. Disabilities were looked at as deserving of more attention. One day Wryebo brought home a friend from first grade named André. André's story was known by Fran, Wryebo's mom, who had told us days earlier, in preparation for our "playdate," to make André feel at home and play just as we would play with any other of our friends.

André was a wide-eyed, hyperactive, rough-and-tumbler, just like me and Wryebo. Teachers worried about us, even as early as preschool and kindergarten at the Montessori where we often had to take "time-outs" to sit in the corner and "think about things." But André had had a bad experience as a toddler. As Fran explained it to us, "André's parents are Seventh-day Adventists, which is a religious sect, and they don't believe that medicine is necessary in many cases. André had an infection in his toe when he was little, and it spread to his entire leg. They had to remove it. So you see, kids, he might not be able to run around as much as you guys because he has a wooden leg."

"Wow!" we thought. "How cool! This kid is just like a pirate!"

It turned out that André could keep up with us just fine. He was wild and loud, just like us. And even though his leg made an interesting thumping sound on the hardwood floors of Wryebo's Victorian house, he was every bit as nimble and athletic as we were.

While playing tag outside on the wooden porch, André came at me at full speed, and his prosthetic wooden leg came unhinged and he tripped headlong toward my torso. At once, I dodged to the left and cried "missed me!" as André tumbled awkwardly, smashing into the railing. The force from his impact made a horrid *thwack*, like the sound of a broken baseball bat. As he broke the wooden newel post clean off the deck, we watched his body, several balusters, and broken railing plunge to the grassy lawn below. In the fray we didn't realize that his leg had become detached and it lay on the lawn too among the broken wood spindles and fragments.

"You alright, André?" Wryebo asked. "Yeah, no problem, this happens all the time." We were mostly worried about our own hides. We might be in big trouble. Wryebo and I knew that the real trouble might come not from the professors angry about the broken materials, but rather from the administrators. We were entrusted to be friends with André and not cause harm to the poor kid. We found him strapping his prosthetic leg back on and ready for more. Having destroyed a portion of the front porch, we decided to leave the scene and retire to a more quiet activity inside, thinking nothing of the long-term architectural damage.

"Who the hell broke my front porch!?" Sure enough, the professors were mad. But the Moms viewed it with much more compassion. Was André hurt? Did you boys help him out with his leg (even though, of course, we didn't need to)? He was fine. After all the reassurances, it was chalked up as a bit of collateral damage from a good deed. Friendship to those who need it most was always the most important theme of the day for the administrators. And ultimately, the professors fell in line.

We lost touch with our little pirate because his parents relocated to the West Coast. Los Angeles wasn't even a remote idea in our brains at the time, but our paths would cross again in the subsequent decade. I could not have predicted this tiny rambunctious play pal would go on to become stereotyped as a symbol of a countercultural movement in LA, while I would spend my future as an accomplished professional in that same subculture, albeit bitterly opposed to its vulgar, lowly stereotypes.

We would come to be linked, not as friends, but as character actors experiencing the same tensions in the Southern California punk scene. That world would deal with us separately. But the world of the Graffins was about to split in two.

3
DIVORCE

Second grade was long enough for our family to try and hold it together for the kids. In a split-family situation (the media at the time was fond of calling it a "broken" family) there are two options: (1) either the children will be prevented from seeing a banished parent—which was the case for my father, who never saw his own dad (family lore is mute on this subject), or (2) our situation, wherein the children would have ample experience with both parents even if it meant separate households sometimes separated by miles or even half continents. Although this second option is almost universally agreed to be the preferable one, it doesn't come without its own hurdles. In our case, the family campus, call it Graffin U., was about to get much bigger, and with little communication between the households a double set of expectations would now have to be accommodated.

By all indications, I was a "momma's boy." When that very first custody weekend came, and my brother and I were to spend our first nights at Dad's house without Mom, I was shrouded with foreboding, for no good reason. The hour of departure approached. We waited for Dad to drive up. I clung to Mom's side and wouldn't let go of her as she calmly explained, "You will see me on Sunday night. You're going back to your same bedroom we had when I was living there. All your friends in the neighborhood are waiting for you this weekend." All of it made perfect sense. But the moment Dad pulled up to the curb outside, I couldn't budge. I clung to Mom's neck and shoulders, giving her the hug of a lifetime, feeling an intense, desperate sense of foreboding. My brother walked calmly, dutifully, to the car but I didn't follow. I started wailing, screaming "No! No! No!" It felt like the world was ending. It was the first memory I had of new realities. Two households, two sets of expectations, no parental unity, no clear road ahead. I was mortified, and it was clear that if I had to choose at that moment, it would have been to stay with Mom. Dad had to remove me physically from my firm, terrified embrace. He calmly and firmly tolerated my hysteria, broke loose my headlock on Mom, and stuck me next to my unmoved brother in the back seat of his Rambler American.

The loneliness of that first goodbye stuck deep in my psyche. Inside of thirty minutes we were back at the place Mom used to call home. Now it was just "Dad's house." It was going to be a fun weekend seeing my old pals from the neighborhood, playing games, and starting a new routine that included listening to records before bedtime. My spirits began to lift.

I don't want to overdramatize the situation. The dean and the professor were aligned on many important child-rearing practices and ethical and moral positions. But I also don't want to underplay the significance of having to adapt. If there weren't significant differences in this environment of divorce to adapt to, then what was the need for the divorce? In other words, anything that is significant enough to result in a splitting of a household is serious enough of a rift to acknowledge hardship for the kids, even in this best-case scenario of spending ample time with both parents. It's not fooling the kids to minimize the differences, it's self-delusional to suggest that having two Christmases and two birthday party celebrations somehow makes up for the back-and-forth rigmarole. In some situations, it may be best to choose the first scenario and have no contact with one of the parents at all. The cost of having a person not know enough about one of their parents to make any definitive conclusion about half their pedigree might be worth the value of avoiding the conflicting influences from the other parent. But such was not our lot. Both Mom and Dad were equally competent, loving, and similar enough, despite their differences, to allow Graffin University to function.

Yet to ignore the differences would mislead you to believe that the influences were the same. Indeed, in a conventional home, where both parents, even with widely different worldviews, reside together, there is an attenuating effect on those differences under the same roof. They seem to blend together, and perhaps we can say they are more nebulously displayed to the children. Whereas in two single-parent households, even minor differences tend to be amplified and seem much more acute. Little things like Dad buys creamy peanut butter while Mom always gets the chunky forces the child to ponder, to enter that part of his consciousness that seeks to know the logic behind this mundane daily ritual—the variation in the making of our lunches becomes a cerebral exercise.

In our case there were little differences, like sandwich ingredients, and there were larger differences, like who the parents spent their time with. In Mom's case it was administrators of the university, just like her; it was African Americans from the urban neighborhoods of Milwaukee; it was people she employed and other deans of her equal status. Whenever we socialized in Milwaukee it was more often than not gatherings at Barbara Bender's house. Barbara, like my mom, was a dean in a different department, financial aid. Her children, Jason and Lisa, were our companions, Jason being my age, Lisa a bit older than Grant. Jason was a wild kid, like me. We bonded over roughhouse play, and riding bikes in the alleys and sidewalks around their house. Though it was unapparent to me or Grant, we must have stuck out like sore thumbs as we were the only white kids bumming around these predominantly Black neighborhoods of north Milwaukee. Workplaces, like my mom's administrative buildings on campus, were racially integrated in the early 1970s, but the neighborhoods were not.

Jason was proud to call us his cousins. He loved introducing us to all his friends in the neighborhood. "These are my cousins, Grant and Greg," he would say with a smirk on his face. He taught me our secret handshake, one that I repeated endlessly, and even taught to my own kids: "gim me fye—udder sigh—troo da hoe—sogk my sohl."

At Barbara's house we watched *Tarzan* on television, and we listened to The Jackson 5's *Greatest Hits* record over and over until finally I convinced Mom to buy me that album as a gift to listen to at home. It was one of my earliest memories of having my own record. I memorized the whole album so that when Jason and I got together we could sing along in tandem. I could sing every part. Sometimes lead, sometimes background, sometimes harmonies. "I'll Be There" was a forlorn melody and a big hit on the radio at that time—WOKY in Milwaukee. We heard it all the time in Mom's car. It was through these social gatherings at Barbara's house that my mom met Chuck, a musician and stepfather candidate who gave me my first notion of what a professional musician was like.

Dad's social milieu was completely different. Dad hung around the professors. Peter Martin, the Shakespeare scholar (and Wryebo and Katy's dad), Dan Zielinski, the geographer, and Don Kummings, the Whitman scholar. They all got together each weekend to play tennis, shag fly balls, and roast bratwurst. Us kids gleefully tagged along, got to participate in their athletic warm-ups, and eavesdropped on their erudite, cynical humor and critical social commentary, knowing full well that it was the key to right thinking and inclusion into an elite class of citizenry. This was likely not the professors' intention. But who can say what effect such actions have on the brains of second and third graders?

So by the time I was seven there were two households, twenty miles apart, to which my brother and I were expected to adapt. The campus had expanded into two realms, the professor's in Racine, and the administrator's in Milwaukee. On campuses all across the land, administrators and professors mix like oil and water. It's not unusual for them to self-sequester. Administrators are usually paid better than the professors. The professors are cynical and often contemptuous of those meddling, pencil-pushing administrators. Together they send mixed messages to the student body who are just looking for some encouragement and keys to a successful future.

The professors were not known for their emotional availability. In our case, the administration was where we turned for that. The professors were more about action and performance. They did not like to discuss the softer things in life, feelings, family history, honorific duties, and so on, unless they were couched in some novelistic or dramatic framework; in other words, these things were fine to talk about so long as they pertained to other people.

Although Mom was a certified teacher, she aspired for the better paychecks from university administration. The higher salary came in handy, especially after taking the drastic step of "the big D" and having to run a household by herself. It was clear from the outset that she wanted her campus to be managed by the efforts of three entities: herself, my brother, and me. Us kids were to learn from the dean how to cook, clean, and help out wherever we could. Each one of us had a job to do: hers, delegate authority and earn the bread; ours, go to school; mine, put away the dishes after the dishwasher was done; my brother's, fold the towels; and so on. This expectation of me was a pipe dream that died within the first couple of weeks of living separately from my dad. I hardly ever did my chores. It proves that new circumstances don't necessarily change one who is lazy into one who is industrious. I had absolutely no intention of putting away any dishes. Consequently, the dishes piled up in the sink, day after day. The laundry became a mountain of unwashed clothes vigorously mined each morning for the least foul-smelling pair of pants to wear to school. Despite her knowledge and skill—a five-time grand prize winner in her younger days at 4-H—she was just too encumbered at her job to devote time to homemaking. And my brother and I were still too busy adapting to a new school to care about household chores.

Dad's house was our more familiar haunt. Under that roof we were the "G" men. Three bachelors just out of boot camp entering the proving grounds of a new campaign. Dad used to sing to us in the morning:

This is the army, Mister Jones.
No more private telephones.

You had your breakfast in bed before.
But you won't have it there anymore.

This is the army, Mister Green.
We like the barracks nice and clean.
You had a housemaid to clean your floor.
But she won't help you out anymore.

Ironically, being enlisted at Dad's house carried with it no chores what-soever. He did all the dishes by himself, dried 'em to a hand-shine, took our clothes to the laundromat every two weeks, made sure there were crullers for breakfast every morning, and basically set a compulsive routine of chores for himself that excused us from any feelings that life with him would be anything but fun.

Athletics and activities with our cadre of neighborhood pals was the daily routine every weekend and school holiday at Dad's. Hour upon countless hour back and forth, the ping-pong ball, the tennis ball, the chess moves, the driveway hoops, swings, hits, and misses. We constructed our competitions with an unspoken strategy designed to make life fun through rote repetition. Never blow away the competition. Always keep it close. Better yet, let them lead. All the better to make for the life-affirming drama of a comeback and the glory of winning at the last moment. Bottom of the ninth, two outs, one man on, we're down one run. Ten seconds to go, possession is ours, two points to tie it up. Serving for match in a tiebreaker, but still down one point. Fourth and goal, twenty seconds left, down by six. On and on it went.

We were building a life strategy. A resilient philosophy, actually. Never reveal to your competition what your true talent is until that mo-ment when you really need it to prove your superiority and leave the oth-ers dumbfounded and defeated, realizing that they had been victims of their own hubris, that you had been toying with them all along. It was this sweet physico-intellectual game that made the endless hours of redundant practice and jock mentality of our opponents tolerable. The pleasure is to play, and to exercise your tolerance while strategizing when to reveal your true power.

Being a bachelor had its perks. Canned Dinty Moore stew for dinners. Ice cream before bed. Ping-Pong and a BB gun shooting gallery in the basement for our recreation. And a nonstop stream of chums in the neighborhood who came to call on us for pickup games and outdoor fun. But the house at first looked sparse. Where once stood Mom's old spinet piano now just appeared a blank white wall. The furniture was likewise only half as abundant as before the divorce, and what was added was a military grade cot for guests, a wood-framed davenport suitable for a cottage porch, and a spindle bed for me that sagged worse than the old spinster down the street who sold it to Dad at her garage sale.

Mom's and Dad's neighborhoods were different too. Dad's in Racine was more of a bedroom community without a metropolis. Mom's in Shorewood, on Milwaukee's northeast side, was only a few miles from the industrial valley where the iron boats would dock and the beer would brew alongside Milwaukee's urban downtown. Both neighborhoods were appropriate for middle-class academicians, but Dad's was more intimate. On quarter-acre lots sat neatly spaced single family units (nowadays they call these mid-century modern architecture). Most, like ours, had a central masonry fireplace that dominated the living room. The bricks used were not like the white Cream City bricks of the previous century but rather the hematite-impregnated reds favored by Wisconsin's own Frank Lloyd Wright. Most households like ours used the fireplace but once a year around the holidays. The central heating systems, with their oil tanks hidden away in some dark corner of the basement, were adequate to keep the poorly insulated one-story buildings just sufficiently warm enough for a flanneled person to be comfortable through the long winters.

Around us on all sides in Racine were families whose dads worked at the nearby industries: J. I. Case tractors, Western Publishing (DC Comics), InSinkErator, and Johnson's Wax (SC Johnson). There was never a shortage of fun to be had since kids of my age were only an arm's length away. Next door were Arthur and Robert, exactly the same ages as Grant and me. And an equal stone's throw behind our house were Tommy and Danny, also of the same ages. Anytime we wanted to play ball or board games or do art projects or ride bikes there was a battalion of eager neighborhood kids to pal around with.

In our Shorewood household, our friends lived on different streets, farther away, necessitating a drive from Mom in order to hang out with school pals. The houses in these Milwaukee neighborhoods were born of a different age. Shorewood had Gilded Age knockoff mansions and two-family jobbers from the early 1900s; industrial-era wannabes, generally of ample size, with high ceilings and solid construction. Bungalows and duplexes of stucco and brick masonry, hand built by craftsman of the last century, stood astride narrow lawns that ran along the broad thoroughfares radiating out from downtown. In both Shorewood and Racine we lived mere blocks away from Lake Michigan's adventurous shoreline.

Magnificent Fourth of July celebrations were the focus of every kid's anticipation at the lakefront, and the ample beaches allowed for reckless bonfires that began at sundown and stretched into the evening, long after the reports of the municipal fireworks finale ended. Roasting marshmallows and brats on sticks provided the culinary and aromatic accompaniment to every Racine kid's summertime bliss on such occasions. Divorce required adaptation. But it didn't seem to hamper my early and eager interest in music.

4
MUSICIAN IGNITION

Even though divorce was emotionally confusing, there's no denying that it created a rich, diverse array of experiences. One thing administrators and professors always agree on: you will graduate from this place and be better and more enlightened than before. This seemed to be the consistent theme at Graffin U. Nonetheless, loneliness, even in the midst of constant friendships, seemed to be my constant bedfellow in the early years of the divorce. It stemmed from the feeling that I was only pleasing one, but never both, parents at the same time. Hence, I often felt that I was letting one or the other down. If only I could find a subject they both loved equally, then maybe I could walk the line between the administrator and the professor.

Luckily, the administrators and professors seemed to love music equally. For professors, it was a reflection of their cultural awareness, an ornament every bit as important as their showy library of titles that defined their curricular specialties and literary tastes. For administrators, it was a similar window into their soul, an announcement of their communal spirit and openness, promoting the underdog as equally qualified to receive the benefits of the meritocracy, insisting that the current, popular style should lead the charge and rightfully dictate the preferences of the culture. Often at odds with the professorial tastes, they nonetheless united in agreement that music should play an important role in an educated person's life. In Mom's case, good music was a soothing lullaby for the soul and an expression of feelings too complex to put into words. For Dad, it held a secret message of life's experience, particularly in the poetic significance revealed by gifted lyricists.

In Shorewood, Mom enrolled us at Lake Bluff Elementary. One of the greatest gifts of that auspicious circumstance was a music teacher, Mrs. Perkins. Our second grade curriculum made it mandatory to attend music class a couple times a week. Mrs. Perkins stood at the front of the class and banged out popular tunes on her upright piano, asking students to sing along with her from the lyric sheets she handed out at the start of each class. I just loved showing off to her. Requiring no peeking at the lyric sheet, I had memorized most of the songs from the radio. Mom always played WOKY, Milwaukee's hit radio station, and her Buick LeSabre had big rear speakers mounted on the deck behind the back seat. In those days there were no seatbelt laws, so I could kneel, facing rearward staring at the cars behind us with my head only inches from the rear speaker on my side of the car and sing to all the latest songs. Mom would often sing harmonies and I learned this skill from her. Stevie Wonder's "Sunshine of My Life," Simon and Garfunkel's "Cecilia," Jackson 5's "I'll Be There," Bill Withers's "Lean on Me," and Mom's favorite, "Killing Me Softly with His Song" by Roberta Flack, were all on constant rotation in those days, and also were selected by Mrs. Perkins to play in music class.

Mom was keen to Mrs. Perkins's teaching style and her philosophy of teaching music through modern records and contemporary singer-songwriters. At a teacher's conference, Mom learned about the grade school choir. Every morning, one hour before classes began at the school, Mrs. Perkins opened up her classroom and held choir practice. Anyone was welcome, and Mom thought Grant and I would benefit from more music in our lives. Plus, Mom knew we were both good singers, and so she encouraged us to listen carefully to our music teacher's wisdom. Mrs. Perkins quickly noticed my enthusiasm for singing and ability to harmonize. She assigned me to sing solos on numerous occasions with the twenty-five other kids behind me singing the background parts. I didn't think much of it. It kind of felt like completing an assignment. If you were to ask me at the time: "Is this something you'd like to do for the rest of your life?" I would have probably answered, "No, I think I'd rather hit baseballs, catch footballs, shoot baskets, or race cars." In other words, singing and listening to music felt like part of my emotional expression. It was a natural part of me. But if I had to think about an activity that brought me notoriety, in the pursuit of fame (as all young kids dream about), I considered things that required more practice, coaching, and that were seemingly more unachievable than the relatively easy-to-manipulate skills of music that felt innate to me.

Even though I didn't consider it a privilege at the time, Mrs. Perkins arranged for scholarships to the annual summer music program at the University of Wisconsin–Madison. Our school was given two scholarships, and for three years in a row she gave the awards to me and Grant. At the week-long music camp we lived in dorms on campus, went to training and rehearsal sessions all day long, ate at the dining halls just like college kids, and learned what being in an elite group of the state's top music students felt like. We had a lot of fun, but I was constantly homesick. The grand finale of the summer music program was a weekend concert with over 150 singers and an orchestra with about a hundred instrumentalists, all set inside the largest concert hall on campus. Parents from all over the state attended, and even though I didn't sing any solos during these events, I got my first glimpse of what being on a big stage in front of a thousand strangers felt like. It also was satisfying to know that Mom and Dad both were in the audience. Despite the rifts between the administrator and the professor, music made Graffin U. whole.

Dad's record library was large and well-organized, alphabetized neatly across two shelves that spanned about six feet wide. Mostly classical recordings from the 1950s and 1960s, he also had more contemporary popular artists mixed in. Often before our bedtime, he broke into the Johnny Cash albums and played them loud for us. I remember how excited Dad got when he cranked the volume on the live album, *Johnny Cash at San Quentin*. His enthusiasm was infectious. I loved singing along, and really paid attention to the words and melody. At that age I had no appreciation for the excellent musicianship of the backup band, nor the production techniques. The only focus was the "man in black" on the album cover and the way he could stir up the audience and evoke unbridled emotion from my dad's professorial demeanor.

He also played us albums by Elvis Presley, The Weavers, Pete Seeger, Joni Mitchell, even The Velvet Underground and other heroes of the 1960s. Then there was Bob Dylan, who I believe Dad kept for himself. I discovered a well-worn *Highway 61 Revisited*, but he never played it for us. I think it was a personal favorite of his, from comments he made later in life about the master lyricist, and probably didn't think it would appeal to us kids. He was right. I snuck a listen when I was by myself. There was little in it for a second grader.

But Johnny Cash was different. Not only did my brother and I love to sing along, but Johnny seemed to represent something more symbolic to my dad, and I could sense the connection. We never knew Dad's father; he was absent, like so many American fathers of the mid-twentieth century; so maybe something in the rebellious way Johnny treated his own personal hardships came through in the lyrics and spoke to Dad's estrangement. Whatever the case, I could see that music broke people down by softening the emotional mortar that holds fragile emotions in check. I was attracted to that power. More important though, at that age, I needed some kind of nurturing medicine, since that house was void of maternal warmth, and Johnny's songs were as good a surrogate as I was going to get.

Dad's method of exposing us to music was very conventional, showing good taste in music by collecting a good set of records, going to live concerts—he took us to see Arlo Guthrie at Summerfest—and paying attention when the musical guests performed on variety shows on TV. Mom encouraged all of that too. But her involvement in music was deeper, more overtly emotional. She performed in citywide choral concerts with the group called Bel Canto. She also performed in the choir for a production of Gilbert and Sullivan's *The Mikado* in Chicago. And given my sensitivity to her emotions, my desire for her maternal comfort, I paid very close attention to her relationship with music, and with musicians.

A cursory study of Mom's record collection in 1972 included many of the top-selling albums from the Billboard charts. Her records were not neatly organized, nor alphabetized. Often strewn about the record player console, albums were open, sleeves were missing or torn, and discs were sometimes stacked to the side of the turntable; all indications that this was a very actively utilized set of records. The collection was small—she had not much money to spend on them—but more current than Dad's, which had been accumulated over decades. Titles included *The Age of Aquarius* by the 5th Dimension; *Talking Book* by Stevie Wonder; and *Blood, Sweat & Tears* by the band of the same name. But by far, her favorite artist was Roberta Flack and her albums seemed to be on constant rotation: *Chapter Two, First Take, Quiet Fire,* and *Roberta Flack & Donny Hathaway.* Mom wasn't introducing us to this music, she was living it herself. She played these records and got lost in their emotional seduction. In a sense, she was discovering her new identity. The soundtrack to her new life was soul stirring, and I could see her becoming more and more enriched and empowered when she sang along with it. I think it gave her a kind of strength as a woman raising two boys in a new and challenging role as a single mother and breadwinner. I naturally gravitated to the hit songs on these albums and learned to sing along with them, because I thought if I could tap into Mom's joy by participating in song, she might hold more affection for me. But Roberta's cover of Leonard Cohen's "Hey, That's No Way to Say Goodbye" was a sad discovery for me. I was drawn to it as a tragically appealing soundtrack to the divorce that was the first true heartbreak in my life.

One of the crossover albums in her collection was *Bridge Over Troubled Water* by Simon and Garfunkel. I call it a crossover because I think it was a minor player in her rotation, but Roberta Flack did a version of the title song, and Mom was likely curious about the original. On my own, I listened to a lot of Simon and Garfunkel. One song really struck a nerve with me, and I listened to it over and over again: "The Boxer." I couldn't interpret the meaning very deeply since I was too young, but the song's sad minor-chord progression and lyrical images of a lonely person beset by abandonment and absence of a home really affected me. Emotional songs like that one and "The Only Living Boy in New York," as well as Roberta's duet with Donny Hathaway, "Where Is the Love?" and Stevie Wonder's "I Believe (When I Fall in Love It Will Be Forever)" gave me a feeling of comfort during this confusing time. I thought I was tapping into my mom's psyche by studying these songs and the emotions that they evoked, and that seemed like a safe, reassuring place.

A premonition of things to come, I discovered perhaps the most personally influential record of all lurking low in the pile: *Jesus Christ Superstar*. It was intellectually challenging and stimulating to see the story of Jesus framed as a cult of personality. It was my first indication of countercultural style in music. It was educational. The curriculum at Graffin U. was devoid of biblical mythology. All the stories I'd ever known about the Bible came solely from that collection of songs. It displayed incredibly proficient musicianship and masterful lyrics. It set a standard for what greatness sounds like. The notion that religious followers are blind was not only a counterculture clarion call, but a profoundly influential concept for me to take in.

I soon learned that Mom's relationship to her favorite music was in concert with another relationship in her life. His name was Chuck, and he was an African-American jazz musician who was highly talented and played gigs throughout the Great Lakes club circuit. Mom and Chuck seemed very happy together. He started joining us for dinner a lot, and soon he was staying overnight even though he had his own apartment across town. It wasn't long before he essentially moved in with us, spending more time at our place than at his own. He brought his records of Ornette Coleman, who he resembled, and also his subscriptions to *DownBeat* magazine. He was fun, funny, talented, and we got along great. He called my brother "fingers" when he was taking guitar lessons. He called me "Sammy" all the time. He was cool, had style, taught me to call eating "greasin'" and talking "jaw-jackin'."

Mom and Chuck hung out at Barbara Bender's a lot and brought me and Grant along with them. We goofed around with Jason while the parents relaxed, cooked, and listened to music. Mom and Barbara both were great in the kitchen, and they shared a mutual appreciation for Southern cooking. They made collard greens, fried chicken, and other "soul food" and we ate it all up. It really felt like we were making a new life even though it was only twenty miles away from my dad's house.

On Dad's days we were back in the old neighborhood of our preschool years hanging out with friends who had never even talked to a Black person. It was rare in those days for schools and districts to be integrated. Even though all my friends spent their days in complete isolation from the Black neighborhoods, nearly all the people we admired were sports heroes and most of them were Black: Kareem Abdul-Jabbar, Oscar Robertson, John Brockington, Wilt the Stilt, Tommy Harper, Muhammad Ali, and Henry Aaron. These are the guys we emulated on our weekend pickup games outside Dad's house. There never was a discussion about their "Blackness." To us, they were simply heroes, personas whose achievements transcended any normal human capabilities. We simply didn't pay attention to their race or skin color. We were fortunate that our social milieu avoided foisting such heavy racial burdens onto us kids. Skin color played no role in our imagination. Chuck's skin color was just a side note to his cool personality as far as I was concerned. And my friends never spoke of it to me.

So when the day came for Mom and Chuck to come back into Dad's neighborhood to watch me play Little League with all my friends, there was no gawking nor attention paid to the "mixed couple" in the bleachers. Chuck may have been the only Black person at the park, but I just wanted to show off and hit a homer for him. The history books say that racial tension was everywhere in the early 1970s. But my mom and dad never spoke of it, didn't think it was worthy of our concern, and instead did everything to prevent it by actionable integration.

For Mom, it was more than integration; it was love. That our lives were shaped by Chuck and his "Blackness" wasn't really an overt factor in our daily routines. His musicianship, however, played a big role in my exposure to live performance. Often Chuck would practice around the house playing horns, sax, trumpet, and flute. He was incredibly gifted. Sometimes Mom and him would duet, her on the piano and Chuck on the flute. One of the most beautiful things I ever saw was their version of "Colour My World" (off the album *Chicago II*) with Mom on our spinet piano and Chuck on flute. It was like a wedding dance! But as will be seen, no wedding ever materialized.

Playing and singing together was natural for us, and it made me feel like we were a whole family. I got similar feelings when we got together with Mom's brother, Uncle Stanley. He always brought along the banjo and guitar at Thanksgiving and taught us to play and sing along to great "old-time" music and country tunes. They were raised in a conservative religious community in rural Indiana and sang in the church choir. Despite rejecting the oppressive expectations of the church later in life, Mom and Uncle Stanley retained a love of religious songs throughout their lives and taught us to appreciate them too. When they sang "He Will Set Your Fields on Fire" my brother, my cousins (Annette and Julie), and I felt like something magical was happening. Music validated our kinship, and harmony cemented the closeness we felt with each other. Music was our family glue.

When Mom and Chuck sang and played together, I saw how happy it made her, and that made me feel secure. Her happiness was procured by the decision to leave the professor, to make music with another man, and to create a household with music as its core. She seemed to find her true love in a man who was a musician. The divorce actually started to make sense to me, thanks to Chuck.

A dark and smoky jazz nightclub somewhere in the mean streets of Milwaukee around 1972 was no place for a seven-year-old boy from the suburbs. But that's where Mom was going to pick up Chuck at his regular gig, and where she went regularly to listen to, and hang with, his band. Given the newness of the divorce, and since I was emotionally still attached to

Mom with an invisible umbilicus, I felt extremely uneasy at night when she let us know, "Boys, I'm going to get Chuck, I'll be back in a while." We were used to being by ourselves for hours at a time, but something about her going out to the club—perhaps a feeling that she loved Chuck more than me—made me insist that she take me with her. I remember clinging to her leg as she tried to leave the apartment one night. After that, she relented and took me along every time. I was embarrassed that I couldn't be left alone like my brother, so I expressed the shame by hiding on the floor of the back seat of the Buick LeSabre, pretending not to be present. Usually, on weeknights, she simply pulled up to the club and Chuck got in, and he pretended not to notice me. But one night, she wanted to hear some of the music and she brought me in with her.

The euphoria I felt was intense. Maybe it was because Mom brought me in as her companion, but the biggest impression on my memory was the sound, and the smoky aroma mixed with liquor, and the visual experience of spot-lit reflections from brass horns, lacquered drums, and sparkling amplifiers together producing a foggy kaleidoscopic radiance from the stage. The music of Chuck's saxophone sweetly resonated through the show of lights. The kick drum thudded at intervals and shook my whole torso. The bass was soft and lilting, the piano was lively and smooth. I recognized none of the jazz standards that were coming off the stage, but I could listen and observe without pestering my mom while she watched with joy and got lost in the music. For the first time in her life, she found a place where she could enjoy herself far from the watchful eyes of a congregation or an administration, or from any obligation.

After a few songs, the band took a break and Chuck brought us over to meet them where they were all enjoying some drinks. Mom said, "I brought along one of the monsters." Chuck smiled approvingly and looked at me and said, "Sammy, this is Geechy, he plays keyboards." I thought I had never heard such a cool name before and Geechy had a floppy hat on his head and was wearing mirrored shades! "What's happening, Gregory? Let's have Lil bring you a drink from the bar," he said to me. I felt like I was one of the band at that moment, and a Shirley Temple appeared in front of me.

Unfortunately, my joy was about to end. Since Chuck had to play another set, Mom insisted we leave before it started. "Your father is coming in the morning and you have to go to bed!" Chuck arranged a ride home later, and Mom and I split out the side-stage door. But I held my head high knowing that I was acknowledged as a VIP and had drinks with the band.

On the way home it dawned on me that Chuck was a success, and Mom adored the achievement as well as the man. This was my first memory of seeing Mom's adoration and deep respect of a musician at work. I knew that I wanted her to adore me too. So I became driven, at this young age of seven or eight, to pursue an avid interest in music. What began as a feeling for the affectionate attention from my mother turned into a lifelong calling. From that early age, I knew that musical performance was a worthy goal and was something that was going to be in my future.

5
THE DEEP ORIGINS OF BAD RELIGION

Religion was a foreign concept at Graffin U. Not to my mom, but to me, my brother, and my father, scarcely a breath of the Bible or any stories from its pages were ever mentioned.

Mom was raised in a rural church tradition in central Indiana. She had a strict but loving mother whose father was an important minister in the Church of Christ. This predominantly rural congregational sect is found in small towns all across the United States, and its history spans the nineteenth and twentieth centuries. For much of that time, our country was nothing more than a patchwork of small towns, and throughout central Indiana and southern Illinois, my mom's family grew up as devotees to the Church of Christ. A Bible literalist, my great-grandpa E. M. Zerr wrote a six-volume Bible commentary still used in the Church of Christ. The Bible says, "Sing to God, sing praises to his name . . . " (Psalm 68:4) but says nothing about musical instruments. Therefore, despite its long tradition of

music, the Church of Christ banned musical instruments to accompany the
choir. Choral music was a big part of the Church of Christ, and the songs
of the Christian hymnal were sung to perfection at every service. The artists who defined rhythm and blues of the late 1960s and 1970s formed the
bulk of Mom's record collection, and nearly every one of them cited Southern church music and the Christian hymnal as being highly influential to
their musical styles. Like Mom, all those artists grew up in churches and
choirs that sang songs with thoughtful, heart-wrenching lyrics, and deep
conceptual—even philosophical—meanings about life.

Being raised in a devout Christian household had its unintended conse-
quences. As an adult, Mom had no love for her grandfather's church. Even
though he was a famous, noted preacher who traveled the entire country
giving six-week Bible studies wherever he roamed, and he was a beloved and
caring grandfather, nonetheless Reverend Zerr's church "brethren" were
hard, uncompromising, and strict. If you followed all the rules, they welcomed you with open arms. And their warmth and hospitality was so attractive and comforting that it made you feel like they were angels. But they
had a penchant for public shaming too.

Mom, before she was known by that label, had to get up in front of the
entire congregation and apologize to them for her transgressions when she
was in college. Life at the "Big City Teacher's College" (Ball State) in Muncie, Indiana, led her to many activities and groups that were "unapproved"
by the church and the small-town sensibilities of Grandpa's congregation
back in the hometown of Anderson, Indiana. This act of apologizing for activities that she thought were moving her life forward, including meeting my
dad in graduate school at IU in Bloomington, was humiliating for my mom.
The stern, small-minded people of her hometown congregation soured her
to religion. She decided it was not worth the comfort nor the hospitality
nor the love from a community if the conditions for that affection were so
rigorous as to stifle growth, self-expression, and self-determinism. After a
final public apology, around the time of her "unapproved" marriage, she left
the church and never went back. A woman who could quote Bible verses by
heart, and recite phrases with ease, and know the 1,189 chapters in order

made the conscious decision to change her life. She decided to completely insulate my brother and me from any religious influence whatsoever. Our houses were full of books, but a Bible, if it existed at all, was either out of sight or tucked away hidden from view on a high shelf. I never saw one, yet I distinctly remember other titles of literature proudly on display.

Great-grandpa Zerr died before he could learn that his granddaughter gave birth to my brother and me. His daughter (our grandmother, affectionately called Momo by us), was a wonderful loving and supportive elder to me, but I knew that she had a silent lack of approbation toward my mom. I never could figure it out, but I'm sure it was due to her disapproval that Mom raised us without any knowledge of the Bible. She lived with us for three months every year after Mom and Dad's divorce. Always a picture of perfection, my small-town grandma cooked for us, read to us, showed interest in our schooling, and held her tongue when visiting us "heathens" in the big city. She watched Billy Graham on TV and enjoyed our company tremendously. I think back to how she must have had to use all of her strength and willpower to compose herself when I revealed to her my proudest moment as a teenager: our first Bad Religion album depicting a real life Sodom and Gomorrah—Hollywood, California—with the title words "How Could Hell Be Any Worse?" She smiled, quietly nodded, and said in her slight Southern drawl, "Oh my land!" She died in my mom's house long after we kids flew off to college. We buried her at her hometown cemetery after weeping uncontrollably as the Church of Christ choir sang her favorite hymns in the small country chapel of her youth. Mom never returned to that building. Her break with religion was complete.

6
PROG RELIGION AND POLITICS

My brother and I were still freshmen at Graffin University. By fourth grade we had settled into a pretty comfortable routine. Mom established herself as an exceptional administrator at UWM as dean of learning skills, Chuck was a busy musician working nearly every night at this or that jazz venue in Chicago or Milwaukee, Dad was teaching English at UW-Parkside and serving on committees for the state qualifying examinations, while my brother and I attended one of the best grade schools in the state. Weekends, vacations, and summer breaks were spent back at the old homestead at Dad's house, full of pals from the old neighborhood who were always eager to see us.

Across town from our school, our nana was always ready to receive us to give the parents some time to themselves. She loved her son, Dad, as a prince, and my brother and I were treated as little kings. Each night, morning, and noon, she cooked food in the German tradition. Her maiden name, Koch (meaning "cook"), definitely labeled her correctly because not only did she make dinner, but there were always leftovers and streusel coffee cakes to take home for the week. Each night in her care, my brother and I would walk with our grandpa, "Papa," to the local butcher, Roundy's, and pick up the freshest meat for dinner. Back then, Milwaukee was separated into segregated neighborhoods, each with its share of small grocery stores, filling stations, and taverns on nearly every major street corner. Everything was walkable.

Sometimes Papa would have us pop into his favorite tavern on the way home from the store. "Now don't tell Nana we stopped here, okay kids?" was his usual request. My brother and I just thought it was cool because as he got to drink his favorite late-afternoon cocktail, the tender would draw us up some Baumeister Root Beer, and that erased all sense that we were doing anything illicit on our grocery errand.

Nana loved our family so much. She was heartbroken about the divorce but continued to love Mom and us as she did before. She was an old-fashioned type of grandmother, equally fond of her "early-American" home furnishings and old-German traditions. I never considered her as anything but a solid rock of love and ancient ways. But she must have been more sophisticated than I could understand because 1974 Milwaukee was a place of change and she had no outward animosity toward that change.

One indication of her willingness to embrace modern culture came at Christmas that year. This holiday meant more than any other in our households. Whereas in past years her gifts were conventional, such as the usual socks and underwear, cool Hot Wheels, and special wooden toys made by Papa in his basement workshop, in 1974 I opened a couple of gifts that were like no other: records. I thought to myself, "How did Nana know how to buy a rock 'n' roll record?"

She had seen a television commercial for K-tel records and thought, "The kids are really getting into music these days," so she gave my brother and me the latest release advertised, called *Heavy Metal*. In the history of the genre, I can think of no earlier use of this term than this K-tel album. I am absolutely sure that Nana had no idea it would become a genre of music, nor that some of the bands on that album would one day play concerts at festivals on stages that I would share with my own band. Nonetheless, my surprise and excitement upon opening the album gift was the pleasing result Nana hoped for. I studied the cover and liner notes but had to wait to play it, for Nana had no turntable. I'm quite sure that she was perfectly content not having to hear what was hidden in those grooves.

This album contained an eclectic mix of classic recordings from bands like Deep Purple, Black Sabbath, Jimi Hendrix, Alice Cooper, Allman Brothers, T. Rex, MC5, Buffalo Springfield, and the Eagles. Clearly, the album title had no intention of classifying a genre. But the one track that I paid particular attention to, and that set the tone for my budding interest in unconventional music, was "Starship Trooper" by the band Yes.

To say that this had an influence on my musical taste would be an understatement, because it also formed the core of my social life to an important degree. Yes became a nexus for me and a small set of my schoolmates. I made a friend in choir, Jeff, whose tastes in music I emulated. We spent countless hours hanging out after school. Jeff had this studious intensity about everything, including music. He entertained me with his adept reading of music and knowledge of songwriting. Through discussions with him, I began paying more attention to how songs were crafted. "Here's a song that was actually written by Paul Simon, but I'm going to play you a version that was recorded by Yes," he said. The song was "America," and when Jeff played me the Yes version of the tune, I heard what was like a rock orchestra with numerous sections that seemed to stray away from the melody at times. "I suppose it was just strummed on acoustic guitar by Simon and Garfunkel during these lyrical sections," Jeff would interject at the top of his voice as the song blared from his stereo's speakers. It was my first realization that the recorded piece is always an interpretation of the writer's imagination.

My first ever "jam" session was with Jeff, and it entailed me playing his mom's small Wurlitzer organ while he strummed an acoustic guitar. He had the sheet music for the Yes song "Perpetual Change" and showed me the keys to play. The first few bars of the song are only keyboard and guitar, and we sounded just like the album version!

Jeff had a large record collection, and he studied it song by song. He played records constantly, showing off his impressive stereo components and cranking up the volume. Sitting in amazement as a fourth grader, on a plush couch in his finished basement, I listened intently. Jeff had crafted this room into a den of wonder with shag carpet samples glued to the floor. The walls were painted as murals depicting his favorite album art. On one wall, Mahavishnu Orchestra's *Birds of Fire* formed the backdrop to his stereo speakers, turntable, and tube amplifier setup on a low shelf. Meanwhile, Pink Floyd's *Dark Side of the Moon* light prism adorned the other wall. Behind us was a massive Yes logo by the artist Roger Dean that Jeff had masterfully copied and painted in fluorescent green and yellow letters that mimicked the album *Close to the Edge*. A bank of black light shop bulbs clung to the ceiling and, when the vinyl was spinning on the turntable, we were bathed in the odd glow of the black light bulbs that made certain colors and materials emit a magical radioactive radiance. A fluorescent red fishnet was loosely suspended and draped across the entire ceiling of the room. It too came alive and shimmered in the black light. Basically, Jeff had created an acid queen's fantasy den, but we were fourth graders and unaware of such mature themes. The music mated to the environment that Jeff created was inspirational, otherworldly, life-affirming, and psychotropic in its own right. We sat rapt and drifted off into our own imaginations as we listened to the magical sounds coming from his stereo. John McLaughlin, Steve Hillage, Todd Rundgren, Yes, Floyd, ELP (Emerson, Lake & Palmer). You would have thought we were deep into drug experimentation. But we were just thrilled by the music, the lights, and the comradery. We were being fed by the taste of Jeff's neighbor, Wes, who was older, in high school, and really into pushing progressive rock to the kids on the street. Having "good taste" in music was a key part of being sophisticated intellectual kids of parents who were academics (in my case) and in the legal profession (Jeff's parents). But in reality, it gave us a sense that we were cool, because we could relate to much older cool kids. By sixth grade, Wes let us accompany him to see Yes at the Milwaukee Arena. I was offered a joint that was being passed around the crowd, but I declined and instead focused on the concert and the green lasers that flooded the audience. "Just like Jeff's basement," I thought, but on a grander scale. I was hypnotized by the sensory onslaught: five musicians, each playing different parts of an orchestrated whole, in sync to an incandescent stage irradiance that shimmered through a billowing manufactured mist whose haze was pierced by countless needle-thin beams of green laser light. I sang along with the incomparably clear-voiced singer, Jon Anderson, at the top of my lungs. It was as close to a religious calling as I can ever imagine.

I got a thrill from knowing that only me and a few close friends in our age group really enjoyed progressive rock. It was music for older kids in high school and college. My experience with Yes and with our little "secret society" of listeners was an initiation of sorts. It gave me the feeling that it's cool to like music that isn't mainstream.

But the truth is, I loved mainstream music too. In 1974, Milwaukee's hit radio station, WOKY, played all the hits. The song "The Loco-Motion" as covered by Grand Funk Railroad was played numerous times a day for five months (!) during this period. This Todd Rundgren–produced classic had elements in it that got the whole car rocking. Mom loved it, Chuck loved it, even my brother clapped along. I paid attention to the lyrics mostly, but undoubtedly those hand claps at the beginning, with their famous long reverb tails, were instant cues for me to say, "Turn it up, Mom!" We had no idea that twenty-five years from that moment I'd be in the studio with Todd making my own distinct record with bandmates from California, which at that moment, in 1974, could not have been more foreign to us. It would take a series of drastic events to get there.

Politics was a major concern in both households. Mom and Dad were solid, Midwestern Democrats, in contradistinction to their parents who were conventional Republicans. The 1950s and 1960s saw a rising tide of citizens concerned for the equality of all people. At Graffin U., the administration and faculty agreed on most issues of equal rights and affirmative action. Integration, especially of Black and white students, was tantamount to a successful university. But it didn't stop there. Women's rights and women's issues were forefront on the minds of many, especially divorced, working moms like our own. So when the nightly news came on, both my parents, who worked such long hours putting into action these important issues of the day, and seeing microcosms of national political strife first-hand on campus, tuned in to hear updates of the day's major events.

The anchors, aka news readers, were trusted like parents. For thirty minutes, around 6:30 p.m., we had to clam up and surrender our expectations of any parental attention to hear every detail of concise reportage coming from the network. We didn't go to church, whose Sunday sermons might have bored us to tears. Instead we had thirty minutes of preaching every single night by clergy of the airwaves that infused by osmosis the pressing concerns of the adult world. As I suppose we would have had to in the house of God, we sat on our hands and zipped our lips and watched our parents be moved, intellectually and emotionally, by the information coming from the boob tube.

It should come as no surprise that when, in 1976, the Sex Pistols were covered on national news, it legitimized punk in our house. If Dan Rather is covering this new trendy phenomenon in London, then it's probably best that we pay attention to it. The Sex Pistols were seen as a fascinating cultural emergence. "Wow, something, hey?" said Dad. "Look at the way the audience dances." Another great topic for the professors to discuss over sheepshead that weekend!

Because of the nightly news ritual that sewed together values of our disparate households, Graffin U. was whole. The common threads that could be discussed openly in both households were current events and liberal politics. The news provided the environment of appropriate discussion about the outside world and "big picture" topics that helped to shape the intellectual complexion of our family.

But it was the professor's job to turn news into action. A photograph adorned the shelf at Dad's house, one of many depictions of family life framed and displayed with pride. It showed Dad in his professional garb, light colored blazer, patterned tie with decorative peace symbols, acting as a chaperone for a celebrity on campus. This, however, is no ordinary Hollywood star, but rather the noteworthy author and literary provocateur Norman Mailer. Dad was his host during a lecture tour in 1971 when Mailer was riding high on his Pulitzer Prize–winning book *Armies of the*

Night. The photograph was hung in the living room and has remained there among the multitudes of accumulated family mementos and framed snapshots ever since.

Parents often don't realize the effect that things displayed have on the subconscious development of their kids. I saw everything Dad displayed as a secret message, a tacit suggestion of the things he wanted us to value. As Mailer himself said, describing himself in the third person, he was:

> an egotist of the most startling misproportions, outrageously and often un-happily self-assertive, yet in command of a detachment classic in severity (for he was a novelist and so in need of studying every last lineament of the fine, the noble, the frantic, and the foolish in others and in himself).*

Could such a blueprint of traits exude into the subconscious brain from a mere photograph? Yes or no, I believed that some kind of emulation of that man was the key to gaining the respect of my dad. In the photo, Mailer is expositing on some serious topic as Dad, by his side, gazes out at the gathering crowd he is to address. The image spoke to me: "Son, it's an honorable thing to have something important to say. It's the only worthy kind of celebrity." What Dad found attractive is that Norman Mailer represented an analytical type of social critic. He was a polarizing figure, and even though I couldn't put it into words, I had intuition that this was something desirable. I had no formal understanding of the particulars, but to grow up seeing that photo every day gave me an awareness, an aspiration as Mailer's place in society became more canalized and my own education flourished, to challenge conventional wisdom because it was cool to question authority.

But it was years before I would put this practice to work. These early mental rumblings were fleeting, as we spent only weekends under the gaze of Norman Mailer on the shelf. Soon it would be months of absence from Dad's house each year. Graffin U. was in for a seismic shift.

---

* From Norman Mailer's *Armies of the Night*, 1st ed. (New York: New American Library, 1968), 54.

7
TRANSCONTINENTAL JOURNEY

I n the spring of 1976, Mom announced that she had taken a new job as the dean of learning skills at UCLA and that we were moving to Los Angeles later that year. As an eleven-year-old my prospects of a transcontinental odyssey were as an astronaut preparing for first steps on the moon. Filled with anticipation yet having no idea about the realities of change that were in store. I was soon to be going from a Midwestern dairy-loving, rust-belt, purebred, popular schoolboy existence to a multi-culti, big-city megapolis minion soon to be lost in the vastness of cultural insignificance. The journey was to take five days, each leg ending at family friends' houses scattered across the country. Being as car-savvy as I was, having traveled every back road of Wisconsin between Milwaukee and Racine for the last four years each weekend, I nonetheless had never witnessed anything other than green forest, cabbage fields, and cornfields in the summer, and winterscapes like those books on Dutch painters in Dad's library.

Our trips to Grandma and Grandpa's down in Indiana didn't provide for much variation over what we had in southeastern Wisconsin except maybe fewer cities, and even more cornfields.

I was not afraid. I felt that our road trip would be an adventure. I suppose it's no exaggeration to say that it's age appropriate to assume that I could foresee nothing beyond the next few hours ahead of me, and they seemed upbeat. We had been saying "so long" for so long each Sunday night to our friends and Dad that it all felt quite natural. No way to know what it would feel like to spend months rather than days between those goodbyes until we'd hug "hello" again.

"Got yer grips? Mom will be here soon." Goofing around was the order of the day every weekend transition from Dad to Mom. But this particular transfer felt a bit heavier because there was a more somber tone to Dad's admonitions. Mom drove up in her dented 1969 Buick LeSabre just as she promised, but where was Chuck? She had dropped him off at Little Richard's, the burger joint up on Douglas Avenue, because she must have known how hard this goodbye was going to be for Dad. Dad and Chuck got along fine, but they were not intimately close, and Mom wanted to insulate her new man from her old as she single-handedly, and courageously, entered the driveway to disband the G-men.

Without question, this was to be the singular event that would determine the course of the Graffin family for generations to come. We were moving to LA. The two campuses of Graffin U. were soon to be a half-continent apart. We hugged Dad as we always did on Sundays. But something was different this time. From the back seat, I watched Mom walk in follow-step back toward where we left Dad at the garage side door. Instead of just turning and going back inside, I could see he lingered there, watching. Then, I saw something so foreign that it shocked my senses. My Mom and Dad embraced. It was the only time I ever saw my parents hold each other. Such a joyous thing, a parental embrace. In our family, however, it's only associated with sadness. When Mom came back to the car, she had tears in her eyes. She wiped them clear, tried to shake off her fragility, and said, "Let's go, kids. I left Chuck at Little Richard's." At that moment, I knew this was more than just a usual Sunday transition. No fear, just emotional weight overcame me, yet I felt safe in the care of my mom who must have known what was best for us. I couldn't have known that the coming odyssey was not merely a five-day transcontinental journey, but a new life different from anything we had come to understand as normal. A completely new trajectory awaited us, complete with undreamed-of situations, tragic upheaval, and scrapped plans. Such were the humble beginnings of a punk rock odyssey.

A mere eleven miles from Dad's doorstep was I-94. Along sidewalk-bordered streets of concrete, we cruised and hit every stop light, pausing without talking amidst the receding August sunlight. Taking in the lingering sadness of a parting and incipiently fracturing family, the on-ramp finally appeared and the hopeful force of V-8 acceleration shoved me back in my seat. A new scene, with fresh and inviting landscapes, was to be found every time I poked my head over the front seat and glanced at the oncoming pavement outside the windshield. A stir of excitement had begun to help erase the boredom of gloomy reality in the rearview mirror. I-94 to I-80 to Des Moines and who knew where else? West was all I knew, and that meant each day of travel I'd see the sun set in front of us, dipping below the ribbon of superhighway and destinations whose names were the responsibilities of the captains in the front seat.

Some will remember the days I am describing, of long, seemingly endless stretches of interstate highway, only recently delittered from years of abuse by careless motorists who used it as their mobile trash bins. There were no guarantees, only surprises, when the navigator decided to pull off at the next exit. Some off-ramps had filling stations, some had country markets like Stuckey's. If you were really fortunate, there might be a waffle house or a Denny's or the crème de la crème, a Big Boy. Each state had a different nomenclature for this restaurant franchise. We learned to navigate based on this variable. If we saw Marc's Big Boy, we knew we were still in Wisconsin. If we saw a Frisch's Big Boy, hallelujah! We'd made it to Indiana. Of course, on the day of our departure from Marc-land, we had no inkling that what was waiting ahead for us in California was the alliterative Bob's Big Boy.

No GPS data existed, nor neat devices nor screens depicting services in the next ten miles. Only a portfolio of huge, printed maps and out of date road guides from the American Automobile Association accompanied us, strewn about the front seat across Chuck's lap while Mom sang to the radio and steered us to our next waypoint somewhere in Iowa.

The first night brought with it a longing sadness for home accompanied by the awkward feeling of being in a strange neighborhood, arriving after dark at the house of one of Mom's colleagues who was all too welcoming but still put out by our presence. We greeted the next morning with optimism as we departed Iowa en route to Denver.

Our commander decided to head south from Iowa to pick up Interstate 70 at Kansas City instead of staying the western course of I-80 out of Des Moines. Perhaps it was because KC was having a "renaissance." The city had invested millions of dollars in PR marketing campaigns, claiming a contrast to the perception of it as the Capital of Cows in the USA to a shining metropolis worthy of hosting the Republican National Convention. In August of that year, within a week of our journey, a Californian named Ronald Reagan made his way to the podium at the Kemper Arena and gave a speech that launched his national political career, which ultimately catapulted him all the way to the White House. Still, Republicanism was no attraction to Mom, so it had to be some other reason we took that cursed route.

I-70 had been in the news that year. It was the newest of the interstate highways, having been completed in 1970, and only that year of our journey had it merged with US-50, a project that required millions of dollars of restoration and resurfacing. Mom was a shrewd and intrepid captain who loved to drive and disdained poorly maintained country roads. She always preferred I-94 between Milwaukee and Racine during our divorce commutes rather than the more-direct but bumpier State Highway 32. So I could see how she may have opted for the smoothest, newest route into Denver available at the time. And that was I-70 through Kansas City. Besides, Kansas was considered "Midwest," just like Wisconsin, so a curious Indiana traveler should have little trepidation in her decision to use that state as a friendly bridge to the West on her family's Midwestern exodus.

But perhaps Kansas City held another kind of magnetism for my music-loving administrator and her music man. Perhaps its reputation for being the birthplace of an essential style of jazz was a comforting attraction to Mom and especially to Chuck who had never ventured to that city before. Certainly the people there must be open-minded and share our family's love of music and humanistic values. Right? Well, jazz sacredness be damned! The sour flavor of Kansas was soon to visit us and color any sweet memories we had of that state. Whatever the motivation, Mom didn't realize she was heading into a land that harbored hostile truckers who prided themselves on terrorizing "mixed" race couples.

In 1976, the highway system didn't provide travelers with the same niceties we have now come to expect, such as name-brand "traveler service stations," "rest stops" stocked with picnic tables and barbecue grills for the family, or "automobile-friendly" truck stops. Most off-ramps were devoid of consumer activity, serving instead as crossroads of major thoroughfares, or county or state highways. Some had filling stations, and one might obtain candy bars or some bread and cold cuts perhaps and, in some Midwest states, the ubiquitous "homo gals" of 2% milk, homogenized for safe consumption and transport. The truckers knew where the greasy spoons were and, in many states, these were insider clubhouses of an elitist society that communicated along closed networks of CB radios. Families were not unwelcome per se, but they also were not sought out as regular customers.

Just outside of Kansas City, we gassed up at a filling station that happened to be situated across from a busy diner whose lot was filled with dirty big rigs idling in the hot sun. While Mom pumped a tankful of leaded "ethyl" into the old LeSabre, Chuck wandered across the street to try and scare up a couple of milkshakes or something to hold us over in the back seat. Now, I can't testify as a matter of documented fact what I'm about to report, but from what I could see from my temporary front-seat vantage point peering out the fly window, I would bet a fair wager that he was the only Black man for miles around. The innocence of our integrationist, equality-minded, liberal upbringing kept my brother and me immune to the possibility that Chuck's mere presence in that diner could be as inflammable as leaded fuel vapor in the presence of a spark. We had no idea what the cultural norms were, and it turned out that Mom was all wrong in ascribing generosity and kindredness to the people we met at this particular off-ramp. This was rural Kansas.

Mom had not lived outside of the northern Midwest, but she was keenly aware of the racism in the country and had worked hard as a chief administrator on campus to balance social inequities and include women and men of color on her most important academic projects and task forces. She was an early adopter and enforcer of equal pay for women on campus and affirmative action to benefit minority workers years before these topics made it to the nightly news. She was not ignorant nor innocent of the potential problems her interracial relationship might cause. And yet, she was intrepid, showing no fear nor hesitation in heading west, through untested routes. My brother and I were never briefed on any possibilities that an undercurrent of hatred existed among some people, or that resentment and jealousy drove many people in our country to violence toward those who engaged in interracial marriages.

Chuck came back to the car with a few snacks and a look of perturbed distress as he urged us to press on and hit the highway. After Mom reached cruising speed, Chuck was clearly uncomfortable in the passenger seat as we noticed three semi-trailer trucks coming up from behind us. Mom looked anxiously in the rearview mirror. She was never one to raise alarm, but I could sense that she nervously added some pressure to the accelerator and grabbed all the muscle the 401 V-8 engine could give her at seventy miles per hour. I turned around and saw that a couple of Kenworths were trailing, quickly gaining on us. Always trained in the academic tradition of rational analysis, I wondered if they were just in a hurry to get somewhere. In furthering my assessment of the situation, I took into consideration Mom's worried glance while remembering that we were used to passing trucks in the slow lane rather than having them accelerating to pass us on the open road.

Humanity comes beset with certain historical incompatibilities. Religion and science, education and slavery, racism and liberalism. When

trying to reconstruct my anxieties as an eleven-year-old along I-70, I run
into perhaps the most universal incompatibility of all: fear and rationality.

There was nothing but open rangeland all around. The oncoming traffic
was far across a wide, flat interstate divide of prairie grass. It seemed as
though we were the only passenger car for miles. When I felt the forward
surge of deceleration, my fear began to surface. Mom had to slow down because both lanes on our side of the highway were now blocked by a couple of
slow trucks, side by side, coordinating some kind of wrathful choreography.
"The old Texas roadblock," said Chuck. Mom issued a "Jesus Christ!" and
that meant all rational explanations were exhausted. I curled up in the back
seat, mortified, and pulled my trusty travel pillow over my head. When I
peeked out of the back-seat window, towering above me was the cab and
driver of one of the speeding trucks from behind that had now caught up
and begun to overtake us on the right. "They're boxing us in!" cried Mom.

I was used to idolizing trucks in those days. Hours of my "quiet time"
at Dad's house were spent on my bedroom desk table, drawing and col-
oring machines of all kinds—tanks, airplanes, race cars, and, of course,
the ubiquitous trucks that we would pass on I-94. My friendly association
with trucks was sorely tested as I peered eye to eye at the driver of a Mack
that pulled alongside our speeding LeSabre. Cruising at what seemed like
eighty miles per hour, the truck drifted to within inches of my back-seat
passenger door and the driver looked down at my face that was frozen with
fear and bewilderment. Tears and terror radiated from my countenance,
but this did nothing to soften the hateful rage I saw in the bearded fat man
who drove that truck! His face was contorted, his teeth were clenched, his
squinted eyes peered vengeance. I had never felt hatred, nor sensed pent-up
rage such as this. I was bewildered. He seemed intent on killing me along
with everyone in the car.

With a slow truck in front, and the black Mack on our right, a third
truck came up on our rear bumper and it seemed like it was going to ram us
from behind. No better sea captain in a tempest could have matched Mom's
composure as she carefully tried to avoid collision with these CB conspira-
tors who were trying to cause an incident on I-70. After what seemed like

an hour—but probably was less than a minute—the bearded trucker pulled alongside Chuck's front-seat passenger door, rolled down his window, and simply pointed his finger, waving it back and forth in his direction.

In another instant, the Mack swerved and would have clipped the front fender had Mom not cranked the wheel to the left in concert. We drove off the road onto the bumpy median. Locking the brakes, skidding, Mom created a lagging cloud of rusty buff sand that slowly grew and would soon engulf us. We all thudded against the doors as the seats pitched from the uneven deceleration, the tires locking then releasing as they feebly searched for purchase. Our unbelted bodies pitched wildly to and fro. Noisy clanks, as gravel spattered inside the wheel wells, were pronounced but immediately got drowned out by the blowhorns emanating from the sinister trucks that sped off into the western horizon having done their dirty deeds.

The car finally halted. We all sat motionless; Mom was gasping and clasping for Chuck's reassuring embrace. Not much was said, but Mom always was one to help her boys understand what was going on. "Mom, what did you do to get those guys mad?" I asked. "Nothin' honey, they were just prejudiced," she said. I never imagined what the reason for such behavior could have been because I was never introduced to the concept that racial "mixing" was forbidden by some people.

As the dust cloud descended all around us, I could see Mom's face reflected in the rearview mirror. Her eyes had that faraway look when one ponders their own existence and takes in the significance of a confrontational moment. She must have been beset by all sorts of heavy thoughts. Only two days into a journey, the trepidation of the unfamiliar became obvious. We were heading into a culture unknown. Would the teachings and lifestyles of Eastern academics translate out West? Would the escape from a stodgy Midwestern religious upbringing and a stifling marriage finally come to fruition in California, a half continent away from its source? Would an interracial union blossom into a life of unfettered love and find a fertile habitat in Los Angeles, or would it wither on the vine from constant social stigmatization? And would these kids benefit from spending their lives in constant biannual travel between summers in Wisconsin and school years in Los Angeles? At that moment, in the middle of a nameless stretch of Kansas interstate, a solitary gray whale stood stranded on a man-made beach, a hundred yards wide, bordered by two ribbons of pavement. Across the median was safety, the way home, and we could drift back east, and in a couple short days we'd be back in familiar waters. But Mom gathered her resolve to guide the beast farther westward, to deliver us to the uncertain future that she'd set out to discover.

Still, freedom from her family's watchful scrutiny and stifling religious expectations, from the narrow-mindedness of small-town Midwestern existence, from the bonds of an unfulfilling marriage, was at this moment met with the heaviest of burdens. The exasperation on her face, though only fleeting, was worrisome to me. But she composed herself and redoubled her determined drive toward a better future, enriching us beyond our awareness at the time. There was a rational side to her escapism: the hopeful familiarity of the university awaited us. It was, after all, our family tradition, fomenting our faith in place of a religion.

After a minute or two, idling on the lonely median, Mom reengaged the shifter after the dust settled. The LeSabre bounced up to speed and climbed back onto westbound I-70. Mom and Chuck spoke few words to each other, but they knew what the potentially fatal act of road rage meant. The mere presence of their love for one another was socially perilous in some parts of the country, and no amount of verbal analysis would aid in sheltering us kids from the realities of racism. We never openly discussed the facts or implications of their relationship. We were always taught that race was not as important in the world so long as human suffering was one's focus. We were taught to view humanity as a diverse family, and prejudice was anathema to this teaching. So Mom did not use this moment to voice her anger and disappointment at the racist individuals who just wronged her and tried to bring her and her family bodily harm. Doing so would have highlighted the intended racism, small-mindedness, and social hatred that she was ethically determined to nullify. So, with remarkable resolve, she did what seemed best for her family in a moment of crisis. She simply changed the subject. "How many more miles to Denver,

Chuck?" I'm sure that she was hoping, at that moment, that our new home out West would be more welcoming.

In the back seat, my overactive imagination was getting the best of me. My fear was blunted by my mom's intrepid confidence. With the rousing of my emotion came, however, an introspective ponderance that became my constant companion. I began to accept, from this early age, that a world of circumstances exists "out there," and my mission in life was to accept it and do something with it. I began to notice that no matter how much I wished for safety and the security afforded me back in the familiar surroundings of Dad's house and neighborhood, there were more powerful forces drawing me away into another world full of unknown perils and adventures. I began to feel powerless and yet, surprisingly, despondency quickly gave way to a hopeful disposition as our gas guzzler came up to speed. The world was big, the journey long, and I felt exuberant as my captain's chief officer. On her shoulders the heavy burden lay—the divorce, the interracial relationship, the western emigration. Perhaps, as well, the albatross was most ominous for the copilot, Chuck, who privately must have recognized the inescapable taboo of his interracial romance in such a racist world. Our anxieties notwithstanding, the constant push westward and the soothing pitch of the V-8 at speed provided the only solace. Away we sped from the site of our heated encounter.

Leaving behind a life of pleasant and ancient tranquility on the stable Midwestern craton, I peered forward toward a new reality at the unforgettable first glimpse of the approaching Front Range. Real mountains! Directly ahead, out that windshield, my life and future, gaining fast. No turning back. My fate was to be played out in the tectonic upheavals of the West.

8
LA PROVED TOO MUCH FOR THE MAN

There's no telling the kinds of stresses that Chuck carried around on a daily basis. Looking for regular jobs in LA at the time, 1976–77, was tough. Probably even tougher for a Black man in the cozy confines of Canoga Park, the West San Fernando Valley, middle-class enclave of Los Angeles where we settled. Inflation was rising fast, and even menial jobs were all filled. Chuck was a college graduate and a Navy veteran, and still this stingy job market had nothing to offer. Chuck had to be true to himself too. He was an artist. He came to LA to play music, but all the best clubs were twenty-five miles away in central LA or Hollywood. We had only one car, and Mom needed it every day, all day to commute twenty miles each way to UCLA. Chuck landed some sporadic weekend work at jazz joints, but these lounge gigs didn't pay much. He hid his stress well around the house, practicing horns every day, never abusing alcohol or pills in front of me or my brother, but the dam was about to break.

In 1978 I was thirteen. An unlucky number perhaps, but another thirteen was on the minds of most California residents. In June of that year Proposition 13 was passed by popular vote. The so-called People's Initiative to Limit Property Taxes became an amendment to California's state constitution. This controversial initiative had the effect of reducing state revenue by 60 percent, which naturally had a devastating effect on all aspects of public education, particularly to the University of California system, where Mom was a dean. At this time, house values were also being reappraised all over Los Angeles. In an unprecedented climate of inflation and wage stagnation (coined "stagflation") some houses, including ours, were doubling their value every few years. Modest houses like ours were purchased at about $60,000 in 1976, and by 1979 they were valued well over $100,000. To make matters worse, mortgages were saddled with interest rates around 15 percent at that time. Without any wage increases, and the gutting of university budgets, Mom must have worried incessantly about the ever increasing cost of running a household, especially if Chuck couldn't find work to contribute to it. These worries must have added stress to their relationship. Two teenage boys, a sometimes-employed jazz musician competing for gigs in the world's most musical and talented city, and a breadwinner mother in the demographic crosshairs of a ruthless stagflation. Chuck probably got read the riot act and Mom probably told him he had to start pulling his weight financially. This is just a post hoc assessment because, as a kid, I didn't pay attention to matters of bill paying and Mom's stress was never foisted upon us. But a sudden eruption of inexplainable violence made an indelible imprint on my memory that I have spent a lifetime analyzing.

If you've ever been shaken out of a deep sleep, you know how disorienting it is. Fear hormones rush through your body, scrambling your wits so you don't know which way is up, where the door is, or what room you are sleeping in. You are paralyzed but for two basic instincts: fight or flight. And yet, one sure thing remains: in that instant you know thyself. And soon thereafter, in my case, you know who your mom is.

I remember being stirred at first, hearing hushed tones of bitter resentment followed by louder booms of drunken protest. Still in slumber, it could have been a dream, so I stayed put under my covers and curled to my side. But the next burst of noise was too horrible to ignore. It sat me straight up and forced my conscious brain to fire its synapses and get a grip on the shuddering fear that was overtaking me. Upon my disoriented waking awareness, I heard Mom down the hall utter a kind of strained, panicked grunt followed by thuds of feet, like they were bracing, struggling to maintain balance as if a scuffle was going on. Suddenly, a thunderous boom shook the whole house and Mom squawked like a running back might when he is taken down by a devastating tackle.

At this point, the fear and disorientation had completely paralyzed me. But something was crystal clear: Mom was in trouble. Were we being robbed by burglars? Was this a break-in? More sounds of struggle came from down the hall as I heard Mom breathing heavy, and crying. Was that the sound of a fist on a cheekbone? I had never heard what it sounds like when knuckles crush facial flesh, so how could I be sure? Was that a muffled "help" I just heard? Why wasn't anyone helping Mom? My brother was probably paralyzed by fear too in his own bedroom. "Oh shit," I thought, "that means I have to get out of bed and do something to help her!"

I guess bravery is something that no one really knows they have until the worst possible moments in life require it. I rose from the womb of my twin bed, walked to the door, and knew not what I was going to do when I opened it. I had no weapons, no strength, no skills at fighting, no size to overwhelm an intruder, and no experience in de-escalating or disarming acts of violence. I had only a voice to use, and an invisible umbilicus that motivated me to push through my fear and swing open that tiny crack of light that emanated from the hallway through my bedroom door. It was "go time" for better or for worse. What was waiting at the end of the hall had to be confronted. Mom's life was in danger! I had to get out there and experience it with her.

It felt like I was walking to my own execution. Whoever is bringing this violence to our house is surely going to kill me when they see me poke my head into their business. And yet I had to witness the drama for myself. This was life, stark and consequential. Get out there and do something! Like a peristaltic movement, something was pushing me forward. I knew there was only one direction to go. Mom needed me out!

Sometimes, when the inconceivable confronts you, the world becomes a confusing place. I emerged from my sanctuary and beheld an impossible sight: Mom was helpless on her back and Chuck was on top of her. His right arm was cocked and fisted high above his shoulder, and his left arm was straight and groping at Mom's throat. Instead of being afraid, I was immediately, oddly, relieved to see a familiar man, instead of a stranger, responsible for the violence. It was probably the sense of surprise rather than fear that overtook me when I used all the force I could muster to scream at the top of my lungs: "Chuuuuck! What are you doing?"

This was enough. Midway through his right cross he paused, released Mom's neck as if he was caught red-handed, and locked his bloodshot eyes on mine. For what seemed like an eternity, but was probably only a few seconds, we three froze in our positions, not knowing the future impact of the moment, each individual equally disheartened and astonished. We said not a word. I, paralyzed in my stance, awaited instructions. Mom somehow mustered her composure from her prostrate position and serenely said, "Go back to bed, baby."

I tucked myself in, contented that the violence had ended. Mom's command was all I needed to reassure me that she was going to be all right. I cried a little because life in LA wasn't all it was supposed to be. I thought a dad should be in the house to handle things like this. But then again, Mom wanted Chuck to fill that role, or so I thought.

After about a half hour, Chuck came in and sat down by my bedside. I had no fear of him because I considered him part of the family. He wasn't there to hurt me. I'm sure that Mom demanded that he go and "make it right" with me. So I was treated to my first dose of that all-too-common language of bullshit spewing from alcoholics: drunk sincerity. "You know I would never do anything to hurt your mother, right Sammy?" "I know," I said. Of course I would have said anything just to get him to leave. He reeked to high heaven of alcohol and smoke. "So you don't worry and just get back to sleep." "Okay," I agreed. But I didn't sleep much that night. From that moment on I shuddered whenever an unusual sound emanated from somewhere unseen, even the slightest creak from a door or a cat fight in the backyard. I remained constantly vigilant.

The next morning, it was the normal routine at Graffin U. west campus. Us boys got ourselves ready for school and Mom was in the bathroom preparing for a normal workday. My brother and I never spoke about what went on the night before. He must have buried his head in the pillow, and I didn't blame him because that's what I wanted to do too. Strangely, Mom didn't mention it either. Chuck remained behind closed doors, sleeping off his hangover.

The most devastating vision imaginable is seeing your Mom trying to cover up marks of physical violence. Mom had purple marks around her neck, so she put on a turtleneck. Her left eye had the most ghastly ring around it. Black and purple at the same time, there was no way she could go out in public with a shiner like that. She slipped on a pair of oversized dark sunglasses to hide the bruises on her face and the sadness in her eyes. Thank goodness Mom had a very good "support group" of close confidants and family friends. I'm sure they helped her get through her days, and I know she spent nearly all of her free time in their company. Mom and Dad taught me and my brother that the value of friends is nearly as important as family, and that it is worth putting a lot of effort into friendships. It was times like this when I saw that wisdom come to fruition. Our family friends were there for us, even though we never spoke of our personal hardships openly.

What was extremely out of character for me, I told no one at school. I didn't even mention it to my dad on our weekly phone calls. My brother and I seemed to have an unspoken agreement to leave it unspoken. Even Mom never mentioned it to us until much later in life when we were adults. But one thing was made clear by the events that followed: violence in our household would never be tolerated.

Mom saw to it that our family would not have to endure any more nights like that one. It may have seemed like a draconian measure and a drastic action, but she told Chuck to "get your shit and hit the road." Of course, I'm paraphrasing because I wasn't privy to the conversation. But the fact remains, Mom was the dean of this campus, and she remained so even in her bruised and battered state. Chuck, however, was gone after that night of terror. He never stepped foot in the house again and we never saw him after he left. When we got home from school, he was gone. He moved to an apartment not far away. Mom had a few interactions with him, but he very quickly became a thing of the past.

To say I was relieved would be inconsiderate of the truth. Relief, yes, that no more violent interactions could occur; relief, yes, to discover that my mom was strong enough to be in control and guide our family. But relief was nowhere to be found in reassurances that our family was headed somewhere good. I loved Chuck. I thought it was cool having a musician in the family. As a child, I wasn't sophisticated enough to understand the seriousness of his transgressions. So I started to question authority. The professor and the dean were supposed to be in charge and confidently steer the direction of Graffin U. even if it met with obstacles. The dean was in charge out West, but the wildly unpredictable landscape—riddled with active fault lines that constantly crept along, turning stable bedrock into powder—was taking its toll on her aspirations of a tranquil home. I couldn't help but wonder if she would have been more successful back on the stable craton of the Midwest. It seemed like now she possessed a resolute, private determination to see this thing through, even if it shook the family to its core. Meanwhile, back in Wisconsin, the professor's curriculum was intact and comfortably predictable. Homelife was dependably routine there, whereas in LA it was "anything goes." There were no guarantees that this entire episode—the western expansion of Graffin U.—would actually pan out.

Getting beat down with violence is bad enough. It took a Wonder Woman's resolve to shake it off. But within months Mom's next life-changing beatdown would come at the hands of a regressive societal backlash that was sweeping the entire country and that affected working women particularly.

8A. A WOMAN'S PLACE

"What are you ladies doing in this class? At this university?" the professor asked, in 1960 at Mom's chosen graduate school, Indiana University Bloomington. "Don't you know that you are taking the spot that should be reserved for men?" he spouted from the lectern. The reasoning of this bigoted view was that graduate school was meant to educate those who were heading for professorial jobs in higher education. K–12 teaching jobs were appropriate for women, and indeed Mom's undergraduate degree from Ball State's Teachers College in Muncie, Indiana, prepared her for that. But university jobs were earmarked for men, generally speaking. Back then it didn't matter how smart you were. A woman's place was in the home. College professors were supposed to be trained to think. Thinking is an all-time job, not just nine to five. Women teachers (like my grandmother, Mom's mom, Elsie Zerr Carpenter) could hold down an elementary school job and still make it home to tend the house in the afternoon and cook dinner at night. Professors, however, had to remain on campus, bring their work home with them, retire after dinner to the reading room, and wake up early with deep thoughts about the day's lecture. It was all very prescribed and predictably routine. No sir, women were not supposed to be in graduate school learning how to be professors. But Mom was there, after a life of academic excellence and skipping grades in the K–12 years, after winning multiple blue ribbons and gold medals in the 4-H competitions each year, and after memorizing the entire Bible and reciting it from memory as required by her grandfather, she was better read than many of her professors. She wasn't going to let some disparaging, bullying man with a PhD guilt her out of school or get in her way. She sought achievement at the highest level and learned to ignore the demeaning, chauvinistic small-mindedness of her unsupportive professors.

It was this drive for achievement that led her to the deanship, first at the University of Wisconsin–Milwaukee, and then at UCLA. Mom reached her academic apex in the 1970s during an era when women were part of the landscape of the diversity initiatives spun off from the equality and civil rights movements of the 1960s. Universities were eager to recruit and hire

women at top administrative positions. In California, her job was to over-
see a department that was created for "learning skills." In short, the program was meant to help disadvantaged students get better grades through
training, tutoring, and counseling. The funding model for this department,
and for the enviable University of California system as a whole, was based
largely on property taxes. When Mom got hired at UCLA, buying a house
meant being hooked into a serious tax responsibility. The only consolation
was that the taxes went to a good cause. The public school system in California, including the world-class universities and state schools, was the
envy of the nation. All those property taxes covered the education system
and plenty more was left over. California had a $5 billion surplus in 1977.
But the conservatives weren't having it.

Proposition 13 was a conservative Republican agenda pushed by the lob-
byist Howard Jarvis. When it passed in 1978, Mom's entire livelihood was
suddenly in jeopardy. Just looking at Howard Jarvis brought back haunting
memories for Mom. "He looks just like those professors in Indiana who
told me that women don't belong in their classrooms." Jarvis spoke of the
"moochers and loafers" in public office who eat up our tax money. His mission was called "tax revolt," and it proves that the subsequent Tea Party
brand of politics was nothing new. He implored people to "show those
politicians who is boss! Cut your taxes by 60 percent!" He found a wide
audience to heed his short-sighted complaining. The initiative passed by a
landslide vote of 65–35.

Proposition 13 put a cap on property tax increases and simultaneously
depleted the education budget. Despite property values in general rising
by 15 to 25 percent annually at the time—resulting in huge tax windfalls
for the state of California to be used for education programs—the Jarvis
initiative limited tax payments by homeowners to no more than 1 percent
annually. All sounds good for many sectors of the economy and society. But
the shortsightedness becomes clearer when you consider education.

The vast majority of Californians live in communities with modest in-
comes and low real estate values—despite what people think, California is
not all glittering mansions, golf courses, and beach houses. They didn't pay

much in real estate tax to begin with, and they were hurt in more significant, long-term ways. Before the conservative "tax revolt," low- and modest-income families could still depend on a good education system, well-funded schools, after-school programs, and high teacher salaries. Living in modest or poor neighborhoods was offset by having access to a high-quality education and a focus on academic achievement, which brought with it a spirit of hopefulness and aspiration for improvement. But after the passage of Proposition 13, huge holes formed in the state's education budget. The proposition also mandated that the state legislature could not raise taxes for any reason without a two-thirds majority vote. This meant that not only schools, but health care, welfare, public works, and even fire departments were soon to be strapped for cash, basically eroding the foundational substrate of society for most California citizens.

Being educated is one thing nobody can take away from you. It takes lots of tax money to create a society of well-funded schools. Using taxes for schools is an ethical and moral proclamation of your community. It says that the focus of our society is centered on improvement, development, and nurturing of the thing that is most important: the people. Living in a society of uneducated people is misery, no matter how rich you are. What does it say about you if your sparkling neighborhood is totally surrounded, soon to be engulfed, by blocks and blocks of squalor and ignorance? It says you must be kidding yourself that your island is any kind of paradise.

Mom's learning skills department was dissolved shortly after the passage of Proposition 13. With its dependency on state funding, the University of California's budget was gutted in 1978. Tuition was increased dramatically, but even this couldn't offset the funding shortfalls, and all "nonessential" departments were affected. Mom's staff had to be fired, and shortly thereafter, her position was terminated. Her career as an academic was over. No offer of recompense nor reassignment was given. Thank you for your service, now pack your shit and get out!

In some ways, in hindsight, the termination of a department headed by a woman in 1979 was par for the course. She was clearly in the crosshairs of an all-too-eager conservative agenda whose misogynist and racist themes have recurred over and over again since the 1960s from the right-wing minority. Taxes are bad, women and minorities shouldn't be in positions of power (they only got there because they have been unfairly favored), and kids don't need expensive programs or community-based support or small classrooms for their education and social development. In short, the conservative agenda had been whispering in Mom's ears all along: *Ladies, you're on your own! So if you want to get divorced, be the head of household, you better be able to wear the pants because we ain't going to help you. Don't come asking your government for handouts to help you with your selfish agenda.*

The western branch of Graffin U. was now decapitated. With its administrator in turmoil, what direction would we go? Mom explained to us that we would have to live very modestly for the foreseeable future. It meant forgoing many of the niceties that she had hoped to provide after the move out to California. Ours would not be a well-funded household: no color TVs, no fancy furniture, nor much extra cash for expendable items. It meant "plain wrap" from the grocery store. Mom did what was necessary: took loans from Momo, depleted her savings, got extensions on house payments, whatever she could do to keep a roof over our heads. My brother and I were expected to get jobs (deliver newspapers, wash dishes, or so on) if we wanted extra cash. But for me, laziness, and the excuse of regular travel back to see Dad, kept me from trying too hard to be industrious. Mom spent the days at a borrowed office space she got from a friend. She would spend the next year writing her dissertation, working toward a PhD, which she eventually received. She wisely enlisted a headhunter to help her search for high-paying jobs, wherever they may be throughout Southern California.

After about a year, Mom decided to enter the private sector, landing a good job as a corporate human resources director. "Academics fight so viciously because the rewards are so meager," she once told me. In the corporate world she would come to find that the objectives were clearly laid out, and the job was much more predictable. Many years later she rose through the ranks, made lots of good friends, and was cherished in her role because of her intelligence and good humor.

But for now, the dean was no longer present at home. Our house became quiet and subdued. After school my brother and I retreated to our bedrooms. Occasionally my junior high buddy Jon would come over and we would listen to records, maybe have a sleepover. But most days of my school year were spent feeling like an alien in a foreign land. I was not a California kid at heart. I didn't have the basic tools to fit in: didn't skateboard, didn't surf, didn't smoke pot; my friends weren't the cool kids. I dreamed of being back in Wisconsin a lot, where it didn't matter who was cool and who wasn't, and I looked forward to school holidays when I could fly back there to see my pals.

One might expect that after such a string of hard luck Mom might have packed up or given up. But she never outwardly complained to me or my brother. She quietly and resolutely persevered and looked forward to her next adventure. Grant and I were along for the ride. We didn't know it then, but we were experiencing a new social reality: the new American society where moms could be heads of households, decision makers, and though husbandless, still serve as respected pillars of the community.

This unwritten social contract required sacrifice of conventional roles, particularly the tender motherly attention of past generations. Of course, I took this as a personal affront, being a mama's boy now in his teens. But the rebirth of Dean Graffin produced a new archetype of the American household. Is it any wonder that *The Brady Bunch* was both hated and yet loved by Americans enough to make it the number one show on television? Women breadwinners like my mom hated it. "Oh God! It is so insulting!" they'd say about Carol Brady and her traditional role as a housewife. Us kids from divorced households watched it with interest, because we could sympathize with the awkwardness of siblings who were only "half" related as stepchildren. Female empowerment TV shows, like *Maude*, *Rhoda*, *The Mary Tyler Moore Show*, or *Alice* were more in keeping with divorced mothers who were rewriting the norms of American society: strong, opinionated women who were the stars and masters of their own situational hardships. Such shows appealed to Mom and she never missed an episode.

For Mom, the divorce, the interracial bigotry, the beating, and the failed dream of a happy domestic partnership became unimaginable hardships. They were all interwoven with a lifetime of workplace bias and regressive conservative judgments about "women's roles" from a society that she had long ago decided needed to change. Now, she was going to have to go it alone. Although none of it was overtly stated nor discussed, I could sense a seething undercurrent of resentment percolating in our home. This conservative agenda, disguised as a property tax initiative, was, in reality, a thinly veiled shroud covering its regressive views of women, and it took its toll on us. It undermined the family enterprise and spirit. Proposition 13 fell squarely on our house, but instead of saving it, it destroyed the breadwinner. Society was full of shit, and it wasn't hard to see that from my vantage point.

The seeds of discontent were planted. In about a year or so they would grow as I emerged from this complicated childhood and stepped onto a punk stage. Their spores I'd release to the wind as lyrics and melodies in Bad Religion.

SECTION TWO

9
THE MORNING
AFTER . . .

After the previous night's Westwood punk adventure, I woke to a typical Saturday morning in the San Fernando Valley: the sun already high and scorching by 10:30 a.m., dogs barking in the neighborhood at the ever-present taunting crows and mockingbirds, lawn mowers buzzing gently from suburban dads starting their chores, the kids next door splashing in their pool. Endless summer to the uninitiated.

My late start to each weekend day as a teen was caused not by hangover but by monotony; a monotony that parallels the aseasonality in the weather. Back in Wisconsin, during the fall, each day edged a little closer to the shutdown of winter. Each spring day brought you a bit closer to that vernal paradise of long day length and perpetual outdoors. Excitement was there each morning and it made getting out of bed worthy of the act. But in LA one cannot trust the weather to be motivating; it's always the same! The will to move, therefore, has to emerge as a force from within. The life force that foments accomplishment had to kick in if I were ever to rise at an early hour.

As a teenage boy in 1981, this was too much to ask. Having not yet determined a life's strategy, and yet having no excuses for laziness, I must have seemed like a louse to the academics and adults in my mom's circles. I didn't really care, but I did feel like I had to prove myself as worthy in some way. I wanted to impress the grown-ups just as we had as little kids when we dutifully repeated jokes we learned from *Monty Python* so that the professors in the other room would laugh and appreciate our precociousness.

I was in a band, but that wasn't enough. A punk band was not any way to gain respectability. Being in a punk riot with the police didn't score any high marks from my mom, so I kept last night's antics to myself. I didn't actually think it was fun, or exciting. The artistic flair of punk rock was in fact respectable in the ethical milieu of my family. But there was nothing artistic experienced last night. Just a world of brutality, injustice, tribalism, and combat, all topics actively avoided in our academic households. Graffin University taught pop art, drama, English literature, and the administration-promoted integration and diversity. How could I reconcile my activities among punk lowlifes with the high standards of my upbringing?

While most of my friends were sleeping off their hangovers that morning, I rolled out of bed and pulled up to my reading table. I had taken on a major, self-imposed, reading assignment. My desk was nothing more than a folding card table with a flimsy Masonite top and a matching desk chair. I purloined this setup from Mom's closet, a rig she used occasionally as a makeshift sewing station. It was wide enough for me to place a row of paperbacks on it, all titles that were to form my budding library of natural history. Le Gros Clark's *The Antecedents of Man*, Bronowski's *The Ascent of Man*, and Richard Leakey's *Origins*.

While I actively skimmed those titles for song ideas, I never actually read them in their entirety from front to back. I felt ashamed that I had no patience to read deeply and completely like I knew intellectuals were supposed to do. So I forced myself to read a massive tome in its entirety, even if I could only spend an hour a day doing so. Luckily, for this feat I chose a great page-turner that would give me intellectual credibility in years to come. It was Charles Darwin's *Voyage of the Beagle*.

Somehow, I was able to read into Darwin's narrative a tale fitting for a punk rocker. Here was a man, groomed by his intellectual, high-achieving parents to join the clergy—even sending him to Cambridge University for that purpose—but who ended up rejecting divinity school and disappearing from society for many years on an around-the-world journey of natural history exploration. Darwin's ultimate "fuck you" came in the form of overturning the theological interpretation of nature as intelligently designed. He did this by crafting the modern secular, scientific view—called evolution—that has no place for gods nor ultimate plans nor purpose.

Every weekend morning I read a little bit more of Darwin's natural history research and it brought me satisfaction. Here was an original course of study little discussed at Graffin U. I became a resident expert. I soon picked up a paperback edition of *The Origin of Species* by the same author and found it difficult to read from cover to cover. But I gleaned what was needed for general comprehension, and integrated it into the biology class I was taking at the time. There was no module for evolution in high school biology at this time in the LA Unified School District's curriculum. So I asked the teacher if I could present a slideshow on evolution, and she agreed. This was my first lecture on the subject and it consisted of a number of skull photographs taken from the pages of my books and presented as a chronology of human evolution. I received an "A" in biology, a field mastered by neither Mom nor Dad; something that made the professor and the administrator proud!

But what of my punk comrades? They were still sleeping off their hangovers as I was probing deep into the Pantanal with Darwin. How could I justify any kind of academic success with the debauchery and recklessness of a punk lifestyle? My bandmates and I got along musically, but they weren't really interested in school.

Luckily, I had a friend named Jodi who was a most enthusiastic supporter of intellectual pursuits. She too had divorced parents, but lived in a more affluent, upper middle-class neighborhood called Sherman Oaks. Jodi drove a BMW to punk gigs, but like me didn't really fit in with the punks' violent attitudes. Jodi had successfully applied for a grant from the NEH (National Endowment for the Humanities) to study some arcane French topic, and she encouraged me to apply as well. "They will give you, like, a thousand dollars to visit the Smithsonian!" she said. I knew of a lot of fossils I wanted to study, maybe add to my lecture material, hmm, and use the $1,000 to buy some boots and a leather jacket! "Okay, can you xerox the application forms for me?"

Jodi got me the forms. But she couldn't help me craft a successful proposal. I was soundly rejected. Jodi had strong letters of support from her high school counselors, whereas I was "winging it" without support letters. I didn't even know who any of the high school counselors were. Although Jodi couldn't help me win the $1,000 grant, she always encouraged me, and she made me feel that pursuing academics was cool.

In my room, I knew that I was one of the fortunate ones. I had a home, a place to escape from the rioting, mean streets of Hollywood—somewhere to collect my thoughts and to process what happened last night. Many punkers were not so lucky. Some of my cohort were kicked out by their parents for not conforming to rigid family standards of decent dress and proper behavior and religious beliefs. More often, they were the kids who suffered most from the police brutality, or violence from other factions. With nowhere to run, they faced the torment and recovered from their wounds in the urban alleyways and cultivated hedgerows of city parks. All my closest friends were safe and secure, but we hung out with many who were hungry and hurt, always using the nightlife comradery of punk to search for their next meal and a place to stay.

Punk was a class war. For all its claim to be egalitarian and communal, in reality, at least in Southern California, it conformed to Malthusian and Darwinian principles, paradoxical at its core. Through struggle, warfare, strife, and conflict came progress. Clearly, my friends and I were able to progress and avoid the scuffle while those without means did the dirty work of the battle and suffered for punk's sake. They were never going to go on and form punk bands. More likely, they would end up on skid row. The paradox of the Malthusian metaphor, progress through conflict, hovered over the creation of this subculture that was marked by the self-destruction of many of its practitioners. Such was the hallmark of the social circles in which I now found myself engaged.

Ponderous thoughts about my social surroundings percolated in my brain and left me craving more learning and creative endeavors. It was a philosophical motivation that kept me engaged in punk and academics simultaneously. The excitement of the street life each evening and the romance of playing music were the tangible assets that made teenage life bearable, and were like a Band-Aid to cover the sorrows I felt from my broken family's recent trials.

10
JUVENILE
DEBAUCHERY '80–'82

Today it's easy to read about punk rock debauchery in Southern California between the years of 1979 and 1982. Scores of writers who lived through that era have now penned memoirs and histories. Some glorify the traits that I found unpalatable. If you don't like to read, there are documentary films galore showing images of youth gone wild and countless bands that accompanied them, serenading the kids to riotous destruction of themselves and others in their wake. Autobiographers have a way of inflating the details of a past riddled with danger and intrigues. The most common motif is "redemption" and, therefore, to make good storytelling the drama is increased when the past ills are more extreme. The redemption is always more sweet when the odds are depicted as unusually unfavorable and unfairly stacked against the protagonist.

But my story is not one of redemption. It's an ongoing puzzle of self-awareness. My level of self-awareness at the age of seventeen in 1982 was almost the same as it was when I was eleven years old. It has evolved slowly and haphazardly ever since. I wasn't attracted to the lowlife associations with punk rock. I saw punk as a creative and exciting outlet. Like other areas in my life, it required some good fortune and proper steering to stay away from miscreants and the penal system alike. Among my friends who dabbled in drugs or alcohol, I was not seen as someone to call up when it was time to go out and be delinquents. I heard stories secondhand, after the fact. "Greg, we made a pipe bomb and blew up a Cadillac!" "Greg, we scored some blow and snorted it only to find out it had bleach in it!"

My bandmate Brett treated me like a younger brother in some ways, even though I had an older brother already. In fact, Brett and my brother Grant were in some classes together at El Camino Real High School. They shared the same love of winning games that required intelligence, such as chess and Dungeons & Dragons. But they didn't play with each other. Brett was worldly and mobile (he had a car or a van at all times), highly gregarious, and loved hanging out. Grant kept to himself mostly. He tolerated my friends, and he had his own friends who were into Devo and Tubeway Army, and played strategy games. They never invited me to join them. Even though I still looked up to my older brother, especially for his intelligence, I wanted more brotherly excitement, and I got that from Brett.

Brett would often try to introduce me to drugs. He once said, "Dude, I have to be high just to be around you," because of my hyperactivity. "Try some of this hash." I felt worldly because he taught me how to light a lump of hash mounted on a pin, then cup it with a highball glass turned upside down, then inhale the cloud as it escapes from underneath as you lift the glass. I liked the smell of it. But having tried it and feeling no effect, I never wished for more.

Sometimes I would go with Brett to score acid from really strange people up in Topanga Canyon. In 1981 and 1982 the area was not far removed from the cultish, reclusive drug subculture of the Manson Family, whose compound was not far away on the other side of the San Fernando Valley. Strange, shadowy figures emerged from Topanga's back roads when Brett pulled over on some predetermined dirt driveway. One of the guys looked like Ian Anderson from the cover of Jethro Tull's *Aqualung* and handed Brett a small package through the open driver's side window, which he quickly passed over to me as he handed the dealer some cash. The guy called Brett "brother," which I thought was like a hippie stereotype. But aside from the paranoia—the guy was swiveling his head from side to side constantly scanning for far-off adversaries—it seemed like a smooth operation to me. Unlike the hashish, some of which Brett had offered to me, this transaction made LSD seem like more serious stuff. There was no way I was going to try LSD, and I was never offered any. Still, it was fun to feel like Brett's trusted accomplice in a true rite of passage: an American recreational drug score, a holdover from the hippie era.

My punk friends in Hollywood had different things in mind. The geographic distance between Hollywood and Topanga Canyon is only sixteen miles. But to this day the two localities exhibit the true extremes of Southern California living. Heading into Topanga Canyon, you get the feeling you're heading back to the Old West. Here you find horse ranches, board-and-batten outbuildings, rocky outcrops, and isolated outdoorspeople who don't want to be bothered with modern fashions or trendy norms. Their lifestyles seem to match those of the outlaws in the movie *Easy Rider*. They came to the canyon to escape the modern world, and didn't care to keep pace. Hollywood people, on the other hand, live on the streets and their vitality depends on the pulse of immediacy going on in the vibrant metropolis. The constant encroachment of tourists and the nightly influx of suburbanites to the clubs and bars and theaters makes for a shifting landscape of uncertainty and nightly opportunity. The Hollywood punk rockers were not interested in the weed-smoking hippies and their antiquated styles. Speed and heroin ruled the streets, and virtually all of my friends were experimenting with them on the streets of Hollywood. But Brett remained mostly in the West Valley, close in spirit and proximity to the adventurous canyons and tumbleweeds, preferring to get high with close friends and enjoy good tunes in the homely confines of the living room, music den, or rehearsal garage.

I too preferred to hang out with friends at home rather than on the streets. But sometimes I found myself in Hollywood after a gig with a rougher crew of users. My confident attitude and projected Midwestern values (I suppose) meant that they never asked me to take part in their drug use. Whenever they scored, they only garnered enough for themselves. My role, in our group—due to my steady hand and interest in biology—was to administer their drugs. They joked that I was "the doctor." These drugs scared me because I never wanted to put stuff in my body that altered my awareness. But I felt a sense of honor that they trusted me with a hypodermic needle, and I had no qualms at the time because I just felt like this is normal teenage behavior for street punks in Hollywood. If I could be the doctor, it would forever establish my role as someone who was not subject to peer pressure to consume the drugs themselves. It was a way to be part of "the gang" without getting high. That suited me just fine.

We were children, running wild without a clue as to the implications of our actions. I felt like I had a role to play in our crew and that somehow I was less of a delinquent than those who were taking the drugs, because I wasn't altering my consciousness with chemicals. This was a juvenile illusion, but it kept me sober. Some went on to quickly develop addictions. Some of them only lived a few years longer. I didn't stop to consider my own role in their downfalls. My only act of resistance was not getting high myself. If they would only follow my lead, I believed we could have a more meaningful relationship and it could keep them from potentially overdosing. I thought maybe we could develop a brotherhood around common interests—movies, sports, or science (just like my best friends back in Wisconsin). But we were SoCal punk rockers hanging out in Hollywood. Style way overshadowed substance when it came to friendships. They were trying to forge an identity, and so was I. You do a lot of stupid shit when you're involved in such pursuits.

This was the tail end of an era when drugs were widely available for teenagers to acquire on the streets, in the schoolyards, and from their parents. Except for the occasional trip up the canyon with Brett, I never saw the deals go down. My friends were always "holding." Maybe they got them from an older sibling, or maybe they stole money from their mom's purse and bought them from the neighborhood dealer. Maybe they bought a weekend's worth to share or secretly stashed away a month's supply just for themselves. It was all a big mystery to me, but the common sight of drugs such as quaaludes, weed, hash, brown heroin, black beauties, and various white powders in small folded paper pouches was such a part of my SoCal cultural milieu that even back in junior high school there were ample opportunities to partake. I was now a junior in high school and I had no sense of taboo surrounding any of these substances.

I was first offered a quaalude in an art class as a seventh grader. The girl who offered it to me was constantly high. A really sweet face and corpulent body, she was in ninth grade and ditched class as often as she showed up to it. She had the aroma of marijuana. It pervaded her clothes, hair, and breath too. She had a crush on me, just like she did on all the boys. But when she offered me the pill in the back room where the art supplies were shelved, on the verge of my first-ever makeout session, I just said no and she took no offense. But she quickly set her sights on another kid who eagerly shared in her altered state. I felt no shame in rejection. I walked with the confidence and security of knowing that back in Wisconsin I had a different circle of friends. I would be spending my summer with them as soon as the semester was over. Back there, our friendships were based on being in the same neighborhood and growing up together from the time we were in diapers. I could never present myself to them as a drug-addled "burnout" from Los Angeles.

Divorce brings a kind of shame to children. Even in the best of cases, the kids are always involved in explaining the nature of their family to other kids. "Where's your dad?" "Why did they get divorced?" Sometimes, it's even harder on the kids when the divorce is "amicable," because there isn't a clear reason why the household is split. When Mom took the job in Los Angeles, I felt a tremendous impulse to report only positive feedback to my friends and family back in Wisconsin each summer. Inside, I was nervous and cautious about life in SoCal. Culturally, Los Angeles was so different from southeastern Wisconsin, especially for a teenage boy. The move to LA meant the immediate cessation of my weekly pickup basketball, baseball, and football games with neighborhood playmates. All extracurricular

sports in the San Fernando Valley were highly organized into Pop Warner leagues that were daunting to me and too time-consuming for my
single-mom household to support. This meant I could not regale my Wisconsin friends with glorious athletic stories from the West Coast.

They say that kids feel guilty from their parents' divorce. I never once
felt culpable for their inability to get along. But I felt a strange compulsion
to always make the best of the separation and report to my friends only the
benefits of living in two different houses with none of the drawbacks. There
had to be some benefit to the extreme geographic separation. There was no
way I could face my friends in Wisconsin, or my dad for that matter, and
spend an entire summer playing sports and spending every waking hour
outdoors, as we often did, if I returned with any kind of interest in drug
culture. It's remarkable how the ubiquity of drugs in SoCal at this time
was matched by near complete scarcity of them back in my neighborhood
of Racine, Wisconsin. Had I been using in LA, it would have been a long,
lonely summer of jonesing when I got back to Wisconsin.

Because of this disconnect in cultures, I had to find something to bridge
the gap. There had to be something unique that was obtainable for me only
in LA. Music was that thing. Even though my musical "career" began before
the move out West—at grade-school choir in Milwaukee—I felt the impe-
tus to amplify my musical interests and skills after the move. There was,
after all, no viable punk "scene" among my friends in Wisconsin. LA was
the heartbeat of the entertainment industry. I could return each summer to
report to my friends that Los Angeles was a breeding ground for attaining
status in music. This could justify our family's drastic geographic boundaries and make sense of the divorce! For the first three summers, however, I
had no band. But I had a growing interest in music and an increasing desire
to go to concerts, and these sporadic activities were just enough to sustain a
narrative of positivity about my life in Los Angeles. By 1982, all questions
about my life in LA would be laid to rest because I returned to my summer
pals with a vinyl recording of Bad Religion's first LP, *How Could Hell Be
Any Worse?* My dad said, "Greggo, this is something you can always be
proud of."

But Dad was not totally ignorant of the debauchery in Hollywood. He had showed me an article from the *New York Times* about the LA punk scene that detailed the commonplace violence, drug use, and general nihilism of punks in the scene there. Dad said, "These better not be the kind of people who come to your gigs, Greggo!" I said, "Don't worry, they're not." But as a dad now myself, I look back and can say with confidence, we both knew I was lying.

Despite my dyed black hair, torn jeans, and new status as a punk singer, summers in Wisconsin were spent, just as they always had been, playing outdoor sports and riding bikes every day, all day with the neighborhood kids. There were no clubs to go to at night, there were no places to hang out or scam on girls. It was like *Leave It to Beaver* but more liberally minded. Life pulsed around diurnal activities. If you wanted more big-city "thrills" you would have to drive a little bit. Milwaukee is twenty-five miles up the road. Chicago is sixty miles in the other direction. Despite the nocturnal excitement offered by these metropolises, we rarely partook in their delights. I was content with the comradery of my pals during the long summer days and the security of my childhood home at night. I felt satisfied that my nightlife could remain as an activity in SoCal where it was a necessity in the growth of my musical life.

The debased activities of a teenage punk rocker in the early 1980s of SoCal would not be complete without a consideration of sexual exploits. It's hard to overstate how different the "health" education of the 1970s differs from that of today. In the Los Angeles Unified School District's junior high curriculum we had a class that taught very openly about the normality and even benefits of masturbation, the need for contraception, the wide availability and safe use of abortion, and the encouragement of consent between sex partners. Even though it wasn't a preferred method by any of us students, the teachers proclaimed that mutual masturbation instead of intercourse was a viable intimate experience. STDs were all treatable at this time. AIDS was not a commonplace concern yet. It was the end of the era of hippie free love, and most kids were taught that sex was nothing to be ashamed of. In fact, the greatest shame among junior high and high school boys was admitting to having no experience with the opposite sex. The girls at my school were often very open about their sexual preferences. There was a tendency for girls to dress very provocatively at this time. Low-cut halters with no bra. Skintight chemin de fer jeans that parted provocatively in the crotch, to produce what us delinquent teens called a camel toe, were all the rage. Many of the girls had regular sexual encounters with older guys. These girls we called "the experienced" ones, and throughout junior high I had no way of ever attracting their attention.

By the first semester of high school, when I was fifteen, I somehow caught the eye of one of these girls in my class, a known harlot who had a boyfriend a few years older than us. Her name was Sue and she seduced me one day by inviting me over to her house after school. I was constantly worried that her BF was going to come in at any time, but she assured me that they broke up and he wasn't interested in her anymore. I wasn't sure of how to proceed, but she was experienced and guided me to a successful first performance, right there on the couch in the living room of her parent's house while they were still away at work. Everything seemed to go smoothly and as I walked home a few blocks away I felt a strong emotion. Sue was so kind and had guided me with gentle authority. I felt indebted and comforted. I figured that this must be what love felt like, and by the time I got home I concluded that I was in love and wanted to let the whole world know. My first impulse was to report to my best friend, Jon, on the phone: "Jonny, I'm a man now!" But somehow, I wasn't able to express to him that I felt love for Sue. She was seen by my friends as a slut, someone who wasn't capable of tenderness. Nonetheless, I told my mom about my emotional connection with Sue (but not the sex part), and Mom said, "That's what being in love feels like, baby."

By the end of the semester Sue was no longer talking with me. Slowly but surely our phone conversations got shorter, our walks home from school together became fewer, and her interest in me faded. She had returned to her boyfriend who was older than me, had a job and a car, and smoked an awful lot of weed. Going back to her old BF made me feel like an experiment. She was just using me to make him jealous or perhaps to dip her toe in a different pond for recreation. I was devastated. Even though everyone else knew that Sue was not a serious consideration for a long-lasting relationship, I honestly believed that we were going to get married. The disappointment resulted in an angry revolt against social norms: I cut my hair short and dyed it pitch black. This was my act of "going punk," and it was spurred on by an emotional disappointment that allowed me to throw caution to the wind. Looking ridiculous and extreme was my way of saying, "Fuck you, Sue!" There were only a few other students at that time who were bold enough to dye their hair. They were seen as radicals and lunatics. I was so angry at Sue that I believed my extremism would cause embarrassment to her. Oh, the twisted illogical folly of youth and inexperience. She not only ignored me for the rest of her life, she simply reconnected with her old social circles, the same people who thought punk was bunk and extremists were losers.

My new punk persona was sufficient to attract the few other punk rockers at the school to begin hanging out with me in late 1979. There were older kids in my brother's class, and they considered me the immature kid brother who was just experimenting with style. Dead Rat Randy was the archetype of a gutter punk. He was exceedingly homely looking and had grizzled facial hair and a snarling countenance all the time. He was way ahead of his time and he even had a go at being a musician for a while. But we never got along or hung out together.

Another guy named Karl was interested in talking about punk. He was a bass player who never cut his long curly hair and listened to Stiv Bators and the Dead Boys. We connected on the level of musical taste, but he was also on the lunatic fringe of conspiracy theories, which he loved to discuss. He believed that our president at the time, Jimmy Carter, was a religious fanatic who hated punk rock. In fact, Karl believed that Carter had a secret agenda to eliminate punk rock from American society entirely, going so far as to ban record stores and radio stations that played or sold punk music. He was a fan of the Republican candidate Ronald Reagan because, according to Karl, Reagan loved punk music and was willing to support punk bands that were industrious and those that exemplified a true DIY ethic, which was more in keeping with the American conservative spirit.

I didn't know much about politics when I was fifteen, but I was almost positive that neither Reagan nor Carter could give two shits about punk rock and that Karl was way overthinking the matter. Needless to say, Karl was a good example of how political conspiracies can really hinder a friendship. Even though we both liked the same bands, Karl's relationship with me was conditional. He couldn't accept that my Democratic leanings were consistent with punk values—no matter that they were imparted by my family's preferences since I couldn't even vote at the time! "How can you not like Reagan when he's the only candidate that supports punk?" I was able to recognize, even at this young age, that some people's reasoning is asinine and based on neurotic obsessions and poorly researched assumptions. Karl and I did not hang out together because I quickly saw him as someone who was best kept as a mere acquaintance.

One of the coolest guys I met was a stylish Bowie look-alike named Doug. Doug loved Tubeway Army and was into photography. We hung out after school and dreamed of being in a new kind of musical band. We weren't content to be hemmed in by the constraints of punk; we wanted to define a new genre. "Let's call it War Rock," he said. Bold idea. But nothing came of it. Like my own, his parents were divorced and both worked hard so they were rarely involved in their kids' exploits. Doug's dad had a condo in Hollywood and one night we were allowed to stay there unaccompanied by any adults. His older sister drove us to the Whisky a Go Go and dropped us off to see Pearl Harbor and the Explosions. Oingo Boingo was the opening band. The music didn't move me, but I was really interested in the skimpy and revealing nightclub fashions of most of the girls. When the show was over, Doug and I took a taxi to his dad's condo and Doug revealed to me that he'd given his address to two girls who were coming over. I considered Doug a magician for having the know-how to secure such a deal. I had no idea how to talk to girls who turned me on. I was still scarred by my failed attempt, one year prior, to ask the sexiest girl in class if she wanted to go get an ice-cream cone after school with me. After she rolled her eyes and sneered "no" I saw her whispering to her crew as class was dismissed, pointing at me as the giggles reverberated down the hallway. This, coupled with the personal affront caused by Sue's toying with my emotions, destroyed my confidence in conversing with the opposite sex.

Sure enough, Doug was not lying. By around midnight, we heard a knock on the door. Two girls appeared. They were probably teenagers like us, but they seemed older and a lot more experienced in sexuality. They were wearing parachute pants and striped shirts that hugged their braless torsos. Bleached blonde hair and lots of makeup adorned their youthful, devious faces. All four of us were all smiles. Doug's dad kept a nice stylish apartment with a classy collection of alcoholic bevvies. The girls immediately helped themselves to hard drinks while I was content to sip my Coke. Doug liked to play the role of the experienced ladies' man, and indeed he was a smooth talker. The girls kept asking, "What kind of games are we going to play?" I had no idea what to say. I liked Monopoly, chess, Risk, and some card games, but I knew that was not going to cut it. Doug cleverly said, "Let's play Dromedary." This immediately appealed to one of the girls, and they exited to the bedroom. I was left twiddling my thumbs with the other girl, both of us unaware that the zoological reference pertains to *Camelus dromedarius* or the Arabian camel that has a single "hump." When I found out later that's what Doug meant, I was so angry that I hadn't thought of it! The other girl and I may have smooched a bit, but it was a classic awkward case of her waiting for me to make a move and me lacking the knowledge, skill, or confidence to move forward. As we heard the bed shaking in the other room, we watched HBO until it was finally time for the girls to leave.

A week or two later, Doug had a party at his mom's house, closer to my own, and he was once again successful in getting some girls to come over in the absence of any parents. While most of the partyers were in the living room smoking weed and drinking, one girl, Melissa, was flirting with me in the kitchen and asking me about the bands I liked. She seemed to know that I was staring at her low-cut, ripped V-neck T-shirt, and she motioned me over to the utility closet in the kitchen. We actually both fit inside of the little compartment that usually stores the brooms and mops and things. I have no idea how we succeeded, but I will always remember it because it was about the oddest place possible to consummate the lovemaking act.

A few days after the party I found out that Doug, too, had had sex with Melissa later that week. "Geez, I thought I was special!" I said to myself. I resented Doug for moving in on my new girlfriend, but in reality, of course, Melissa did not see me as a boyfriend at all but rather just a temporary plaything with which to try out a new sexual position in a seemingly impossible location. Melissa announced to Doug that she thought she might be pregnant, which precipitated an immediate war of finger-pointing between me and him. Doug was on the hook, but he craftily reasoned that since he came a few days after me that my sperm must have fertilized the egg first. I insisted that she would not have had sex with Doug if she already was pregnant with my baby. The comical absurdity of the argument notwithstanding, we were both petrified that we might have to be parents at the age of fifteen. I told no one about this, nor did Doug. We just hoped it would pass like a bad nightmare. It turned out that Melissa wasn't pregnant at all, and soon all three of us lost contact with each other.

Teenage life in the San Fernando Valley was plainly more dramatic and shocking than the lifestyles of the coddled and tame back in Wisconsin. When I went back to Racine for Christmas in 1979 I revealed to my buddy Arthur, who lived next door, that I was no longer a virgin. He claimed in disbelief, "You committed fornication?" I had no qualms about it, but I realized that my friends in LA and my friends in Wisconsin were developing at different rates. What was normal to teenage existence in LA was positively foreign to our gang of Midwestern neighborhood kids. It just seemed like you had to grow up faster in Los Angeles.

11

LOOKING FOR
BAD RELIGION

There weren't many scenesters in tenth grade in the San Fernando Valley in 1979. I was comfortable as a recently converted punk rocker, but I wanted to experience the scene, and maybe find a girlfriend who had a car so we could go to concerts in Hollywood or Orange County. But more than anything I wanted to sing in a band. Nearly all the punks were older than me.

I hung out each day with my pal Jon who was in my grade. Jon understood the differences between the kids in Wisconsin and in LA. He came back east to stay with us at my dad's house one summer. He loved the Dodgers, I loved the Brewers. But he also loved music, the one connection I shared with both my LA and Wisconsin friends. One day that summer, Jon joined me, my brother Grant, and my best friend in Wisconsin, Wryebo, as we ventured to a film festival in Milwaukee, at the Oriental Theater, that showed concert footage and musical shorts of avant-garde bands. This was just before the era of videos on television. Some bands and artists, however, anticipated MTV by shooting their own videos, syncing them to their own recorded music, and transferring the production to film so they could be shown at movie houses around the world. At the Oriental we watched the complete early film experiments of Devo, some grainy footage of Siouxsie and the Banshees, and other bands we had not yet heard of. But the highlight for us was Elvis Costello and his video for "(What's So Funny 'Bout) Peace, Love, and Understanding?"

That same day, probably in conjunction with the film festival, there was a swap meet going on along the sidewalk somewhere near the theater. All kinds of imports from the UK were available for purchase. It was here, on the streets of Milwaukee, where I picked up my first punk import, the 45 version of Sham 69's "Give a Dog a Bone." The highlight for me was the B side, "Mister You're a Better Man Than I." Jon bought *Armed Forces* by Elvis Costello and Wryebo bought Devo's *Are We Not Men?* These records were the original nexus of an incipient music collection that would become the transcendent link spanning the disparate cultural settings of two cities I would call home. This music was cool to my friends from LA as well as here in Wisconsin. Even though the cultures were so different, the music formed a cohesive social glue that was relatable to friends in both places.

It was 1980, and back at school in LA I met and hung out with an older girl named Kerry, already out of high school, who seemed more like a woman to me. She and I hit it off because I think she appreciated my intelligence about culture and art and science. Little did I know that this was all she was interested in. Kerry was a songwriter and guitarist who emulated Chrissie Hynde of the Pretenders, even sporting a little black lace half-glove on one hand. She drove a car, so I felt really excited that she was willing to take me along into Hollywood to see X perform at the Whisky. I never made any moves on Kerry and she never did on me either. I thought, "This platonic thing is kind of lame, but intellectually it works for me." It gave me the feeling of being part of the scene that was vibrant and "happening" outside of the San Fernando Valley. Still, it sort of nullified my status with other girls to be hanging out with an older woman in a purely intellectual relationship. It gave the impression that I was in a serious relationship and therefore "off limits" when in fact I was eagerly "open for business."

Kerry's circle of friends included no other girls. She knew a bunch of intellectual type punk rock dudes, and she was a musician. They liked to talk about songwriting and the meaning of songs. They were the first ones who had their fingers on the pulse of the LA punk scene. They had been going over to Hollywood for a year or more and had been to the legendary Masque club. They were the first to notice an influx of violence at punk shows. They alerted me to the bandanas sported by certain thugs from Huntington Beach, and to steer clear of them. I learned a lot from Kerry and her circle, but I had not yet begun writing music, so even though I tinkered on the piano they didn't really consider me a fellow musician. I was more like a younger tagalong. Still, they took me to some cool shows like X at the Whisky, and once we took a major excursion to Huntington Beach.

What a weird crew we composed. Kerry, the Chrissie Hynde look-alike, a six-foot-five walking stick named Gregg of all things, a former football jock named Scott who was stocky like a fullback with a crew cut, and me. But there we were, driving for over an hour to a dark and dingy warehouse in Huntington Beach called the Fleetwood. I was so excited because I had been listening to *Rodney on the ROQ* radio program every Sunday night for months, and finally I was going to see one of my all-time favorite bands I'd heard on this radio show: Black Flag. This was going to be my first time slam dancing. Gregg and Scott had been to other shows, so they were veterans of the slam pit. Kerry never intended to slam; she liked music for its meaning and style. She didn't have as much desire to release pent-up aggression like us boys did. Scott alerted me that the Fleetwood was supposedly a rough place, although they had never been there. I didn't care about any of that. I just figured everyone in the place was cool and that I would fit right in. We got there fashionably late to catch the end of one of the support bands' sets. It might have been Middle Class or Redd Kross. Regardless, upon entering the poorly lit hall I witnessed not slam dancing but a bunch of fists flying and long-haired dudes running for their lives! I thought, "Geez, those guys must have really pissed off the wrong crowd!"

Soon, Black Flag took the stage. I was one of perhaps four hundred other punk rockers anxiously anticipating their first song. The singer, Keith Morris, was wearing a homemade T-shirt that said "Circle Jerks." That had no meaning to me, since they had not recorded any music yet, but little did I know that they would become some of my best friends a few years later. When they opened the show, the entire room became a holding tank of ferocious energy, people bouncing off one another like gas molecules under high heat. Fists swinging, legs kicking, slamming to the beat of Robo's drums. When guitarist Greg Ginn broke into the opening of "Nervous Breakdown"—the song I had recorded off the radio and listened to incessantly—I joined in the fray and completely lost all sense of which direction was up. I got bounced around and fell to the ground, but I was quickly grabbed by another punk who lifted me back into the fray. My athleticism, particularly my abilities as a basketball forward, gave me stability as I twinkled on my tippy-toes in combat boots, bending my torso at the waist, holding my elbows out and swinging them wildly and alternately like a speed skater, all the while singing at the top of my lungs, "Crazy! Crazy! Crazy! Crazy! I'm crazy and I'm hurt . . . head on my shoulders . . . going Berzeeeerrrrk!" Since I came away from the slam pit unscathed I figured that I fit in just enough to get by. That night, on the drive home I felt like I was part of the scene. My mature and intellectual car-mates discussed politics and how they enjoyed the X show better. I thought they were nuts! This show was way more fun. And it turned out to be notable because it was Keith's last stand as singer of Black Flag—a night never to forget.

When we had seen X play, it was a real downer to me. I didn't realize it at the time, but it too was highly significant. X took the stage, but singer John Doe could barely address the audience. His cohort, Exene, was even more distraught and beside herself. She was crying inconsolably as the band began to perform. This was to be a special night because Ray Manzarek of the Doors was accompanying them on keyboard. It was a loud mess of a show, and the singers were literally wailing in disconsolation because of some tragedy that I couldn't comprehend. Maybe it was where we were standing, but the importance of what they were communicating was lost on me. It turned out that just before taking to the stage, they'd learned Exene's sister had been killed in a car crash on the way to the show. What a terrible night. And as a punk teenager I couldn't really grasp the magnitude of the tragedy. But Kerry and Gregg and Scott all agreed that it was a powerful performance. They loved Ray Manzarek too. I was an impatient punker who wanted some action and some slamming. I was too immature to be sensitive.

"Turning punk," the transformation punk rockers go through when they finally decide to cut their hair, wear more extreme clothes, change their outlook on the world, or make other kinds of changes to their daily lives in order to proclaim their nonconformity with established norms, is hard on some friendships. I lost a few friends, like Kenny, for instance, one of the first guys to befriend me at school when my family first arrived in Los Angeles. Kenny introduced me to some cool hobbies, such as magic. We both got pretty adept at performing stage illusions and close-up tricks because we took lessons and went to weekly demonstrations at Magic Emporium, a local hangout and magic shop. We played a lot of basketball together and had a number of classes together in junior high. His family sort of adopted me because they saw how well Kenny and I got along. They invited me to their Sabbath dinners on Fridays and we had sleepovers quite regularly. On a couple of occasions, they brought me to Palm Springs for weeklong escapes to Kenny's grandma's house during school breaks. I enjoyed the time we spent together, and the things and places Kenny and his family exposed me to expanded my world. When I went back to Wisconsin for the summers, Kenny and I kept up a great correspondence, writing letters each week to monitor the progress of our activities, his at a camp in SoCal and mine in the old hometown.

But as soon as I "went punk" Kenny began to distance himself from me. He didn't like the characters I started hanging around with. I thought it was just jealousy for my attention, but there must have been more to it. Kenny once wrote me a note that essentially chastised me for liking people he considered reprobates, and also criticizing punk music itself as lacking quality and musicianship. The invitations for sleepovers and family dinners ceased. I quickly realized that our friendship was highly conditional, predicated on a unity of superficial norms that I was eagerly rebelling against, namely style of dress and musical preference. I already knew that friendships didn't have to be so conditional.

My friend Jon also saw my transition to punkdom. Even though he didn't "go punk" per se, he was interested in the genre and was glad to learn about the music. He borrowed his mom's car and we went to the punk swap meets at Capitol Records in Hollywood to shop for records from England and other punk accessories. Jon gravitated toward the tamer stylistic dress of Elvis Costello whereas I wanted to look like Cal from Discharge, but we both recognized and bonded over the greatness of punk songwriting and punk's gradual infusion into society at large. Jon proved to me that true friendship was not to be disposed of when one of the parties decides to change. A good measure of the strength of a relationship is how well the friendship can grow in spite of those changes. Hence, a transformation could be a platform for strengthening the relationship. Unfortunately, Kenny didn't agree. He didn't want to acknowledge that "going punk" was anything but a recipe for social disaster. Our bond soon fizzled.

Luckily, there were new friends to be found. Jon and I held court every day at lunch time in the school's courtyard. After I dyed my hair and Jon wore his new skinny tie—emulating Elvis Costello in his *Trust* era—people started taking notice. Two types of people gravitated toward our little corner of the courtyard: those interested in punk music and those who loved harassing punks. Our school was suburban and there were a lot of narcs who policed the place every day. So it was really unusual to have any violence on campus. But once I was accosted in the hallway by the school quarterback who was trying to show his manhood by taking on someone taller than him. He stopped me in my tracks and said, "HEY! What are you looking at, punk?" I said, "What are you, a Dirty Harry wannabe?" He then began wailing on me with his fists, and I quickly used a tactic I learned years ago from my hero Muhammad Ali: rope-a-dope. I just covered my face with my forearms, bobbed my head, bent at the waist, and let the idiot swing away. He missed nearly all his shots and landed some feeble blows on my shoulders. After he tired himself out, his entourage of sycophants paraded him away down the hall and I heard him proclaim, "Punk sucks, you faggot!" The kids who were sympathetic to my plight, mostly the science nerds and the band geeks, gathered around me and saw that I was unscathed. A few of the Black kids who were bussed in to our school from South Central came up to me and said, "Man, why didn't you fight back? You coulda smoked his ass." I was fine, and I was content with my approach to such a superficial scrap with a lowlife. Taking the Gandhi approach is best: Do not lower yourself to the bully's standards. They always do themselves in on their own.

It was fun to see the variety of people who gravitated toward our area each day at lunch on the quad at high school. One day, an older punk rocker named Tom came over and started chatting with us. Tom and I hit it off immediately. He was wickedly smart, playful, and had that mischievous attitude that I really appreciated. We hung out after school once and walked home to his parent's apartment. They lived right next door to a Denny's restaurant that would become a hangout for all the punk rockers in the West Valley in the years to come. Tom was really into girls and they loved him because he was cute and playful. I wasn't so cute, but he introduced me to a few of them and I fooled around with at least one of them in an afterschool smooch session at his parent's place. I soon learned, however, that these girls were more interested in something Tom offered that I couldn't compete with. Drugs. Tom liked to experiment with all kinds of mind-altering substances. He was the first one I saw empty the contents of nameless pill capsules onto his thumb crotch and snort it.

Tom had a contentious relationship with his dad. Having no siblings, Tom laughed incessantly at his dad's attempts to make a respectable kid out of the delinquent he was. Tom tormented his dad by drinking all the beer in the refrigerator. His dad worked hard as a machinist and came home to an empty fridge. "Ahhh, Tom, ya bastard!" were his usual grumblings, which Tom eagerly reported to me as he imitated his father's intonations. Tom often told me that he hated his father. Tom said that the only positive feedback he ever got from his grumpy old man was when he ran errands to the liquor store. The owner of the local liquor store knew Tom's dad and allowed Tom to pick up smokes and booze if it was for his dad. Tom always helped himself to a portion of the order as a service fee.

One day, a few years after Tom left high school, while still living in that apartment next to Denny's, his dad said, "Dammit, Tom, you smoked my last cig. Go pick me up another pack right now." Tom, who had developed a bad heroin habit by this time, took the family car and sped down the street, Valley Circle Boulevard, and at sixty mph crashed into a parked semi-trailer truck, decapitating himself on the spot. But that tragedy was still a few years off.

Around the same time that Tom was hanging out with us on the high school quad, a lanky quiet kid with a buzz cut and engineer boots came over and began to chat. "You guys going to that Black Flag show?" he asked. Jon said, "I can't drive that far with my mom's car at night." "I already saw them at the Fleetwood," I said, "plus I don't have a ride." "I'll drive," said the kid named Jay, and immediately we hit it off. Here was someone in my grade who was willing to hang out and drive to where the action was.

Just a few weeks prior, Tom had introduced me to his friend Brett, who had already dropped out of El Camino. I had expressed to Tom that I was determined to be in a punk band, but I had no idea how to start one. Tom told me that his friend was already in a band called the Quarks, but he didn't think that they were very good. Brett was the guitarist and one of the singers in the Quarks, but Tom thought they needed something more. Tom took me to one of their performances, a dance at our high school auditorium. What I heard was kind of a New Wave train wreck: a guitarist (Brett) who obviously loved the Ramones, along with a keyboardist (Brian) who was kind of like a mix between Billy Joel and Danny Elfman. Both of these guys were looking for more from their band; I could tell that, and so could Tom. Independently, Tom arranged for both of them to meet me. Brian came over to my house and we hung out and played some music on my mom's spinet piano. Brian showed me how to use my left hand to play steady octaves on the bass notes, a trick I had never practiced. He also recommended a "frightening" new album that had just come out by an LA band called the Germs. He said the lyrics were unlike anything that had ever been written. I had heard the Germs on the radio—*Rodney on the ROQ* of course—but anyone who knows that band knows that in order to appreciate the lyrics you must read them on the album's insert, because they are quite unintelligible on the recordings. I took Brian's advice and bought a copy of the Germs's *GI* soon after our hanging out, but I never really clicked with Brian and we didn't see each other after that.

The meeting with Brett was also set up by Tom, but it didn't entail songwriting. Tom had already told Brett that I was a great singer (based on absolutely zero evidence but my own bragging), and I was excited to be hanging out with someone who actually was already in a band and had all the equipment necessary to perform concerts. Brett and Tom came to pick me up in Brett's mom's station wagon. We were headed to the Hollywood Palladium to see the Ramones. What a thrill! Brett's first words to me were, "You ready for a nonstop bop, dude?" I said, "I guess so," even though I wasn't sure what a "bop" was. From the moment that the Ramones cranked up, it was clear that Brett and I were interested in the same musical nuances. I could tell that Brett was interested in all aspects of the band's presentation, from the sound and placement of the amplifiers to the dress and antics of the musicians. I was focused on slam dancing and singing along with the songs I knew. Just being part of the frenzy was pure joy.

The next weekend, Brett's parents were away and he decided to have a little party at their house. Tom brought me over, and all I can remember about that night was the thrill of singing at the top of my lungs through a microphone and PA (public-address) system that Brett had set up in his bedroom. Brett was downstairs entertaining some of the local girls, but I spent the entire time in his bedroom playing with his electric guitar and singing into his PA. Tom took over on vocals for a while and I played some rudimentary chords on Brett's Gibson guitar ("the Paul"). It was the first time I ever played electric guitar at full volume. Even though the normal activities of a parentless party in the San Fernando Valley in those days were focused on getting high and getting laid, I was oblivious that night, and I stayed up late just experimenting with sound. Eventually, after Tom had climbed out onto the roof of Brett's house and rolled around singing like Darby Crash at a hundred decibels, the neighbors complained, and we had to shut down the PA and amplifier. But like the rush of drugs that I imagine must feel great to those who partake, my brain became fixated that night, set to overdrive with the determination to do more singing and songwriting as soon as possible.

12
GENESIS

Early in the fall of 1980, on one of those typical sweltering days in LA when people from the East are naturally prone to expect cooling temperatures and glorious color displays from the autumn leaves, but instead are greeted with the hottest, windiest days of the year as the Santa Ana winds blow dust in your eyes and strip the sycamores of their ugly brown foliage that matches the color of the crispy lawns in the neighborhoods, I made my way to a doorstep where two new buddies were waiting with anticipation. "What's up, dude? This is going to be aachselent!" said the shorter of the two.

This was the house of Jay Ziskrout, a drummer who was already graduated from my high school. Joining him in anticipation of my visit was Brett, who I had met only twice before, at his house for a party and at the Ramones concert to which he drove us in his mom's station wagon a few weeks prior. Both times I had been in the company of our mutual friend Tom, who was like a security blanket for me. Not only were these guys older than me, but they were also savvy SoCal kids who used drugs, had girlfriends and automobiles, and grew up in the California culture—all things that made me feel nervous. Tom kept insisting that we would form a circle of fast friends.

I gained trust in Tom because I honestly thought we made a good pair. We could pal around without judgment. Not only could we go to punk shows and have each other's backs in the slam pit, but we could do kid stuff together too. Jon and I took him along to Magic Mountain to ride the world's biggest wooden roller coaster—it was called Colossus—and everyone in the amusement park stared at Tom. "That guy's got blue hair!" we heard more than once that day. In general, I felt that Tom was a lot more punk than me. Once at school he and I somehow got cornered in the boy's bathroom by a few hardened toughs from South Central who were convinced that we were in some sort of gang. I was sure that we were in for some kind of ass whupping. If it wasn't jocks setting their ire on us, it was the wannabe gangbangers. "What set you from, boy?" They kept pointing to the safety pins on our T-shirts, saying to me with scowls on their faces, "What this be about?" I had no idea what they were asking. Tom understood and said, "We aren't in any gang, it's just punk fashion. Watch this." At that moment he took one of the safety pins off of his shirt, approached the mirror on the wall, and jammed the pin clear through his earlobe! It was a bloody mess and his lobe swelled up. "You punkers crazy!" said the meanest of the bunch. But it was enough to disperse the gathering, laughing and whooping as they left us alone. Tom pierced his own ear with a fat safety pin because he had some inkling that if he hurt himself, the violence of our would-be assailants might be disarmed. It worked. I thought he was a street-smart genius. He never once tried to get me to use any of the numerous substances or pills that he regularly experimented with. Tom seemed to know who I was intuitively, and he accepted me without judgment. So I was ready to follow his lead anywhere, and I really trusted him when he suggested that Brett and I would make a good team.

Upon entering Jay Ziskrout's house I immediately let all inhibitions fall because my eyes fixated on a most beautiful sight backlit by the shimmering golden sunshine coming through the sliding glass doors of the pool deck. There on the softly padded white carpeting of the living room were two towering stacks of PA speakers, six feet high, framing a makeshift stagelike setup with an orange drum kit sitting in the rear. A silver and black guitar amp stood on the floor next to the drums, and a straight mic stand with a Shure microphone was placed front and center. These necessities of band life were totally unobtainable by me—I hadn't the know-how nor did our family have the finances—so it was like I had been invited to participate in a privileged elite world that I had dreamed about my whole life. In my world, stuff like this had to be provisioned by a public institution. Schools and universities had music equipment for students. Usually, you had to sign up for it and it was thrashed from years of abuse, and then you had to return it. But here, I was being given the greatest privilege. My very own microphone! It was like I had been hand-selected by Tom, faithful advisor to Brett and me, to embark on a new journey. I had dreamed about being a singer since I was a child but had no way of putting the pieces together in order to fulfill it. Now, the pieces were in place and I took the role with aplomb and felt a surge of privilege and gratitude to the guys who made it happen.

If there was anything awkward about my first rantings and ravings into the microphone it didn't show. Brett and Jay Ziskrout seemed very serious about their own instruments. Brett gave me the lyrics to a song he wrote on a pad of paper. I sang "I don't have the weed and I don't have the time, and I will tell you why!" The scribbled "w" was really an "n," but for the first few passes of singing this song I just assumed it was about drugs—something my bandmates knew a lot about. It was cool, or so I thought, that they trusted me to communicate this lifestyle even though I didn't partake in it.

I presented a song that I had written, and they played it with every bit as much enthusiasm as they played the other one: "Economy, technology, does it really work? The guy runnin' the government is just another jerk!" After a couple hours of rehearsing these two songs, we had about four minutes of music to perform! We filled our rehearsal time playing other songs from our record collections. I loved singing through the PA. I was good at voice mimicry, so I didn't hesitate to do some a cappella while the other guys were taking a break. I was good at emulating other singers. This is where Brett and I really bonded over our love of ELP. I sang "Confusion—zshun—zshun—zshun—zshun—zshun—zshun . . . will be my Epitaph" from the live album *Welcome Back My Friends to the Show That Never Ends*, and I sounded just like Greg Lake. Brett liked the guitar riff of the Knack's "My Sharona," and I could sing just like that singer as well. We had a lot of fun goofing around, but it was immediately clear that we needed a bass guitar to solidify the sonic blast that we wanted to achieve. But where to find a bass player was a puzzle. Brett definitely did not want to return to his former bandmates in the Quarks because they were too New Wave and not really part of the burgeoning LA scene that we wanted to be part of. Already out of high school, Brett and Jay Ziskrout had not spent much time building their connections with scenesters. Strangely, it fell on me to find a bass player because I had high school friends who might be appropriate.

One guy came immediately to mind: my friend who hung out with us on the quad at lunchtime, the other Jay (Bentley)! Earlier in the semester, he had indicated an eagerness to be part of the growing punk scene that was taking place throughout the Southland (but not in our neck of the woods). When Jay hung out at his dad's house in Manhattan Beach, he rubbed elbows with the beach skaters and surfers who were making names for themselves as punk rockers. Jay seemed like a knowledgeable dude, and he got along well with Jon because they both played basketball together as lanky high school PE buddies.

It didn't take long for me to bring up my most exciting news one day at lunchtime: "Yeah, we've got this band going but we need to find a bass player. Jay, do you want to join?" He was a bit caught off guard. "Uh, I play guitar."

We continued our bass-less rehearsals and quickly grew our repertoire to four songs. I brought in another song and so did Brett. Our set list grew to about eight minute's worth of music: "Politics," "Sensory Overload," "Drastic Actions," and "Slaves." Brett broke out the tape recorder and we made three passes at our set list on three separate tapes so that each band member could take home a copy. I had a cheapo tape recorder, so the sound quality was terrible, but I loved hearing our original tunes coming back off the tape. Even though my voice was totally distorted and the guitar was louder than the snare drum—in fact, it was an incoherent jumble of noise—we played quite well together and I loved the sound of it. Jay Ziskrout was convinced that the sound of the recordings would have been much better if we had a bass, but neither he nor Brett had made any progress in finding a suitable band member. There was an unspoken, unwritten assignment that whoever was going to fill the role had to fit the job's criteria: someone worthy of not only playing the instrument but also willing to help grow the popularity of the band by being connected to the punk scene. There simply weren't enough punk rockers in the Valley to have our own following from mere locals. We were going to have to create inroads to Hollywood and beyond. This made me think again of Jay at school. He hung out with cool people from the beach, he had a car, and he seemed like he wanted to play music because he billed himself as a guitarist.

The next day at school, when he came over to our lunch spot I handed him the tape we had made at rehearsal. "Here's four songs; if you dig them, do you think you could play bass on them?" Even though I didn't intend for it to be one, it was a test of his desires. Did he relish playing the guitar more than having a band to play with? I was offering him a band, but he would have to switch instruments. I had a belief that if you could play guitar, then bass would be an easy adaptation. Jay eagerly took the tape and learned the songs. Within twenty-four hours he went down to Sears, bought a bass guitar and amplifier, and showed up at Jay Ziskrout's house for our next rehearsal.

After the quick introductions to the other guys, Jay played the bass notes exactly to the rhythm and progression required on our four songs. We were so excited! The bass made us a sonic force to be reckoned with. It shook the house and syncopated with the kick drum, and we all had huge smiles on our faces. We were all convinced that we could take this sound to the clubs and be successful. Sure it would take some practicing, but we were committed to doing that every day after school until we were so well rehearsed that we could play the songs in our sleep. It was that very same day that we started thinking about a band name.

Many ideas were batted around. But most of the time was spent just being silly teenagers. Along with Tom, who was officially our first "roadie"—but really he was more than that since he was responsible for getting us together—we all sat around joshing on one another. These guys had wicked senses of humor, and laughter was a constant companion when we were around one another. It was teenage mind emancipation. Brett, Tom, and Jay Ziskrout broke into discussing methods of ass-wiping in order to make sure you were finished on the toilet. "Do you check the paper each wipe, or do you simply have a predetermined number of wipes before you leave the throne?" I never actually gave it much thought until this discussion! Tom then told me of a girl he knew who had a clitoris in her rectum so that she orgasmed every time she took a shit. I was so naive, and he said it with such authority and confidence, that I actually believed him! Brett countered that another girlfriend of his had three nipples. I found that fascinating and worthy of more investigation. I was trying to fit in, not look awkward, but I was also really intrigued and eager to add my own tidbits to the bullshitting. I was good at imitations and impersonations. I had a muscleman act that had the guys in stitches. I'm not sure if their laughter was aided by marijuana—a distinct possibility—but they would egg me on to do the impersonation of muscleman over and over until tears of laughter came streaming down their faces. I was really good at mimicking Tom Snyder (also from Milwaukee) who famously was clueless about punk, but sometimes featured punk bands on his late-night NBC talk show, *Tomorrow*, for totally disjointed interviews. I would break into my Tom Snyder routine: "Okay, guys," (then pause and take a drag from a mock cigarette) "why all the violence?" Jay did a hilarious imitation too. He could walk like Clyde, the orangutan in Clint Eastwood's movie *Every Which Way but Loose*, which brought screams of laughter from all of us. Furthermore, being the lanky one, Jay's emulation of John Cleese's "Ministry of Silly Walks" from *Monty Python* was unmatched.

Our view of the world was nothing but satire, irony, and parody. It's remarkable that Brett and I were ever serious enough to write songs that actually had deeper meaning, because whenever we were around one another there was nothing but cutups and clever commentary about this or that worldly affair, or jokes and stories of the opposite sex.

We all agreed that a band name was a serious matter. So we put down our instruments, took a real break from the rehearsal, and formed a circle around the coffee table for a discussion. But even that was subject to non-stop hilarity. We sat there on Jay Ziskrout's parents' lavish living room sofa laughing uncontrollably at the possibilities. Each proposed name passed through numerous rounds of ridicule. Jay Ziskrout suggested Smegma. I had only heard this word once before, in health class. This mythical substance forms on the penis under foreskin that isn't cleaned regularly. Disgusting and shocking! It even has a slang associated with it, which Brett was quick to offer as another potential name, Head Cheese, which brought on more whoops of laughter. I busted out the announcer voice: "Now, here he is straight from Wisconsin, the singer from Head Cheese!" (It's not slang in the dairy industry!)

After a good ten minutes of consideration, we agreed that anything having to do with the penis was a no go. We were fans of the Dickies and they already had the perfect logo. We wanted something original and unique. So we logically turned to the opposite sex. Tom offered the name Vaginal Discharge. After the howls of laughter subsided, we all privately considered the name for a brief moment. VD would make a cool logo, we agreed. But it could easily be confused with Venereal Disease, which also is a cool concept for a band, but we thought it to be too literal and too overused a concept among high school counselors and health teachers. I was a huge fan of the band Discharge from the UK, almost in a sacredly reverent way. I didn't want to adopt a band name that bordered on infringement of their concept. They came up with a disgusting name to match their shocking sound. I didn't feel like that style fit us. We were searching for something more comical, thoughtful, and ironic.

We turned our attention away from sex-ed topics and looked for another social ill to parody. The family was a good target. Jay and I came from divorced households, while Jay Ziskrout and Brett didn't have any experience with divorce in their own families. Jay came up with Bad

Family, and I expanded it to Bad Family Life. BFL could make a cool logo, and nearly every punk rocker created friction in their own families. There would be endless topics to explore as songwriting material. So for a few minutes we lived with the name. But it didn't really resound with the kind of impact we were looking for. The hoots and hilarity were calming down after numerous rounds of proposals. We could have shelved the discussion at this time, but as anxious teenagers looking for a purpose to keep rehearsing we felt like a name for the band had to be decided immediately.

In addition to our households being run by divorced moms, Jay and I also were sheltered from the rigors of religious education. My mom actively avoided religion for my entire life, and I never knew Jay to attend church or read the Bible. Brett and Jay Ziskrout, on the other hand, were from pretty typical Jewish households. They both went to Hebrew school and had formal education in the ways of those ancient traditions. From one of them came the suggestion: "How 'bout Bad Religion?" Since I felt no offense from the concept, it struck me as nothing personally distasteful. But I quickly realized how religion played a role in the life of nearly every American citizen, be it Jewish, Christian, or other. This, to me, seemed like an endlessly deep well of potential for songwriting topics. It was erudite enough to satisfy the professor, critical enough to satisfy the administration, and punk-sounding enough to give us credibility with our peers. We all agreed on the name and immediately went back to rehearsing.

Brett left rehearsal and got busy that night. He crafted a song that would become our "theme song," using our band name for the title. What better way to promote ourselves than to have a theme song titled with the band's name? But he didn't stop there. When he arrived at rehearsal the next day he was fashionably late. We all sat around waiting for him for a half hour, and finally he paraded into the living room holding a huge drawing of a symbol he had sketched and painted on an eighteen-by-thirty-six-inch sheet of watercolor paper. He came in shouting, "I've got it!" The crossbuster symbol was born: a bold, red circle surrounding a black Christian cross with a red diagonal slash through it. It was to be our band's logo: an international symbol of Bad Religion. We all loved it. It was offensive enough but not hateful. Since the Christian cross is the most recognized religious symbol in the Western world, our logo could be seen as the perfect metaphor for all religions.

It's incredible to reflect on how this image of a negated symbol became fixed in the popular imagination. The 1970s saw the first introduction of the graphic "P" with a red circle-backslash "No Parking" signs in America. Before that, the signs were spelled out with words: "No Parking Zone." The red circle-backslash symbol reached its zenith in 1984 with the smash blockbuster movie *Ghostbusters*, where instead of a "P" the movie's marketing team placed a graphic image of a Casper-like ghost caught in the act of haunting. This symbol captured the imagination of every demographic, and it was widely marketed to kids. The film became a cultural phenomenon and was the highest grossing comedy of all time and remained in that position for the entire decade. The Library of Congress has since placed the film in its vaults and deemed it an American treasure, denoting it as "culturally and historically significant." It's likely that our fortuitous association with this friendly red circle-backslash symbol helped to pave the way for our band's logo over the years. In America at least, I'm sure that the *Ghostbuster* symbol and the "No Parking" graphic image helped to defuse any possible antagonism from religious groups. We were never antagonists—we were simply the antithesis of the symbol we were slashing: you won't find religion in this house.

With only a few rehearsals under our belt, the parental rules of the Ziskrout house became clearer. This was only supposed to be an audition space, not a rehearsal studio. We had to move. There was no way Jay Ziskrout's parents were going to allow a band to take over their living room every day after school. We needed a permanent space where parents could not be bothered.

This left only one option. Although I always hesitated to ask for my mom's help, because she worked long hours to support our single-income household, there was no other choice. I meekly asked her: "Mom, can we use the garage to rehearse after school?" She answered, "I reckon, so long as you guys clear out when I get home from work." This was all the approval I needed, and within twenty-four hours of her response we were loading up all the equipment and moving in to our detached garage on the back alley of Woodlake Avenue in Canoga Park, California.

More aptly described as a dry sauna, Mom's garage was typical for this part of the San Fernando Valley. No insulation, clapboard-on-frame with a tar-shingle roof, about twenty by thirty feet of floor space inside. Much of that area was already spoken for in the way of boxes that had been packed a few years before and remained as unopened family stuff from our move across the country. Here they sat on crude lumber shelves in their perpetual state of suspended animation, baking slowly each day as the typical Valley temperatures reached ninety or one hundred degrees. The garage had no ventilation or windows, just a double-bay swing door that opened out into the alley and a man door that opened on the opposite side toward the backyard. It was detached from the house, so my brother could hang out in the house and not be bothered by us pesky punkers. We moved some boxes and created a large enough space for drums, amps, and the PA. It wasn't much, but Mom's garage would come to serve the purpose for which we needed it: our hangout after school with no parents or siblings, and our staging ground for the band's missions. It became labeled the Hell Hole, an apt term for a band called Bad Religion.

I was filled with emotion, but I kept it to myself. A strong sense of displacement overcame me as we unloaded the equipment from Brett and Jay Ziskrout's vans. Out with the old, in with the new. But the old brought back poignant memories, of only a short time ago; memories that were quickly becoming foggy and yet still moved me powerfully. This garage space was the rehearsal area for Chuck. Only a year or so prior, he would spend a lot of time out here, away from the house, practicing his horns and flute while pacing on the remnant little patch of shag carpet that still lay on the cement floor in the corner. I missed having him around after school sometimes. His jazz saxophone could be heard softly emanating from the garage while I played in the backyard. I didn't really consider myself knowledgeable about jazz but it surrounded me in my youth, so it served as a sort of emotional security balm. Dad used to play it constantly on the car radio during our Sunday evening drives between Racine and Milwaukee. Floyd Brown's jazz showcase on WGN serenaded us as we made that somber journey every weekend, back to the grind of another school week at Mom's. There on school-day afternoons in Wisconsin, Chuck's jazz serenades of flute, sax, clarinet, and trombone were constant companions, calming background music that filled the house from the living room each afternoon before he headed out to a gig at some Milwaukee nightclub. This was the auditory accompaniment to my complex childhood experience. But eventually, Chuck, and all that he represented, was effectively removed from our family's lore after that horrible night of anger. Our family moved on without him. Adapting to the new sounds. The jazz ceased, and the punks moved in.

Moving in were people with whom I would form new experiences, no matter that they would never know the man who only a year or so prior occupied this makeshift rehearsal space and left an emotional scar on me forever. Their understanding of me began fresh at this point in time without care of, or respect to, the previous events in my life. It was better that way, I guess. I could redefine myself, and build a new world with these guys without the burdensome baggage of my emotional insecurities and embarrassingly complicated family situation. As a bunch of punk friends excited to get on with our mission, we never spoke of who or what came before.

13

NOT BOYFRIEND MATERIAL

"**I seen you lookin' at 'em**," she said, out of the side of her mouth. "Huh?" I replied, faking innocence, thinking of how Dad always warned me to watch out for girls who incorrectly use the past tense of verbs. "My tits! Don't pretend you didn't, I caught you! But it's okay," she said as she nuzzled up to me outside the venue; it was the Whisky a Go Go, and the Dead Boys had just played. All us punks were going to head over to Oki-Dog when Jill, a short but sturdy, sweet punk girl from back East, intercepted me in the parking lot. Her bleached blonde hair was cropped but not spiked. To complement her torn, belted blue jeans and black tennis shoes, she wore a "wife beater" white tank top and a lacy bra. And, yes, I was peeking as far down as the plunge of the low neckline would let me see. The gig was viciously hot inside, and it was eighty degrees outside on the sweltering pavement of Sunset Boulevard. The damp air kept her body wet with sweat, giving the shirt all that much more revealing transparency. The V-neck dipped asymmetrically, unmasking a sheer, un-centered cup that no longer held its contents in check, revealing one peek-ing areola that escaped from the elasticated hem. "Well, maybe we can go hang out somewhere instead of going to Oki-Dog," I said. Just then, as luck would have it, Lucky passed by, the famous drummer and my acquaintance from the Circle Jerks. "Why don't you guys come hang at my place? It's right around the corner. Follow me." Wow! So cool of him, I thought. I re-ally wanted to get to know this new girlfriend. We strolled along following Lucky and his girlfriend, making small talk as they sped ahead of us.

"Where you from?" I asked. "San Diego," she said. "We moved here with my mom from back east in Missouri." "Cool, I moved here too with my mom, from Wisconsin." By the time we got to Lucky's place, it was clear that we were kindred spirits, not interested in getting loaded, not interested in fucking shit up, but really interested in each other that night. There wasn't very much talking left to do. When we got to the small apartment, Lucky was already entertaining his girlfriend in the bedroom. The little living room had a pull-out sofa that was ready and waiting, so Jill and I wasted no time in putting it to the test. We did it fast, furious, and care-less as teenagers are wont to do. She smiled at me when it was over, and I felt like I had succeeded in making her happy. And as we were putting back on our recently shed clothing, Lucky's half-dressed girlfriend came out of the bedroom and said, "You guys want to switch now?" This, coming from someone a couple years older than me put a start in my heart. Even though she was sexy and top-naked, I was instantly shocked into think-ing about how Jill might react. We both looked at each other and realized there was much more that we wanted to talk about so we could get to know each other better. "No, I gotta get going. My stepdad let me borrow his car only until midnight," she said. "Yeah, thanks, but I gotta get back, my ride's waiting at Oki-Dog," I lied. I just wanted to spend more time with Jill. Sometimes doing the nasty up front relieves a lot of weirdness in get-ting to know someone.

On leaving the apartment, Jill said, "I'll give you a ride to Oki's, but let's cruise a bit first." We ended up talking for an hour or so. It turned out that Jill was from a pretty typical Midwestern family whose dad was tied to the MLB franchise in Kansas City. This was significant because there were very few people in the punk scene with whom I felt comfortable revealing my love of sports, and my participation in Little League back in Wisconsin. In fact, Jill understood a lot about me just from the revelation that we both had childhood friends who we left back in the Midwest, and we missed them a lot. We missed playing pickup games and riding bikes in the neighborhoods. We bonded over similar experiences in coming to the West Coast and feeling like aliens in many ways. I felt that I had met someone who had the potential to really understand me, and vice versa. We could have been long-term lovers and friends, but it wasn't meant to be.

After numerous phone conversations late into the night, and a few trips to visit me at my mom's house, the relationship tanked. One might assume it was because I was only a seventeen-year-old punk with no car and no accommodations to make her feel comfortable. In fact, the only place we could get privacy was in the Hell Hole, the Bad Religion rehearsal space in my mom's garage. We would spend the night out there on a foam mattress used by day as a sound baffle for the drum kit. One night, after screwing on the garage floor, I implored Jill to spend the night. "You don't want to drive all the way back to San Diego, do you? Just stay here with me. We'll have cereal in the morning!" "No," she said, "I have to get this car back to San Diego." I felt so sure that she wanted to stay, but I could tell that she had made a commitment to her parents. And that too was attractive to me. It was the opposite of so many punk friends who actively tried so hard to destroy trust, ignore rules, and cause chaos in their interpersonal relationships. I wasn't into this kind of punk; in fact, it wasn't punk to me. I had experienced enough interpersonal chaos. I wanted interpersonal tranquility in this world of social chaos. But the 405 was calling, and she had to zip down that ribbon of highway before it got too late or she might not be able to use the car anymore. Then where would our relationship be?

"Okay, but you look so tired. Are you sure you're okay to drive back?" I wanted to comfort her so badly, to make her feel that she needed to be nowhere else in the world but there next to me. I wished so badly that I had something more attractive, more alluring to offer to get her to stay the night. But I had nothing. She was a girl from a household of means, with a good car and nice clothes. She was used to nice things. I felt like I was way beneath her. She was probably aghast to come all this way to visit me, and that I wooed her with a date in a dingy garage, fooling around with carnal desire atop a smelly polystyrene mattress that served other purposes for my band. Jill probably felt really uncomfortable but couldn't voice it. She probably wanted to say, "I like you a lot, and we have a lot in common. But this is kinda gross." There was nothing I could offer her that would change that. I had nothing in the way of material comfort nor graces to be in a serious relationship. I was like a street punk in many ways. I had a cruddy bedroom where I never changed the sheets, a garage behind my house that was dusty, dark, and cluttered, no car, and no job or income. The main thing I had was my band, and my songs that were recorded. But Jill was no groupie. She didn't like me solely for that reason, and I didn't want someone to like me solely because of my status. After rounds of pleading with her to stay, finally she said, "I have no choice. I gotta go. But I'll be okay." "Call me when you get home, okay?" I said.

But there was no call that night. Nor the next day. I was sure that I had blown it with her. It is something that remains with a young man, the feeling of helplessness when he can't put all the pieces together to create a long-term relationship. I had to admit that what I was now enduring was an unmitigated failure. I had not enough maturity nor infrastructural stability to offer another person. Material things were necessary to be in the kind of relationship that I wanted. I couldn't provide stuff for my partner, like a car or a decent place to stay, to nurture any kind of domestic setting that she would need to make a relationship work. I was only seventeen, but I already had lived enough life to recognize that a gaping hole appeared in a person's well-being if there was no tranquility and predictability in their domestic situation. What chance has a relationship if there is no central place for it to grow? Furthermore, even worse, I lived 140 miles away from Jill, so I couldn't even be nearby when she needed me.

Two days later I got a phone call from some dude named Derek, whom I didn't recognize. "Greg, I'm a friend of Jill's. She was in a car crash on the 405, late-night, after she left your place. The ambulance took her to the nearest hospital, here in Mission Viejo, and she's still here now." "Mission Viejo? You mean she almost made it all the way home before her crash?" I asked. "Yeah, she actually had just crossed into San Diego County, near San Onofre, I guess, but they brought her here to MV," said Derek. Jill had suffered a broken neck from the crash after falling asleep at the wheel. I was scared for her. Was she paralyzed? Was she going to suffer long-term damage? Then I quickly realized that Mission Viejo was too far away. It was a major excursion for me, especially because I was so inexperienced behind the wheel: I had only just received my driver's license a few months prior. I could never borrow my mom's car, our family's only vehicle, to go see her. In fact, I had never driven on the freeway except to pass my driver's license test. I was too immature and inexperienced to know what to do. But I knew with all my heart that I wanted to go to her bedside. There was just no way to accomplish this most basic, nurturing gesture to aid this meaningful, budding relationship. I could ask Mom to drive me, but self-pride blocked me from asking. How embarrassing a signal to send to a girl you're trying to impress; that your mom had to drive you around.

Later that day, when she was stabilized, she could speak to me from her hospital bed. Derek called again and I asked, "Can you put her on the phone?" Jill's voice sounded weak, but she was very clear. "Greg? Why didn't you even come visit me in the hospital?" I felt embarrassed and helpless. "My mom had to use the car all day to go to work. I have no transpo." She must have realized at that moment that if this relationship was going to move forward, she would have to do all the work. I had no understanding of how I could meet her halfway. If only she was at a closer hospital, I would take public transportation, the formidable Rapid Transit District, LA's bus system (also called "the loser cruiser" by the kids at my school), to her bedside. Even if it meant spending three hours in bus lane commuter traffic, I was up for it. She was worth it. But the SoCal public transit sector was very poorly organized, especially if you had to cross county lines, as in this case. Mission Viejo was deep behind the orange curtain, in Orange County. There was no transit system that connected the counties in SoCal. I gave up on the prospect, and therein destroyed my chances with Jill. I was too unimaginative, too immature in personal relations, and too lacking in self-confidence to be a boyfriend.

Jill called me about a week later to tell me that she was going to heal without impairment. It was only a minor vertebral fracture. But there was bad news too. She and Derek were going to be a couple. This was her way of saying that I didn't do enough to impress her and that my actions surrounding her hospital stay seemed like I didn't care about her. It's strange how inaction can often be interpreted as precisely the opposite of true feelings. Every bone in my body was motivated to be in a relationship with Jill, but I had no way of acting on these impulses. Distance, as is so often experienced from living in the widely distributed geographic matrix of SoCal, requires a car and a place to put it when you get there. I had neither, and therefore I couldn't ever hope to have a relationship with anyone outside my local zip code. Jill continued on the line. "Besides, Derek has a car, and we live close to each other." "Well, good for Derek. Does he know that these are his most attractive qualities?" I asked. She didn't answer, but we said goodbye.

I was heartbroken. I had all the qualifications of a perfect partner for Jill: similar Midwestern values, a love of sports, and especially a love of punk music. But despite our compatibilities I was lacking in one key area: material necessities of life. I was still a kid living under my mom's roof, totally dependent on her hard work for any semblance of stability in my life. I was a child who had obligations to two lifestyles, only one of which was in SoCal. The other one was back in Wisconsin. I had friends there, and my dad who further supplied me with stability and material needs during the summers. My life was complex, and this is something that never waned. Until I became more independent, I was destined to be a bachelor. Girlfriends had to be temporary, even though I wanted more long-term engagements.

From that point on I viewed relationships with a very practical eye. I was convinced that the only way they could work was if the fundamental daily routines and occupational necessities of each partner were met with financial and utilitarian stability and predictability. In other words, there could be no anarchy in personal life unless you wanted to live in a rotating door of wives or partners. I didn't want that. I'd have very little confidence in myself as a boyfriend from that point on. I needed someone who was so comfortable in their own stability and maturity that they could just fall for me because of my wonderful qualities as a person. In other words, I needed someone mature so that they might be able to love me for my immature qualities. As I came to learn, this is the pipe dream of many professional entertainers.

14
POETRY OF PUNK AND MAKING THE SCENE

After a few weeks of rehearsing at the Hell Hole, we assembled a six-song repertoire of original music. We rehearsed the short, eleven-minute set list over and over. To fill more time we might mimic the "jam" session we often saw at Black Flag shows when they would play "Louie Louie"—the extended version—during their set. Our rehearsals had numerous breaks. Typically, we could only stand about thirty minutes of closed-door sessions in the Hell Hole before we had to open up and get some air flowing through the sweltering furnace that was our rehearsal space. We naturally retreated back into the house, where it was cooler and more civilized. Break time was often spent around Mom's spinet piano, where I often serenaded whoever was nearby with punk songs worked out to simple arrangements on the ivories. Brett was highly entertained by my renditions of ELP songs and he urged me to play more. "Lucky Man" was our favorite sing-along. I had an inexpensive twelve-string acoustic guitar that was hard to keep in tune. It sounded like many of the recordings at the time that used a chorus effect on a twelve string—putting a chorus on an acoustic instrument that already had a built-in chorus effect today seems nonsensical! It was the perfect accompaniment for the beginning sections of "More Than a Feeling" by Boston. Styx, Billy Joel, and Foreigner were also requested by Brett, as he sang harmonies to my rudimentary renditions of popular radio songs. I got more serious attention playing songs by the Dickies on piano. I could bang out a killer version of "You Drive Me Ape." Elvis Costello's "Sneaky Feelings" was about as complicated a piano riff as I could handle in those days. I butchered it pretty well, but the vocal parts came more naturally to me, and I entertained the guys with that one too. I worked out Todd Rundgren songs on my own, for private use only, because I didn't want to parody them and I feared that the guys would not appreciate my fondness for his work. In a parallel way, Brett didn't egg me on to attempt any Elton John songs because of his own reverence for EJ's work.

Pretty much right off the bat we took our job of writing seriously. Somehow, despite all the goofing around and singing cover songs from a different genre, Brett and I had good intuitions of what our band's mission should be. Eventually we wanted to make a record. That would serve our needs as a constitution of sorts, depicting our punk aesthetic. But what of the lyrics? We were surrounded by the poetry of punk and we had to carve out a niche from the myriad of preexisting themes expressed by the SoCal bands we listened to. They spanned from the ridiculous to the profound, and we loved them all:

Absurdist

He was a funny man with the straight black hair, he lost it in an accident but he doesn't care

or

Planes carry people around and around, Trains are late getting in the station

or

Operation, operation, snip and tie, snip and tie

Literal

I don't care about you, Fuck you!

or

Fix me, fix my head, fix me please I don't wanna be dead

Existential

Standing in line we're aberrations, defects in a defect mirror

or

Don't want to drown in American society

Lifestyle

Grab a girl, go for a whirl, head on down to the beach

or

Go-go music really makes us dance, do the pony, puts us in a trance or

> She found it hard to say goodbye to her own best friend.
> She bought a clock on Hollywood Boulevard the day she
> left

Call to Arms

> We're not the background for your stupid fights, get out
> of the darkness, it's time to unite

or

> Let's lynch the landlord man

One of our band contemporaries, Circle One, took few steps toward virtuosity, yet stumbled upon a lasting theme. Despite the seeming short-sightedness of their title "High School Society," and the simplicity of their prose, I perceived an attitude in their words that could last a lifetime: "Fuck the people! They go with the crowd." This encapsulated a theme that could, in the hands of a more artful wordsmith, be expanded to all sorts of critical realms. It was, essentially (I believed), what Charles Darwin was saying to the theologians with his theory of evolution: groupthink is bunk, popular consensus is bullshit, and thoughtless, uncritical populism should be resisted as a personal constitution.

But we also needed attitude. The singer often dictates that for the band, and I had none of the belligerence of many singers I considered my favorites. It was a crucial ingredient. For ignoring belligerence in the aesthetic of punk is to miss the foundational bedrock of the idiom.

There are two kinds of belligerent disruption. The first is that of the common man, the working-class stiff. It is a boneheaded, artless form like the truckers who terrorize mixed-race couples and try to run them off the road. This is a run-of-the-mill kind of belligerence. Nearly ubiquitous in every walk of life, it's always been ripe for sowing the seeds of popular music. It's no surprise that many of the working-class guilds and ways of life have embraced shit kickin' music. It serves the belligerent attitude of the common man. Punk had this same capability. Punk music serves the impulse to "fuck shit up." There is, however, nothing unique about this behavior: it is, after all, so common that punk cannot claim it as its defining hallmark. I wanted something more out of our music.

There is another kind of belligerence. The belligerence of the mind. Ideas can be disrupting, just as outwardly obnoxious behaviors can be. This strain runs deep in the spirit of America just as the working-class style does. The founding fathers of the USA utilized it. They were interested in the disruption of English legal convention and imperialism when they created our own national constitution. Instead of using tactics similar to the brute belligerence of the lowly working class, they committed words to paper, words so shocking to the Crown back in old Blighty that warfare was precipitated in due course.

Taking all this into consideration was easier than actually putting words and music to it. But like a swaying, wavering compass needle around the neck of a mountain wanderer, it pointed us toward a conceptual goal and gave us our marching orders. We had our direction.

There were plenty of people at Oki-Dog, every night of the week, who wanted to talk about music and had bands, some of whom were making names for themselves. Jay and I hung out every chance we could get, which was every Tuesday after the Starwood had a punk show, and usually Friday and Saturday nights as well. Jay had a Toyota pickup truck and he drove me everywhere in it. Before he left high school for good, he drove me to school each day as well. We made the rounds in Hollywood in that truck, going from Sunset Strip "legit" venues such as the Whisky or the Starwood (which was actually on Santa Monica Boulevard), to underground places like the Hideaway—always to see punk shows or just to hang out on the sidewalk where the action was. Our desire was to get Bad Religion more widely known. I wanted to be invited to play at some of these venues we were frequenting. Jay and I spent most of our time hanging out with other people who were in bands and yet had not made names for themselves. But some were on their way up.

One of them was the most sociable fellow with the same first name as mine, Greg Hetson from the Circle Jerks. His band, newly formed, included Keith Morris, the singer of Black Flag, who I had seen perform at the Fleetwood. Greg Hetson was already accomplished, having been in the original lineup of Redd Kross, a band that Rodney Bingenheimer played frequently on his radio show, *Rodney on the ROQ*. Always interested in chatting about music, "chicks," or cultural events in LA, if you wanted to know where to find an aftershow party or a "happening" place on any given evening for fun, Greg from the Circle Jerks was who you asked. The Jerks wasted no time in becoming famous. They recorded an instantly classic first album, shortly after forming in 1980, called *Group Sex*. It featured stunning drumming and memorable guitar riffs that became engrained in every punk band's rehearsal warm-up. Keith's vocals were startlingly aggressive yet melodic. The songs became snapshots of the Southern California punk scene, critical of the fashions, descriptive of society's superficiality, and glorifying of the seediness in Hollywood.

Greg Hetson and I hit it off immediately because he could tell that I had a wide and mutual appreciation for things he enjoyed outside of punk rock. For instance, he liked to travel, and by the time the first Circle Jerks album was out, he had embarked on a tour with the band that visited nearly every city with a punk scene in the USA, and even some that lacked one. Greg was the first punk musician I met in LA who actually knew where Racine, Wisconsin, was—the Jerks even played a show in downtown Racine to a mostly empty Memorial Hall! He had a keen understanding and tolerance of people from different parts of the country (he was born in Brooklyn, but moved to LA as a child, like so many others in the Southland of California). This made him likeable by many, and, to me, he felt like a trusted adviser when I was looking for someone who knew the ins and outs of punk culture in LA—someone well connected but still willing to do activities that were fun and disconnected from punk culture. Greg followed sports, and he knew that I loved playing basketball, baseball, and football in those days, and that I always favored the Wisconsin teams. He kept me apprised of when the Wisconsin teams were in town to play the LA teams, and he was always up for going to games. We went to see the Angels play the Brewers out in Anaheim, and shortly thereafter I started inviting Greg to come "jam" with us in Bad Religion whenever it was convenient. The idea of a jam session in punk was not very consistent with our concept of crafting precise, succinct short songs, but I considered Greg a local celebrity and was really glad that he started to take up my offer to join us with his guitar in hand.

One of his first appearances with us was during our second appearance on an obscure, "public access" kind of local TV show called *New Wave Theater*. At our first taping, in 1981, we showed up at a soundstage in West Hollywood and had no idea what to expect, and it was indeed odd to take the stage without an audience. Amidst the numerous video cameras, strewn about the floor, were other bands setting up their equipment, waiting in line to shoot their own ten-minute performance segments. The show revolved around a loose, somewhat existentialist narrative spoken in free-form poetry by the Harvard-educated master of ceremonies in New Wave dress, Peter Ivers. His introductions to the bands were from left field, but they added to the show's disjointed flow from the juxtaposition of loud-and-fast bands such as the Circle Jerks or Fear to the synth-rock art explorations of bands like Mnemonic Devices. In those days it was not uncommon to find such mixtures of eclectic bands making up the LA club scene. Ivers introduced us as "high-speed tough guys from Purgatory Beach," which was a clever way of summarizing our sound and lyrical style. But we thought he was a kook at the time, which was an honest reflection of our immaturity. The show was actually an important moment in the history of television. The blend of video with stock footage of film and the way they were edited together made each episode visually compelling. As punk kids, we weren't impressed by these "artsy" elements of the show. We just wanted to hear and see the punk bands. We didn't realize that this production was in fact far ahead of a trend that would later appear in broadcasting (typified by MTV) and in theater (performance art)—outlets that gave no recognition or credit to the show's creator, David Jove. Bad Religion, with our unique view of society spelled out in the lyrics to our songs "Oligarchy," "Bad Religion," and "Slaves," fit right in to the writer's intentions and the emcee's stream-of-consciousness introductions. The show's creators were trying to predict the future of a society run amok. The irony is that Bad Religion would go on for decades making a career out of this kind of social criticism, but we were too young and immature at the time to recognize that Jove and Ivers were our comrades in that quest.

For our second appearance on *New Wave Theater*, Greg Hetson made a cameo appearance as a featured soloist on the song "Part III." After that, he became a de facto member of the band, playing with us whenever it was convenient at gigs and showing up to record some solos when we were in the studio. A number of years later, he would join us full time.

After the release of our EP we acquired a significant local fan base. Punk rockers from the San Fernando Valley, although dispersed in small clusters, began to take notice along with some clusters of Hollywood scenesters who were friends (from hanging out so much in their neighborhoods). A pal named Peter took over drums from Jay Ziskrout, who unceremoniously quit the band for personal reasons.* Peter brought with him some friends who knew other friends, and before you knew it, the Hell Hole became a bit of an after-school hangout location for punk rockers from the most distant parts of the San Fernando Valley. I would have preferred it if the nexus had grown to accommodate even larger numbers of new friends, but two things conspired to keep the crowd small: (1) no place in the garage to sit and watch the band perform—it was just too damn small and had no chairs; and (2) no creature comforts to characterize it as a cool place to hang out—it was just too sweltering and unaccommodating. Because of these limitations, the space itself was not a good hangout. It was more of

---

* Jay Ziskrout believed the band was not consulting with him enough on group decisions. He took a stand and left the band, a move he now cites as juvenile indignation.

a Bad Religion "headquarters," serving as a meeting place to make plans so we could meet up later, after rehearsal, at a concert, club, or the trusty Denny's restaurant next to Tom's apartment. The growing network of Valley punk rockers always knew where they could find us on any given school-day afternoon.

Word of mouth spread far, and one day we were visited by the most famous fanzine writers of the time, Al and Michelle from *Flipside* magazine. They were from Fullerton, way out by Disneyland in Orange County. It was a real honor to have them come to this far end of the Valley, since they had to travel about sixty miles from their neck of the woods. I had met Michelle at a gig in Hollywood, and I'd given her my (Mom's) phone number. She said she was a writer for *Flipside* and I told her that we were a band from Canoga Park. She said, "Where is that?" To which I replied, "Call that number and come to one of our rehearsals."

I had a crush on Michelle because she said she was a writer. This proved to me that people outside my immediate friendly circles, from other punk scenes, were intellectually motivated, giving me hope that I could find not only a girlfriend but maybe also a community of like-minded people with whom to hang out. My punk friends from the Valley were pretty cool, and intelligent for the most part, but they loved drugs and drinking as part of their lifestyles. These substances and the activities that go with them secretly frightened me. For all I knew, they led inextricably to unconstrained anger and family violence. I swore I would never experience that again.

I really longed for a community of friends, like back in Wisconsin, who loved the punk lifestyle but shunned the self-destructive aspects of it. Michelle gave me some hope, and she reaffirmed my suspicion that there were punk rockers in Southern California who cared less about the party and more about the intellectual aspects of the scene. It was with great enthusiasm that I answered Michelle's phone call and invited her to come visit and write about us.

Luckily, her boss, Al, was willing to make the trek. They had heard our EP and we must have made an impression. Being featured in *Flipside* was a big deal to us because we had been ignored in the press up to that point. Despite our success on the radio when *Rodney on the ROQ* played our tapes—one of our songs, "Politics," even charted on Rodney's published monthly rankings—none of the local press nor fanzines paid much attention to Bad Religion. We always thought it was due to our geographic association. The Valley just wasn't extreme enough, gritty enough, cool enough, degenerate enough, or anything enough that it could be seen as worthy of note to a punk rock journalist intent on crafting a vivid portrayal. Famous magazines like *Slash* and *No Mag* were focused on a more mature audience, people in their twenties or thirties rather than teens. These magazines were more dedicated to the first wave of punk, along with its more artful nuances and stylish practitioners. We were just a bunch of snotty, wannabe, copycat punk musicians to them. How could there be anything original in a suburban incarnation of a scene that matured and became a fixture in the "dirt" of Hollywood? But our music spoke to the growing readership that *Flipside* appealed to, and we fit perfectly into the demographic that they seemed most interested in highlighting, namely, the growing suburban clusters of teenagers who rejected the music of the 1970s, brandished a new look, perhaps less stylized than the older punk rockers, but more functional, composed of remnants from Dad's closet combined with accoutrements for a skating and surfing lifestyle, combined with a new attitude appropriate for the new decade.

It's a great irony that I craved intellectual recognition but our first published interview reads more like a comic strip. Michelle asked, "Is this one of your guys' house?" I replied incredulous of the question, "You're in my MOM's house!" thinking to myself, "I'm only sixteen, does she really think we can afford to live on our own?" I could tell that Michelle wasn't that into me. She was older, maybe nineteen, and didn't seem to care much about the meaning of our songs. Furthermore, it was quickly becoming apparent that this interview was a "getting to know you" bit, and kids living with their parents in the San Fernando Valley wasn't much to write about. But I was still motivated to give her a good interview, and I knew that *Flipside* could become an important relationship to nurture for the band's future success.

Al and Michelle had driven from where they lived, and Michelle was making comparisons with our neighborhood and theirs. "This is so far away! What do you guys do around here?" This made me scratch my head in disbelief. Was she suggesting that we lived in the boondocks? Her question implied that the kids in their suburban wasteland, Fullerton, had more exciting prospects than we did here in Canoga Park. Anyone who has visited the Southland in California knows that the so-called communities, each with a different pleasant-sounding name, are actually just street-bordered squares in a patchwork of unending quarter-acre lots with ranch houses, garages, and maybe some grass and a pool in the small backyards. Seemingly endless rows of houses stretch in every direction, creating unbroken stretches of neighborhoods that blend into one another imperceptibly. Cross a particular street and bam! You're in a different zip code. But the suburban landscape remains the same for hundreds and hundreds of square miles. Southern California wrote the book on "urban sprawl." To suggest that one community was somehow "out in the boonies" was absurd. Even as a teenager I saw through such a premise. The only place to be, as far as I was concerned, was in Hollywood or the neighborhoods near it, because that was where the concert venues, theaters, and clubs were that could make your band famous. The notion that suburban clusters of punk rockers had their own unique qualities that ranked as a "scene" was ridiculous. All of the SoCal neighborhoods had more shared qualities than differences. Nonetheless, our San Fernando Valley community was stigmatized as being nowheresville.

I wanted to impress our interviewers with music, so we rehearsed our set. Afterward, we showed them around to some of the local establishments, such as Phases, the disco that held New Wave dance nights once a week, and told some wistful stories about our desire to play more shows in Hollywood. We also demurred. We didn't want to let on that we had recently appeared on a TV show called *New Wave Theater*. Despite the other punk bands invited to play on the show, which would have proved we were in good company, we didn't want it to appear in print that we were associated with something bearing the name "New Wave." Our teenage brains were extremely self-conscious, to a fault, and we desperately wanted to be known as a punk band.

We strove to display a style that would be accepted by punks, even though we were inexperienced at public relations. Our early interviews and our first appearance on *New Wave Theater* depict innocence and silliness. But by 1982 and the second appearance on *New Wave Theater*, we were more experienced. We had made two records, a six-song, seven-inch vinyl recording titled *Bad Religion*, and we'd followed it up with a full-length LP called *How Could Hell Be Any Worse?* If our first appearance on *New Wave Theater* seemed fearful and immature, this second act showed us as jaded, overconfident, snarling punks with a purpose, almost as if we were doing THEM a favor by appearing on their shitty show. We didn't even bother to talk to Peter Ivers after our two songs ("We're Only Gonna Die" and "Part III"). We felt like we were headed for bigger things than just a taping on a local TV show (*New Wave Theater* later was "picked up" nationally by USA Network and integrated into their *Night Flight* music show). Luckily, we didn't burn any bridges back then, because the truth is we benefited by learning from and participating with older collaborators who had more experience than us (such as Jove and Ivers) in turning their creative visions into a finished product.

Nowhere was this more evident than on our first LP. The album insert reads "Produced by Bad Religion," but an older guy named Jim Mankey deserves at least partial credit as producer. Jim's girlfriend at the time, Johnette, worked the front desk at a world-famous mastering facility called Gold Star Studios. We all took an immediate shine to Johnette when we decided to walk into that place for the final mastering touches on our first record. Johnette was so enthusiastic and friendly it made me feel like our band was somehow special. She showed us around the place, introducing us to the personnel. "This is Stan. He's going to be the mastering engineer on your record," she said. Stan Ross was a legend in the industry, but at the time I didn't know anything about him, nor the process of mastering recorded music. Johnette gave us all a lesson. "Stan taught Phil Spector the art of production," she boasted. This immediately drew Brett's interest, because Spector had recently produced the Ramones album that we all loved. We knew we were in good hands. Stan was like your favorite shop teacher. He showed us every piece of equipment in the studio. I listened as a student and observed his techniques. Mostly I was intrigued with the way vinyl master discs were encoded: literally carved out of electromagnetic vibrations from the recorded music on the master tape by a stout needle attached to the electronic signal output of the tape machine. It was all magical and I felt privileged to be there.

On our way out, Johnette said, "Hey, you guys should think about working with my boyfriend, Jim. He's a wiz in the studio and he can help you when you're ready to record more songs." We kept in close touch with Johnette and when the time came to record our first LP, we took her suggestion and started planning with Jim, who is the opposite personality of Johnette—he's soft-spoken, a bit withdrawn, and definitely not the "loudmouth" in a creative situation. He gave quiet, thoughtful counsel about the logistics of making an album and was experienced in the world of recording. Jim had recorded albums as a founding member of the band Sparks in the 1970s, and had made a record with Todd Rundgren. He taught less as a professor and more as a quiet practitioner of a secret craft. He simply stated his preference, and we complied. Jim told us to book time at a studio where he knew the staff. We couldn't afford a top-tier studio like Gold Star, so Jim suggested a second-tier room with top-tier equipment—Track Record Studios on Melrose—and he came up with a great idea to help with budgetary constraints. "The staff will allow me to work with you guys after hours. So let's book a week of time, midnight to 6 a.m., and that should be plenty to get started."

We didn't know anything about running a twenty-four-channel recording console, nor a multitrack tape machine, nor any of the outboard effects and compressors that go into making an LP. Jim handled all of it. In reality, Jim did way more than engineer. He actually had a vision of how the record should sound. Even though I wrote songs on piano and acoustic guitar, it was Jim who had the idea to use them on the album. This decision created some of the album's most notable features, such as the acoustic guitar as a layered effect on "We're Only Gonna Die," and the punk piano that I played on "Fuck Armageddon . . . This Is Hell." Johnette and Jim went on to form the well-known alternative band Concrete Blonde, and it wasn't the last time we would collaborate together.

With two records under our belt, you might assume that the Hell Hole and Canoga Park had become some kind of budding punk rock scene by early 1982. But both remained isolated outposts. The nightlife was all in Hollywood or somewhere around there within a ten-mile radius. Orange County to the south, the Inland Empire to the northeast, and the San Fernando Valley to the northwest were diffuse sources of punk rockers and bands. All of them made nightly excursions to the roughly seven mile stretch of nightlife that went on between West Hollywood and Downtown LA. Local clubs could be found in other regions—Costa Mesa had the Cuckoo's Nest, Huntington Beach had the Fleetwood, and San Pedro had Dancing Waters, all legendary nightspots for slam dancing. But in order to have a chance to be written about by important music critics at the time, you had to play at the Starwood, Whisky a Go Go, Palladium, or any of a number of multipurpose auditoriums within a stone's throw of these Hollywood establishments. These were the places frequented by writers of the *LA Times* and the *LA Weekly*. Literate punk rockers everywhere recognized the quality of the reviews in those publications, and whether we were willing to admit it or not, we jealously watched as other bands were mentioned or reviewed in them and wished it had been us. One of these bands, Mad Society, from Hollywood, was fronted by an eleven-year-old with a mohawk named Steven. No one in the band was older than fifteen, save for Cathy, one of the musicians, who seemed like the band babysitter. They wrote songs about being "hit by napalm" in Vietnam, which was believable because they were kids of immigrant parents. We were friends, and we hung out in Steven's mom's apartment near Oki-Dog nearly every weekend for a stretch of time in late 1980 and early 1981. Despite not having particularly well-crafted songs, nor having much of a serious fan base, they had something we did not: a manager. Her name was Daphne, and she was older, maybe in her late twenties, and had been around the LA punk scene for a few years. She made sure that

Mad Society played the important venues around Hollywood. She got them high-profile gigs that were covered by established music journalists. Her connections to these writers and other musicians helped her create an illusion, through cheerleading, that Mad Society was notable and deserved to be taken seriously. In reality, they were notable for really one thing only, being extreme; extremely young, extremely obnoxious onstage, and extremely stylized. Who wouldn't take notice when you have a little eleven-year-old in a mohawk screaming at the top of his lungs, "When I was a boy in Vietnam, we were hit by napalm!" "Napalm! Napalm! We were hit by napalm!"? Steven was born around 1969. He was a boy still when he sang this song. Nonetheless, it was believable enough that he was singing about his own experience as perhaps a toddler, which seemed captivating and noteworthy. His look and punk attitude made headlines in a feature article for the Calendar section of the *LA Times* in 1981.

Being part of a growing punk scene felt natural, and it was our diurnal rhythm. But there had to be something more. To me, this was the beginning of a great creative experiment. My intellectual influences were all academic. I had to be worthy of the academy, it was in my blood. The only things worth striving for were the immortal ones, the words and ideas that went into the songs. I was supremely jealous of Mad Society because they were formally recognized as making an important contribution to the punk scene by the *LA Times*. Meanwhile, we were not even recognized by promoters in our end of the San Fernando Valley. We had to rely on invitations from our friends' bands there to play.

Our closest club, called Valley West Concert Club, was just a few miles away, on Ventura Boulevard and Winnetka. When they decided to start having punk shows, we, being local, assumed that we would be on the short list of bands to appear there. Somehow, however, the club's booker had gotten in touch with the Adolescents and Agent Orange from Orange County, and we found out through them that they were to appear. No one even called us to perform at our neighborhood's premiere venue for punk rock. Dismayed and feeling disrespected, we nonetheless happily agreed to play as a supporting band for Agent Orange because they recommended that

Bad Religion appear on the same bill. When we got the call, we were over-joyed with the prospect of playing in a concert venue nearby, but even more excited that our friends the Adolescents, who regularly played in Holly-wood and had received critical praise from the *LA Weekly*, decided to make the trek to our end of the Valley to visit us.

On the afternoon of their concert, Tony and Steve and a few others in the Adolescents crew came over to the Hell Hole. I was so excited. The venue was only about five minutes away, so I told them that they could hang out until sound check if they wanted. We rehearsed a little bit, played them a couple of songs, but the real fun began when we retreated to the living room and I decided to serenade them with piano versions of their own songs. "Kids of the Black Hole," "No Way," and "Amoeba" were all amena-ble to nice piano arrangements, and they appreciated my stylized render-ing. These songs seemed to have it all: poetry, defiance, sing-along melody, and even backing harmonies, all accompanied by virtuosic musicianship. Their friendship was heartwarming, but more than that, the experience was inspiring. But friendship in punk often led to the notion that you don't need any help from "outside" forces. We began to think, through friend-ships such as these, we could achieve our goals on our own terms.

In fairness, there's nothing about DIY (do it yourself) that is intellec-tually unpalatable. Sure, if you can reach your goals on your own, then go ahead and do it yourself. But hardly any of the bands that we strove to emulate actually achieved anything without the collaborative efforts of other entities such as record labels and promoters, writers and record stores. It didn't take much scrutiny, even as a teen, to note that. None of the writers that we read, nor movie directors that we admired, nor ath-letes whom we idolized, could do it alone. They were all trained by experts, apprenticed by masters, promoted by agents, and became established in a formalized way. That's why we had heard about them in the first place. We went to movie theaters, concert halls, book stores, and baseball stadiums to see their greatness. After all, the Ramones, Clash, Sex Pistols, Circle Jerks, Dead Boys, X, Fear, and Sham 69 all worked with producers, agents, promoters, and managers who were part of the music establishment and oversaw the activities of these bands by conforming to a structured, formalized methodology. I saw punk music as similar to the way a student is guided by teachers, advisers, counselors, and in graduate school apprenticed by masters and doctors, to achieve the status and ability to make lasting contributions to society. There was really nothing DIY about it. If you want to contribute to the edifice of usable knowledge, the hallmark of your civilization, even if it means overturning the cherished beliefs of yesterday, the way to do so is through formalized institutions, and building on the accomplishments of others.

The Circle Jerks were among our best friends in 1982. Not only had they given *Rodney on the ROQ* our first recorded tape to be broadcast on the airwaves, they also gave us some opportunities to play concerts by recommending us to promoters. We knew that promoters were the key to getting shows. If you could get invited by promoters, and prove to them that you were reliable and had a bit of a following, they would call you time and again and again. One of the most notable early promoters was Gary Tovar of Goldenvoice Productions. In those days they began booking Bad Religion because we were reliable and eager. We didn't hesitate to get in Brett's van, Jay's Toyota pickup truck, and Peter's Mazda, and drive to a gig whenever they called. Their preferred venue at the time was a small warehouse-like room called the Community Center in Goleta, near Santa Barbara. Other notable venues hired us as a support band. We played the grand opening of a venue called Godzilla's that was to be the San Fernando Valley version of the Cuckoo's Nest or the Fleetwood. Specializing in punk rock, billing itself as a kind of "culture center" for the genre, with pool tables and a bar, we played the opening night with Fear and China White in 1982. Later that year we played the same venue, having proven our worth with a reliable following, opening for the Damned from the UK. Gary from Goldenvoice recognized our commitment and reliability, and he kept us in mind whenever he needed an opening act. We were far from an established act. But our words and ideas began to be heard thanks to the collaborative spirit of a vibrant community of punk rock enthusiasts, promoters, and fellow bands. Unfortunately, the "scene" took an ugly turn.

15
INTO THE UNKNOWN

There is a video clip—film, actually—on YouTube depicting a 1984 Bad Religion concert at the Olympic Auditorium. You cannot tell from the clip that we are only third on the billing. I am singing and playing as if the entire audience was there only to see Bad Religion. I am in more ways than one in a world of my own, oblivious to the business of music, content with the relational qualities of the music, and motivated solely by the intellectual pursuit of the creative experience.

I'm buoyant, upbeat, and jocular, displaying none of the classic punk traits that singers before me stereotyped in their stage presence, such as menacing scowls, self-importance, righteousness, and over-confidence. My hair is long; I'm wearing a Guinness hat and "Fuck 'em Bucky" T-shirt. Showing no awareness of the tragic lives carried out by the throng of soulless suburban wasted youth who made up the audience, I string the songs together with mirth, sarcasm, and the lightness of a party host. My friend and fellow college student John sits at the side of Peter's drum kit onstage— acting as a de facto roadie—with a face that shows fear, recognizing the hoodlums, drug addicts, miscreants, and useless no-goods who continue to pile onto the stage and slam dance and stage dive. He does nothing to dissuade them. High as a kite himself, the entire scene he experiences as a dreamscape. There was at least one killer in the audience with a gun, I found out later, who shot an innocent kid for some unknown reason after we had left the stage. John was right to be worried. But my nervousness always morphed into comedy. I displayed it on *New Wave Theater* when beset by questions from Ivers about the meaning in my song. I had not prepared any answers. I was annoyed and frightened by his desire for an intellectual response, so I simply retreated to familiar waters: What would Bill Murray say to this question? "Back off, man! I just write the words!" I said. Ivers was generous in his response, letting me off the hook and coming back with a funnier rejoinder to my statement. He said, "Oh yeah, you don't write the thoughts!"

Punk had morphed into a monster by 1984, and I entertained that monster without accepting its ugly reality. Any of my friends from "the scene" who were still punk at that time were strung out on drugs or drinking heavily. I only saw them occasionally, whenever we played concerts like the one at the Olympic Auditorium. It was easy to separate myself from this group of former friends because they were not at all interested in anything I had to offer in my daily life. This was a period when I began to feel like an entertainer—not a comrade in arms—to the troops of punk rockers who had little in common with me. My days were spent on campus at UCLA going to classes, meeting new friends, new comrades who were, like me, getting trained in field geology and biology. The shreds of punk culture that persisted in me were purely musical fragments that could be called upon in creative reflection or meditative moments to write new music; and the desire to play it never left me.

Perpetual scenester Greg Hetson continued to tour with his band Circle Jerks during this period. They were morphing themselves away from their former punk personality and toward a more lifeless form, melding heavy metal and mid-tempo rock together with a roadworthy touring schedule that avoided much of the decay in the SoCal scene. Whenever they were

on hiatus, Greg would call me up and say, "We should play some shows."
He knew the people putting on the gigs, most of them in and around Hollywood. The nightlife had become less about punk music and more like
nostalgia, resulting in a flawed perception of the original punk scene: a glorification of violence, drug use, and general sleaze. I was willing to lend the
name Bad Religion to this audience because I believed in the goodness of
the music, although the band lacked two of its key members during this
period. Brett and Jay were off and uninterested in performing. If not for
Greg's constant mining for something to do when the Jerks were on break, I
probably would have simply stayed put on the Westside and never gone into
Hollywood at all. But I didn't stay put. I still saw potential in the music
of Bad Religion and I believed that there was a good reason for it to be
heard, even though I recognized that most of these fuckups in the audience were not there to hear good music. These poorly advertised shows
were still truly alternative to the commercial and more popular music going on at the time: hair metal. In spite of waning public interest, however, I
still believed that punk had plenty of potential because it was still the only
musical genre where social criticism played to a young audience, which was
perfectly appropriate for intellectuals and bohemian wannabes like myself.
But the sad fact remained that nearly every slam pit had devolved into a
disjointed jumble of drunk or speeded-out former jocks randomly bump-
ing into or tackling one another in a mad dash to try and get on stage for a
stage dive in a scene that can best be described as a deranged sausage party.
Women, by and large, avoided these gigs. So, given this shit show, there
had to be something of merit to these events. I found motivation in the
weird juxtaposition of extreme intellectualism in the songs alongside brute,
mindless imbecility on the dance floor. This, in itself, was an interesting
satire of the human condition.

I was in my second year of college, so exercising my mind and pursuing punk shows as a philosophical experiment—kind of as a lecturer in
front of apes—was an interesting challenge. Punk music, at this stage,
could not translate to or compete with the more popular, and more creative, hair metal scene blossoming in LA at this time. Ratt, Mötley Crüe,

W.A.S.P., and other rising stars had songs and melodies that were easier sing-alongs than anything created by LA punk around this time. Furthermore, the hair metal bands embraced the "badass" image of drug abusing, street smart, oversexed creatures of the night that were hallmarks of the punk rockers who frequented Hollywood's clubs in years past. This meant that the tug of nightlife still remained in Hollywood for kids from the surrounding suburbs. But without the confrontational stance adopted by the police toward punk rock, the metal shows were a safer bet. Many punk rockers, both male and female, got sick and tired of the violence, nihilism, and cop harassment that typified a night out, and they grew out their hair to join bands or join in the revelry of the new fashion on the Sunset Strip. Costumery and accessories that were previously popular with punks—safety pins, leather jackets, bondage pants, boots with bandanas, chains, and British textiles—were discarded in favor of a more American arsenal of products that metalheads favored: leather vests, headbands, Aqua Net (a hair spray to make bangs and hair tops stiff and pompadourous), lip gloss, costume jewelry, tight pants or bodysuits of spandex or leatherette, gloves with knuckle cutouts or fingerless, and specialty footwear. It seemed fun and creative, and I could understand why the women all seemed to emigrate from the punk shows to these more welcoming and colorful displays of musical talent. Our shows were depauperate of the fairer patrons, and were attended by a dwindling leftover cohort of speed freaks and drunks who wanted to hurt someone, or hurt themselves. Meanwhile, just across town or down the street were metal concerts whose lines stretched around the block, with fans who felt energized from witnessing a new form of nightlife, and in the process actively creating a reimagined vision of the Hollywood music scene.

Whatever this new scene was, it lacked social criticism, and its fans seemed fickle to me; former punks going any way the wind blew. What kind of punk would just grow out his hair and start following bands whose singers are wailing on subjects as inane as being "too fast for love" or having the "looks that kill"? This meant that the punk ethic, however you define it, never really resonated with many fans of the music. They just abandoned it outright and started listening to something else, much more alien, much more pop-oriented, and adorned by much more feminine caricatures.

With respect to hair metal, punk truly was an alternative. It remained a different way of presenting musical ideas. I thought it was still possible to continue the tradition of punk songwriting. I felt that it was a worthy cause to play concerts, continue writing, and thereby extend the intellectual tradition of Bad Religion even though it was effectively background music for a lot of fuckups and thugs. As a selective force, I believed it would attract a few discerning listeners nonetheless. Little did I know just how few it would become over the next few years.

When the ball dropped on New Year's Day 1984, it wouldn't be inappropriate to say that Bad Religion had lost its way. The previous year saw band members adrift from one another, me in college spending my evenings studying, reading, and hanging out with a steady girlfriend. The trauma of punk violence, first from the police breaking heads to disrupt and dissuade concerts, then from scene hoodlums themselves, made going to clubs an activity only for the desperate. Drug addicted or sex-obsessed creatures of the night could still score at Hollywood dives such as the Cathay de Grande, but I had exams to study for and luckily, I wasn't interested in getting high.

My connection to the scene at this time was just a phone call away. Greg Hetson was a scenester who somehow managed to gain in popularity, even as the punk scene withdrew in importance. His band, the Circle Jerks, continued to expand their popularity even through the downturn in the LA punk scene at this time. No single band did more for the popularizing of SoCal punk across the country in the first half of the 1980s than his band. They were punk royalty and their touring business model was one that other bands strove to copy. Nearly every thousand-cap venue in America welcomed the Circle Jerks at that point. Greg would head out on tour for weeks at a time and come home with pockets full of cash. I was so envious. I wondered if Bad Religion could ever be so successful. We were perpetually an opening act. No promoters took us seriously enough to believe that we could headline our own show. The Circle Jerks, however, ran their tours like a business, with an accountant for a drummer, a cynical but serious booking agent, and even a band lawyer for occasional recording or merchandising negotiations. I was in awe of what the Jerks were able to accomplish at a time when the LA scene had morphed to a darker, underground selection of less-popular bands and uninspiring dive venues. The Circle Jerks were, at this time, entitled to play concert halls instead of holes-in-the-wall. Their audience seemed to be growing while ours continued to diminish in size and quality.

The previous year, 1983, saw tumultuous changes in the band. Brett and I decided to write an album that no self-respecting punk wanted any part of. Jay refused to play bass on it, and he quit the band sometime in the early rehearsal phase. We found some friends, musos, not punks, who were willing to record the songs. We titled the album *Into the Unknown* and released it in November. It was a culmination of all the musical influences that Brett and I had loved before we were punk. In some ways, it was entirely a "fuck you" to a dwindling scene that had turned toward meathead violence and nihilistic, misogynist attitudes and away from the tolerant and intellectual attitudes that we perceived and celebrated in the former scene. The album began with a hopeful song, "It's Only Over When You Give Up," that intimates a belief that there was a shred of the former scene's spirit still alive in my mind. The problem with the album is also its greatest legacy: it sounded nothing like punk music. When the only way to attract punk fans at the time was to get harder and more nihilistic in attitude, we went the other way; more musical and elaborate, with songs that resounded with our old favorite themes—philosophy, the environment, and the prospect of humans realizing our potential despite the grim outlook.

The truth about the lack of interest in our new release came quickly. No one bought the album. Copies were being returned by distributors. Furthermore, we had secured a two-night headline billing at the famed Mabuhay Gardens nightclub in San Francisco, which was a major achievement. Not even when we had released our previous album, *How Could Hell Be Any Worse?*, which was well received and sold thousands of copies, were we offered our own headlining show in San Francisco.

But now, because that previous album continued to generate interest, the Mabuhay bookers took a chance on securing two nights for us. Little did they know that we were a totally changed band. Instead of a wall of guitar amps and shredding rhythm section, we unloaded the van with a synthesizer and two clean-cut music school friends ready to play their first gig in a punk club. Brett and I were shocked to find out that they had sold only two tickets in presale. Nonetheless, we played the headlining show on night one to a walk-up crowd of maybe fifty people who had hoped that we would avoid playing the new album. They were disappointed to find out that our new musicians didn't really know how to play many of our previous songs, since they had recorded only this latest album with us. Night number two was a bit better because we had taught the new guys to play "We're Only Gonna Die" and "Fuck Armageddon," two of our more popular punk songs from the previous album. But still, only about fifty-five or sixty people were in attendance.

From an outside perspective, with the benefit of hindsight, the more generous, or philosophical, observer might rightly sum up *Into the Unknown* as a juvenile attempt by amateurs to explore a variety of stylistic interpretations nicked from previous hit albums of the 1970s. Even more generous reviews might claim, as the Bomp! Records president, Greg Shaw, did when he refused to help us distribute the album, that "This album is just a bit too far ahead of the direction that music is trending these days," predating post-punk and a sound that REM came to perfect. The most typical reaction was summarized in a published review: "Into the unknown and out the window!" by *Maximum Rocknroll* fanzine in San Francisco.

The depressing truth was in plain view. No one was really into our new direction. Greg Hetson summed it up best, even though he was not present for the concerts. "Fuck 'em if they can't take a joke." Feeling less like a joke and more like a musical adventure, I coped with the reality of unpopularity by moving further away from the punk scene and redoubling my efforts as a university man. I was more interested in expanding my mind through education instead of taking biochemical holidays to distant shores of perceptive experience. Even though I took every opportunity to play concerts whenever Bad Religion was asked, the word on the street was that Bad Religion had "sold out" and tried to make a commercial record with synthesizer and guitar solos on it.

This was a good time to exit LA, and my acceptance to the University of Wisconsin as a transfer student couldn't have come at a better time. College was an important distraction from the punk world. For some reason, most punk rockers of the early scenes avoided college. I never asked them why, but most of my friends in LA seemed to be more interested in going to clubs than going to classes. Some of them took the idea of DIY way too seriously. They saw it as some sort of sellout if you had to depend on a big institution to educate you. I heard statements like "The street is my teacher" or "I learned from the university of hard knocks." Be that as it may, I never had any lofty aspirations about going to school. I wasn't doing it to justify some false notion that it would make me better than anyone else. It simply was the next thing to do after high school. Probably the most important thing it allowed me to do was avoid having to get a regular day job. As long as I was going to school it was easy to get on-campus jobs that could allow me to pay for expenses while pursuing evolution, a field of study that was quickly growing into a life philosophy for me.

In the early summer of 1984, Jon, my best pal from junior high school, was back home in LA after spending freshman year in Wisconsin. Of all my LA buddies, he was the only one who ever made the visit to my state of origin. He visited me during my summer sojourn in Racine and liked the place so much that, when the time came, he decided to apply to the University of Wisconsin. He was accepted and joined the NCAA Div. I crew team there. I was his roommate that year, but I put in for a transfer to UCLA and in the summer of 1984 I was back in LA. We both had to have a productive summer. He prepared as an athlete. I was going to school to learn zoology and evolution. Punk rock was an occasional fun distraction whenever Bad Religion was asked to open for this or that band at this or that awkwardly named venue that had just popped up. But mostly, punk remained as a mythical place in my mind that inspired me to write songs for a scene that seemed mostly dissipated.

Upon his return to LA that summer, Jon and I chummed around as usual. His coach instructed him to use UCLA facilities to keep in shape and I rode along with him on his daily commute to campus. I loafed around at the student union or wandered the displays in the libraries while he ran the stadium steps.

One day heading back from UCLA, upon the crest of the Ventura Freeway at Mulholland Drive where the entire San Fernando flatland spreads out in front of you as you cross "over the hill" at Sepulveda Pass, Jon was blasting the radio in his mom's K-car. The cheesy stock radios in those cars weren't very good. But Jon, whose musical taste was always in step with mine, let the volume rip on what he claimed was his favorite station.

In 1984, KMET was starting to play harder rock in a big way. Jon proclaimed, "I love heavy metal." He was no different than a lot of punk rockers, even though he was not committed to the punk lifestyle. People who loved punk music lost interest in it simply because by that year there was very little of it being recorded. The small music labels, few and far between, had no power to get their music heard. The major labels had direct lines to the radio stations and were hawking a new commercial sound. Even though "metal" had been in the musical lexicon for quite some time, now it was starting to be sold in big numbers as "headbanging music."

KMET always prided itself on being a lifestyle station. Their DJs believed that rock was a way of life. By 1984, some of them decided that metal, in its general form, fit this bill. Most of the bands they played, Triumph, Scorpions, Dio, and especially Quiet Riot, were a blend of an older, classic, dark metal sound, heavy with guitar chords, simple melodies, leathery accents, and English sensibilities. But a newer sound was being highlighted as well: bands with a flashy look, featuring guitar solo–oriented ballads à la Van Halen, whose singers verged on crooning with emotional vulnerability. The transition to this "new metal" could be easily summarized by listening to Black Sabbath from the 1970s and comparing it to Ozzy Osbourne's solo albums from the early 1980s. There was a change, but it was still obviously metal. Instead of Tony Iommi, now the hard rock guitarists were influenced by Eddie Van Halen and Randy Rhoads.

By 1984, this sound was in its full commercial flowering. People who liked hard music were still out there. In fact, the sound of hard music, rock or punk, was in no way sounding dated. On the contrary, distorted guitars were the sound of FM rock radio. People were filling the auditoriums to hear hard, and sometimes fast, music. If there was any "lifestyle" attached to headbanging music, it was a shallow one. Being "more metal" than the next guy seemed like a ridiculous thing to base a lifestyle on. But I was uplifted by the fact that songs with distorted guitars, raucous drums, and melodic big voices was a popular formula. Regardless of the cultural peculiarities, I still believed that punk rock had yet to find its true heyday.

"Rainbow in the Dark" and "Last in Line" by Dio and "Bang Your Head" by Quiet Riot were on the air, and Jon turned up the tunes. I thought, "This is ridiculous song material." But sure, it was fun enough to hear it on the radio while we cruised home with the windows down as the sun set in front of us on the way home from Westwood. Jon was pumped from his insane athletic workout, and I was full of deep thoughts, having emerged from inspiring meditations in the college library.

16

ACADEMICS AND PUNK

Perhaps it was because I was never introduced to the origin stories of the Bible, but as I read more about evolution, particularly with respect to human beings, I began to make sense of the world around me. There are a lot of technical aspects to the science, but there's also a pleasing big picture view of the world that emerges. No individual is born to fulfill any kind of destiny or cosmic purpose. Every day of life is an adaptive process. The environment is constantly changing, and for humans that includes the social environment. Therefore, no one is in their rights to judge you because you are, just like them, constantly trying to make the most of the situation you've been dealt by factors beyond your control.

It began to dawn on me that some people could use this coarse-grained philosophy to do harm and accept no personal responsibility for bad deeds. That didn't feel right to me. It was an unsatisfying conclusion to try and do harm to others. Similarly, it was not satisfying to sacrifice my own happiness to bring others out of their suffering, as might have been the case if I became codependent with my drug-addicted friends. We were all given a unique set of circumstances, and I felt obligated to try and do as much good as I was able. Where that sense of obligation came from is mysterious, but no doubt it was heavily influenced by observing my parents in their methods of dealing with life's struggles.

Studying evolution became an endless source of information and discovery that would deeply influence my desire to write and share ideas with the world at large. The best way available to me was through music. I was convinced that intellectual study and discourse could easily meld with music and songwriting. Therefore I had to keep Bad Religion active in spirit while at the same time attending school. I could not see any hope of taking a nine-to-five job and achieving my ambitions. So there was no way I would refuse the opportunities to get on stage and sing the songs that I believed might provoke people to use their most precious human adaptation: their minds.

This belief in helping humanity was a lofty goal. In practice I had no way of knowing if my studies, songs, fieldwork, research, or concert tours would ever pan out. Still, I believed that if my songwriting had a unique worldview, it would make the band all the more interesting. Anyone can write a popular or catchy song. But that's the beginning, not the end, of a legacy. To have a significant impact, I felt that an artist must embody a holistic, thoughtful profundity in their work that encapsulates their life journey so that they might bring their fans along with them in a communal experience. This was heady stuff for a freshman university student. But I reached this level of insight from reading about Charles Darwin, the father of modern evolutionary theory. Darwin's life was filled with torment and hesitation because he discovered the facts of life, recognized their profound implications for society (particularly religion), and anxiously, carefully, pondered whether or not to publish his results. After two decades of hesitation, in 1859 he finally released his famous book *On the Origin of Species by Means of Natural Selection*. It became known as the preeminent condemnation of creationism, and to this day serves as the fundamental scientific challenge to those who wish to favor faith over facts. Darwin's dedication to natural history taught me that experimentation, observation, and extrapolation were lifelong pursuits that can form one's evolutionary worldview. Likewise, I adopted the long-term approach to being a singer and I furthermore decided that songwriting could mimic the experimentation process of a scientist.

Some experiments and observations lead nowhere, but the process of their undertaking is valuable. It teaches the scientist to refine the work, learn from the mistakes, and craft a better experiment next time. The conclusions are malleable, temporary placeholders, agreed upon as fixed only until more data, better observations, or new discoveries come to light. This outlook kept me focused on the long term. Songwriting is a process too, and it's a creative challenge to find interesting concepts. Since evolution is incompatible with religion, it seemed like a limitless well of implications that could run parallel with the anti-authoritarianism in punk songs under the banner of Bad Religion. I didn't get overly concerned about the success or failure of any particular recording or song idea. Each one was like an experiment in what I hoped would be a long process of musical refinement. This was the motivation that launched me and sustained me through my academic odyssey.

I spent most of the summer and all of the fall of 1983 in Madison, the city of my birth, studying zoology and geology at the University of Wisconsin. It was a splendid time to be with my childhood friends from Racine, most of whom were also students at UW at the time. We hung out together every single day, all living on campus and eating in the dining halls. I had a job as an ice cream jockey at the famous Babcock Hall scooping out sundaes and cones of the ice cream manufactured on campus by the ag school. For me, it was a dream job. Dad had taken us for ice cream at Babcock Hall as kids numerous times, and I always wished I could have that job because I'd just live on ice cream and water. As penniless students, we employees were allowed to take all expired cartons of yogurt and/or cottage cheese that we wanted. Day-old dairy tasted the same as fresh to us starving sophomores, and I treated my friends to all they could eat.

Being with my childhood pals was deeply rewarding. We even relived the glory of our neighborhood pickup games when we formed an intramural football team and won the coveted UW-Madison intramural flag football championship of 1983. But there was a hole in my creative life. I missed being onstage with my band. I missed the status of being a musician, even if that status had taken a great hit because Bad Religion was on so many punk rock shit lists at the time. I actually felt strangely rewarded that my friends in Wisconsin really appreciated the songs on *Into the Unknown* despite that their opinions meant nothing to the punk elites who decided which bands got to play onstage and which didn't back in LA. But still, I wanted more of a musical career and I knew that it wasn't going to blossom in the Midwest. I wasted no time in transferring to UCLA for the start of the winter quarter in January of 1984.

At this time, the Olympic Auditorium in downtown LA was actively showcasing punk bands that could bring in larger audiences. The ever-expanding Goldenvoice Productions was in its adolescence at this time and they saw the Olympic as a place for serious bands, such as those from England who were used to headlining world tours. The UK Subs and PIL were among the most popular shows of 1984, but equally well attended were shows by the only two LA bands that could separately headline the place and pack it full, the Circle Jerks and Black Flag. The Circle Jerks had their share of offers from Goldenvoice, who placed them right alongside those aforementioned acts as headliners themselves. The Circle Jerks may have stood alone as the only LA punk band at this time that continued to amass a national following of fans and attract the interest of regional concert promoters. The Circle Jerks were a band that promoters didn't have to be afraid of: theirs was a tamer style of punk that got softer and more "mainstream" with successive album releases. Tapping into a more rock-oriented audience proved to open up invitations to parts of the country that previously had never seen an LA punk band.

Interrupting my studies at UCLA was the occasional phone call from Greg Hetson: "Get the horns ready, call the band members! We can play next Wednesday at the Cathay!" We assembled a makeshift band that stayed together for a couple years for the sole purpose of playing those haphazard punk gigs that came up from time to time. Newer music fans who had missed out on their chance to see the original lineup of Bad Religion were treated to an authentic sounding live rendering of our first album and EP. Peter had moved on to another band, so we had our friend John, Peter's occasional roadie, take over on drums and Greg Hetson's friend Tim from the South Bay play bass. Our gigs were only sporadic, usually on weekends at makeshift halls, or when someone at Goldenvoice needed a local "name band" to support an act from the UK. Greg Hetson could always find a spot for us at the Cathay de Grande in Hollywood. They had an ongoing Wednesday night showcase, "six-bands-for-a-buck!" Obviously, payment was not a consideration. Keeping the band together was a labor of love. Singing those songs and feeling like they mattered was my only motivation.

Most of the people who watched us were skeptical, or downright cynical. Punks wanted more harsh lyrics, faster songs, more rage, sleaze, and grime from their front men in order to distinguish their tastes from the more glitzy and unapologetically polished thrash metal that was taking over the clubs at this time. The punk scene was smaller, more violent, less diverse, and less tolerant in general. There was always the suspicion that their favorite band would "sell out" by a secret desire to make themselves more popular. Bad Religion straddled the line. Our songs were of various tempos, some heavy and plodding, like "Drastic Actions," some mid-tempo, like "We're Only Gonna Die" and "In the Night," some faster, like "Damned to Be Free" and "Fuck Armageddon." But all were melodic. Fast or slow, I always infused melody into the music, rather than worry about rage. Furthermore, I wasn't a preachy-type lead singer. I didn't have any rabble-rouser in me. I just sang with a passionate delivery and focused on getting the notes right. I found myself daydreaming on stage. Looking out at a bunch of dudes, angry, drunk, or on speed, taking any opportunity to come up on stage to disrupt the performance, steal the microphone, goosestep or slam dance their way to the edge of the stage, and dive back into the sparse slam pit. Where once a punk rocker could expect to be supported by a sea of humanity in a packed punk club when he did a stage dive, now the audiences were so sparse that a stage diver more frequently ended his act with a dull thud on a concrete dance floor because there was no one there to catch him. Between songs the clubs were dark and silent. Shirtless dudes panting from their inebriated, anaerobic desperation wishing only for a fast drum beat to motivate them further toward collapse. "Shut up and play!" was a common rejoinder to my narration or introduction of the next number. "Faster!" was commonly heard when someone succeeded in wresting the mic from my hand during a slow song. Since we tried to keep the audience entertained, we stuck to a short set list, avoiding *Into the Unknown* entirely. We risked getting beat up onstage if we so much as even breathed that title to the angry crowds.

Even though my "day job" at this time was to be a student at UCLA, I held a secret belief that Bad Religion was a worthwhile endeavor. I had a full schedule of classes, studying, and a new relationship with a girl from San Diego who I was trying to impress—my future wife, Greta. I didn't want her to see me singing for a bunch of thugs and drug addicts in some dingy warehouse, so I told her that Bad Religion had been a featured band at the Whisky a Go Go only a couple years ago. She wasn't really into the Hollywood nightlife, but she had been to her fair share of concerts at the Whisky.

Unfortunately, one of her first experiences seeing me perform with Bad Religion was far from noteworthy. It was in the fall of 1984. I showed up with Greta at some no-name, marquee-less dance hall in a featureless suburban wasteland called Sun Valley. The place looked like it had already been brutalized by the riot squad: broken window in the front, bashed-in metal doors on the side where the bands loaded in. By the time we got there, our drummer John was already stoned, and I introduced him to my new better half. John had this ability to remain calmly observant and hilariously witty with his remarks, even when high—in fact, I was never really aware that he was using drugs at the time. It only came up many years later when he told me so. The audience was sparse, mostly male, and generally drunk or high, showing more scowls than smiles. John said, "I think we're the opening band for a gang fight."

As was typical, there was no backstage catering, no room to hang out and chat with other musicians or guests, nothing that could be described as comfortable accommodations at all. The chill of the autumn night matched an equally dark, brooding, leather-clad cadre of patrons staring each other down, figuring out who would fight who while John and I tried to hide our displeasure with what the punk scene had become. A couple of forgettable bands were on stage before us, hollering into the microphone between songs, "Punks unite!" and "You don't have to fight!" But it was clear that the only thing the audience was interested in was bashing each other senseless as soon as the drums resumed another pointless exercise in rhythmic mediocrity. The stage was just high enough to delimit the audience from the band, but slam dancers readily approached the singers of the opening bands, grabbed their microphones, and shouted nonsensical (presumably gang-appropriate) slogans while the drummers just kept on playing. These slogans led to more violence, and what the bands believed was enthusiasm for their next pointless number was, in reality, frenzied gang fights leading to numerous broken heads and bloody faces.

By the time we started playing, around 9 p.m., I thought that the violence must be over due to attrition from the casualties of the previous acts. I was wrong, although somehow, probably due to the "elder statesmen" status of Greg Hetson on stage, there were fewer attempts to steal my microphone. There might have been 250 people in the venue, which was too few to create a packed feeling on that dance floor, but just right for landing arm-length punches and two-step kicks. Every song we played was interrupted by someone getting knocked out cold on the dance floor. I spent much of the time retreating back toward the side of John's drum kit to stay away from the hand-to-hand combat ensuing at center stage. While singing, I often looked over at Greg—playing his guitar jovially as always, pretending the violence didn't matter to him, which was a useful strategy—with my angry countenance and furrowed brow as if to say, "This is another fine mess you've gotten us into!" My new girlfriend was disgusted, at times saying, "Let's just leave." Even though I agreed with her, I would never leave in the middle of a show—as again, believing, perhaps naively, that there were some people there who really loved our music and deserved to hear the songs they came to see. Still, I was embarrassed that punk had become such a nihilistic, ugly, and artless thing.

As we were loading out to get the hell out of that nameless venue of this nearly forgotten show, John and I exited from the backstage door, heading to where our cars were parked. John noticed that there was a slippery wetness on the filthy alley pavement shimmering in the poorly lit night. It had not rained, so it couldn't be water. Then we realized what was underfoot: so many battered and bruised patrons had been escorted out of the building that night that we were tracking their exit marks, stepping in their pools of blood. It was a long time until I felt confident bringing Greta to any more shows. What used to be fun (going out at night, slam dancing at punk shows) now had become bizarre nightmarish forays into dark venues populated by ugly leather-clad creatures intent on causing bodily harm. It was simply too stressful to be a punk.

17

THE MANUFACTURE
OF DISSENT

Punk was ripe for exploitation. Outlandish desperados were all that was left of the scene. And these were seized upon by popularizers who were uninterested in telling a more compassionate or empathetic tale about the more worthy aspects of the genre. There are guys who wait their whole life for someone close to them to finally kick the bucket just so they can say, "He didn't suffer fools"—calculating bastards who memorize such phrases and use them opportunistically to inflate their own reputations without giving due credit to those who came before. Such artless saps love to throw shit at the wall and see who is interested in what sticks. This is what happened in the early documentary period of the punk scene in SoCal.

Certain promoters and people behind the scenes started telling stories about punk, and the consumers of mainstream media listened. Storytellers were emerging who were trying to make a business out of the punk scene.

In the spring of 1984 my friend Phil invited me over to his recording studio, Spinhead Studios, one day after classes. His pal Dave, an aspiring film-maker, often hung out there too, and he had just brought over something for us to watch on video. "There's this new film coming out by BYO. It's supposed to be about the scene from a couple of years ago. I've got a copy of it!" We watched together as the opening credits ran the title: *Another State of Mind.* "Cool," I said. "I know these guys. Maybe it will be about something positive other than the violence and thuggery and drugs."

The movie depicts a national tour by Social Distortion and Youth Brigade in 1982. Despite its good intentions—the band Youth Brigade was narrating throughout, interwoven with blurbs from other punks in scenes from other cities in North America—it failed to offer punks much hope for a unified intellectual narrative vision. In fact, as the movie went on, I got more and more disheartened. It starts off depicting a huge punk audience slam dancing over the narration of Youth Brigade's singer, claiming, "This movie is about music by kids for kids," which was bullshit because those kids on the film were not slamming to any music made by Youth Brigade. I'd been to shows by Youth Brigade. They couldn't draw that many people to their shows. So, strike one. I protested, "This isn't even a Youth Brigade show, so why is he talking over this first scene in the movie as if he had anything to do with drawing those kids together?" Within the first two minutes the singer-narrator was revealing that some sort of mission is behind the counterfeit concert footage. He was singing the praises of his "organization," the Better Youth Organization (BYO). "Jesus Christ!" I said. "This is a propaganda film?"

Next thing to catch my attention was an interview by one of my heroes, Keith, from the Circle Jerks. I respected Keith greatly. He inspired me. He wasn't a "kid" and he didn't write music for kids. He cowrote and sang some of the most important punk songs ever to come out of Los Angeles. But you wouldn't have guessed that they even knew who he was. Not only did they fail to mention how important he was to the LA punk scene, they didn't even list his affiliation with the Circle Jerks during his interviews or credits. The film kept harping on how bands have to "do it yourself" if you want to be heard. But the filmmakers showed the opposite strategy. They essentially asked for help from others to make their film! And they did so with no intention of crediting them. Is this really supposed to convince anyone that somehow this is an example of a "Better Youth" or "good" aspects of our punk scene? "This is turning into a real shit-pie," I uttered.

And furthermore, "Better Youth Organization" sounded like some kind of eugenics nonsense. I was reading about the dangers of genetic experimentation and social engineering in my evolution classes. Real tasteless shit to anyone with an intellectual bent or knowledge of basic history. This, I chalked up to poor taste, but perhaps let it slide as artistic license. Strike two.

But where the movie finally struck out was when it showed a packed concert featuring images of the Circle Jerks and Bad Religion on stage but choreographed to the music of Youth Brigade over the footage. These were by far the most dramatic sequences of the movie: elated punk rockers dancing to music that they loved by the Circle Jerks and Bad Religion. Two bands never mentioned in the film! The disconnect was that these images were accompanied by overdubbed music from Youth Brigade, a band that never elicited such enthusiasm nor drew that many punks to their shows. This rendered the entire project a sham piece of propaganda as far as I was concerned. "This is video plagiarism!" I yelled. "Is there such a thing?" asked Phil. I didn't know, but it sounded good to me, and both Dave and Phil got a kick out of my film review.

I remembered the uncredited Bad Religion concert well. It was such an incredible turn out. Over a thousand punks, or so it seemed. I took a pause between songs to say to the large punk audience: "Let's switch places. Everyone in the audience up on stage, and when we start the next song we will do the world's largest stage dive!" (That moment is captured in the film at about forty-four minutes in.) At that moment we broke into our song, "We're Only Gonna Die," and mayhem ensued. I didn't know that anyone was filming it, but I'm glad it was captured on camera because it's one of the truly breathtaking moments of satisfaction I had onstage at that young age. That song was played on *Rodney on the ROQ* and the entire

punk community seemed to embrace it at the time of this particular concert. Unfortunately, by the time the film came out in 1984 it felt like whip-
lash. Not only were we uncredited in the movie, but the punk scene itself
had devolved, and had shrunk to a fraction of its size. By that time, punk
crowds that used to number over a thousand were now averaging around a
hundred. The legacy seemed to be dying, and these storytellers seemed only
intent on self-aggrandizement.

I felt then as I do today: If you're trying to point out how "good" your
community or your organization is, you should start by giving credit to
those who helped build the scene that you're claiming as your own.

This experience was par for the course. Around this time, there started
a trend where self-appointed punk experts began to outline their vision of
punk morality. As if some kind of mystic rule book had been lying in wait
for a prophet to emerge to decipher it and let all punks know the score. Like
the attention given to televangelists and old-time religion, the mainstream
media was only too happy to feature these teenage punk philosophers, and
it came across as some kind of attempt to form a new religion. Sweeping
statements. Bold generalizations. No data. "If you don't fight society, society will win!" "You gotta do your own thing because nobody in this society will ever help you out." It was something that would eventually build
into a national pastime. Whoever had the camera on them could claim just
about anything, and a certain portion of the viewers would believe it without question.

Some of us refused to listen to false mandates and knew how to spot
them. But others failed to recognize propaganda. The propagandists
themselves failed to realize that when they spouted off about what is or
isn't punk, they flunked Authority 101. Prescriptive thinking undermined
their own oratory, and lost anyone with half a brain. Plenty of punks, it
seemed, were all too happy to voice their beliefs and conscripts with the
expectation that others would follow blindly. Sadly, the unwashed masses
didn't want to do the work of learning how to think. They just wanted to
be told what to think. There were all too many punk bands who craved
such a following, any following. Sure, I wanted one too, but I preferred it

to be a microcosm of society, a microcosm of the university, an enlightened bunch. For this, we had to assume we were playing to an intelligent audience and give them something to nourish their minds.

I wasn't interested in hearing about my cohorts' unexamined beliefs, and to be frank, I didn't care if they thought I was punk or not. I clung to the notion that music was sufficient to express an interesting point of view, even a defiant one. If that was liked by punks, all the better. For many years, I wasn't interested in doing any more interviews or sharing half-baked philosophy with the fanzines. I was content to acquire knowledge rather than disseminate it at that point in my life. Bad Religion was in the midst of a three-year hiatus between albums. Neither I nor Brett wrote a single punk song. I was glad to be getting trained in informed opinion at the university, restricting my thinking, honing skepticism, trying to focus my thoughts and make statements validated by factual data. Read the independent thinkers. Intellectuals. Darwin and Haeckel, A. S. Romer and S. J. Gould, Ernst Mayr and E. O. Wilson, Sagan, Bronowski and Leakey, Chomsky and Hardin, Hesse and Nabokov, Kesey and DeLillo. Seers. Masters of their disciplines. They're who I admired, and their achievements in arts, letters, and science were aspirational motivation for me.

Punk was becoming stereotyped as having no intellectual merits at all. As if punk was associated with all of society's ills, TV shows highlighted its ugliest aspects. *The Phil Donahue Show*, the popular daytime talk show, featured punk runaways and downtrodden kids. *CHiPs*, the nation's top primetime police drama, featured punk criminals. Even the feature film *The Decline of Western Civilization* by Penelope Spheeris focused more on the violence, nihilism, and teenage rebellion rather than making any kind of coherent sense of the film's title. I watched the movie wishing to hear more songs, see more performances from my favorite bands, but instead had to sit through interviews with punk scenesters, many of whom were acquaintances, being elevated in their portrayal as some sort of philosophers. It was totally depauperate of intellectual focus. And most disappointing, the bands were portrayed to look more like a freak show and less like an artistic community cemented by great music.

The punk follow-up by Spheeris, *Suburbia*, wasn't any better at adding either nuance or general interest to the punk scene. It merely capitalized on and hastened the formation of a seedy, negative stereotype. Loosely scripted, actual kids from the punk scene (rather than trained actors) were asked to act out scenes in the telling of a story about homeless teens in the Southland. Drugs, alcohol, family dissonance, runaways, and so forth. I felt like screaming when I saw it: "Yes! We get it! But what does punk have to do with it?" These things are so commonplace in American life that I suspected that the director was simply exploiting the kids on screen. Getting them to "play themselves" in roles that were stereotyped was just sad to me.

But nothing saddened me more than the onscreen image of André, that kid with the wooden leg who Wryebo and I befriended as schoolboys back in Racine. All his youthful exuberance gone. Now he appeared as one of the film's characters, a drug-addled runaway being exploited for his disability under the thinly veiled premise of storytelling. He was playing himself, but was being used as a symbol of an incorrect and unflattering stereotype. Even though I had lost touch with him a lifetime ago, I still felt a sense of friendship and loyalty, and I believed that he deserved better treatment. We made friends as mere tots according to the dictates of our academic upbringing. Due to the strong urging of our mothers (the administrators), we befriended André in the spirit of humanistic, compassionate values that they instilled. What I saw on screen was a breach of humanism, a glorification of vulgarity.

I always found it puzzling that Black Flag was depicted by Spheeris as some sort of deeply philosophical cult. The truth is, a punk had to make a choice when he decided to go see them play. While the cops were busy bustin' heads outside the venue, inside was a parallel, unconscious, contradictory absurdism only apparent to the thinking person. Black Flag concerts always were dressed with a one-man police force—a roadie named Mugger, crouched in front of the band, mad-dogging the audience, daring any punker to test his might and come up on stage for a celebratory stage dive. "Not on my watch" was the posture of this most famous bodyguard of the LA punk scene. Getting punched in the face for wanting to stage dive was somehow deemed acceptable by many punkers at the Black Flag show. So, basically, if you weren't getting clubbed in the head by the LAPD outside the venue, you risked getting punched in the face by Mugger inside at the concert. None of this was touched on in *The Decline*.

Nowhere in these films or features did they talk about punk as being musically and lyrically compelling. They failed to touch on what made punk so attractive that it could fill concert halls just a couple of years ago but now struggled to fill small clubs. They didn't give enough attention to the essence of what made the SoCal scene unique: the multitude of bands that sprung from the Southland and the songs that made them great. The music was in a quagmire. Bands stopped writing good songs. So began a period where preaching about proper conduct in the punk scene overshadowed the music of the scene. Punk went into a sort of hibernation.

18
INTELLECTUAL TRANSITIONING

Any thoughtful kid of college age needs brain food, new mental challenges, if he wants to expand his intellect during his life's journey. Those old songs didn't pack the same wallop for me in 1984 that they did a few years prior. The punk scene in 1985 hadn't produced any newer bands that contributed much quality material to the punk songbook as far as I could tell. I was compelled to add to it, but I needed newer themes to feed my rapidly expanding worldly outlook. I was interested in writing songs that could expand on and update my experiences stemming from the stagnant drabness of the suburban moment.

Southern California, arguably the largest suburb in the world, was at the height of its population growth rate. With over a hundred thousand new residents coming to the Southland each year, it saw influx from all walks of life. But despite this upbeat metric, no intellectual grist was being served in the punk scene. No wonder "Richard hung himself," as the spin-off band

DI sang at that time. Nihilism was rife and it became synonymous with Southern California punk. There was nothing on the menu to offer any later generation of punk rockers.

The anti-intellectual flavor of conservative thinking, so prevalent throughout the Southland, especially in Orange County, championed stereotyping, factionalization, conspiracy theorizing, combat rather than negotiation, competition rather than symbiosis. In short, gang mentality thrived in this anti-intellectual climate. The stereotyping of punk rock as a nihilistic, hopeless community of drug-addled, lazy ne'er-do-wells intent on breaking laws and smashing property had reached its apex, and most punk concerts at the time were filled with fans who were only too happy to live up to the stereotype.

I consciously sought to counter these stereotypes. I had an inner drive that always brought me back to songwriting as a means of cathartic expression. The natural world, its laws and principles, and the unceasing creativity in natural processes required study, and inspired observation and reflection. The result was an unending list of interesting subjects for song material.

My determination was slowly hardening into a personal resolve to continue the band's tradition even though it was in the absence of Jay and Brett and despite the detours that the punk rock scene decided to take. I had my own detours to explore.

At UCLA, my instructors were field geologists and field biologists who sent us students out of town and into nature as often as possible. We had use of the fleet garage vehicles, mostly Suburbans or fifteen-passenger vans, that shuttled us from the classroom to the outcrop. School for me was a chance to go camping as much as possible. Study of geology and biology meant seeing the textbook examples in the field. Weeklong excursions to the Sierra and Inyo ranges with Professor Clem Nelson (a legend of California geology), birding trips to Mount San Jacinto and Malibu with Professors Tom Howell and Martin Cody (ornithology legends), or weekend collecting trips to San Diego beaches, the Coachella Valley, or Transverse Ranges with Professors Ray Ingersoll and Ted Reed were par for the course every semester during my training as a naturalist.

An entire semester-length class, the Field Biology Quarter (FBQ), was spent away from campus, in tents and campgrounds collecting data on species distribution and environmental conditions and identification of birds, snakes, mammals, plants, and insects. Field Geology was a series of classes that spanned years of the undergraduate curriculum. Each academic quarter, a different region was chosen for us students to spend as much time as was needed for mapping, collecting hand samples, and identifying the myriad minerals and rocks in the structurally complex backcountry of Southern California.

One of the instructors of FBQ was a shit-kicking, guitar-playing, fortyish, longhaired, mustachioed, salty-dog professor named Laurie Vitt. Not the typical-looking prim and proper faculty type, more like a badass Tommy Shaw from Styx. Laurie spent most of his time in the wilderness identifying and studying the behavior of reptiles and amphibians in the Amazon basin and in the southwestern USA. On all of our excursions he carried his trusty six-string guitar in the back of his field vehicle, a 1970s Econoline van. An accomplished guitarist and singer, he perpetuated the mythology of the campfire sing-along and appreciated my singing ability and interest in music. Laurie took a liking to me and sort of took me under his wing when we were in the field together. He showed me how to snare lizards (humanely) and how to pick up venomous snakes. One of his favorite areas was the Coachella Valley, especially because of the large number of pristine areas that supported a great lizard biota, but also because the mountains that flanked the southwestern portion of the valley contained a particularly interesting species of snake, a subspecies of the rosy boa (*Lichanura orcutti*).

Laurie liked to call me "flake-o," but that was his term of endearment because he truly was a rock 'n' roller who, like me, found a path of coexistence for academics in his life. Like a true original, he didn't think much of punk music or the guitar playing of Neil Young, or anything resembling a copycat. He simply championed talent and curiosity. His philosophy was shared from the driver's seat if you were lucky enough, as I was, to ride shotgun on the way to the next field site. He told me lizards in the wild are pretty much

the perfect model for all animal studies. They even demonstrate charac-
teristics from which human traits were derived and from which humans
have not successfully diverged in our evolution. "That lizard over there,
see him on the rock? He's doing his amphiplexus (pushups) because he's
demonstrating visually to all other lizards within eyeshot that he's the king
of the territory. He has access to all the females within this area. When
a musician is on stage, he or she has the rapt attention of everyone in the
auditorium. Simply by virtue of their position onstage, like the lizard on a
rock, they are exceptional in the population. Humans haven't been able to
decouple this basic lizard social phenomenon from their lives: no matter
that consciousness and intellectual rationalization evolved in parallel, we
are still essentially like lizards. The position and privilege of having the best
territory (in our case, the rock and roll stage) means the most evolutionary
success in life."

Aside from the truth or lunacy of his ramblings, I was taken by the ability to use facts from nature and apply them to a philosophy of life that was
meaningful and satisfying. It provided an intellectual framework for me.
Bad Religion was starting to be a comforting intellectual platform that
allowed me to share my observations of the world with a wider audience.
It was just such a shame that that audience seemed to be getting smaller,
more nihilistic, and more drug-addicted as the decade progressed.

I became fast friends with a couple other FBQ students named Jay and
Mark. On a trip to Mexico our class spent a month at a field station in the
middle of nowhere near Chamela, Jalisco. The field station was centered in
pristine tropical deciduous forest, and each student was to find a research
project by wandering around the trails in the forest and looking for something of interest. Almost every student chose to work on some diurnal animal or plant. Birds and euphorbs were common and easy projects. Mark
chose birds, Jay chose euphorbs. Their routine was easy: do some observing
or collecting in the morning and spend the afternoons writing up the data in
the lab. I, however, chose to work on nocturnal ants, a fascinating social animal with lots of interesting behaviors to observe. The only student to work
at night, I observed leaf-cutter ants with my headlamp and notebook in

hand while my classmates were drinking beers and eating dinner in the field station commissary. This meant that my afternoons were free, so I hung around with Jay and Mark in the laboratory while they wrote up their data.

We hit it off immediately because of our similarly cynical view of nearly everyone around us. Our comical and ironic takes on society, especially academic life, made for great bonding. After a long day of collecting and measuring plants, Jay often cranked up the lab boom box to play his favorite mixtapes. Many of the songs were by Neil Young. I had heard many of these songs before, because back in junior high school my buddy Jon had an older brother who played acoustic guitar and would serenade us singing Neil Young tunes in his whiny, high-pitched falsetto. I was always impressed with the songcraft, but anyone who tried to re-create those songs on acoustic guitar sounded almost comical. Jay, Mark, and I often sang them a cappella, and we couldn't help but crack up every time we attempted to do it with a straight face. We would greet each other in high-pitched falsetto: "Hello cowgirl in the sand!" That song would, in a few years, serve as a template for me and Brett's idea for a new Bad Religion album.

Having returned from FBQ fieldwork, and back in LA, one day my friend Phil called me up and asked if I wanted to record some music at his newly renovated studio in North Hollywood (Spinhead Studios). I had written some music that was inspired by Neil Young, and we recorded it with Phil on bass. We got Greg Hetson to come down and play guitar too. These were days of avoidance for us, avoidance from the punk scene that used to be our primary focus. Phil spent more time building his recording studio. I was spending more and more time away, out in the field, doing academic work. We both enjoyed camping. He joined me on some trips geologizing in the Coachella Valley. We both rode motorcycles at the time (it was my primary transportation in college), and his 750 Honda was much newer and more enviable with its electronic starter than was my beater of a cycle, a 450 Yamaha with only a kick-starter.

One of my songs from this period, "Runnin' Fast," really exemplifies my attitude during this time of my life. I constantly felt like I was trying to "keep my distance" from the world of previous acquaintances who were still stuck in the punk scene. Most of them didn't go to college, but rather drifted in a downward spiral of drugs, alcohol, or general nihilism that seemed to haunt me in its constant presence. If I ever wanted to hang out with my friends of old I would have to descend into this pit, or so I felt. So I was "Runnin' Fast" from that world. Phil also went to UCLA (in math and philosophy), so we bonded intellectually and musically. I felt assured by him that not all punks were descending into a bottomless pit of negativity. Phil's friend Dave Markey used "Runnin' Fast" as part of a soundtrack for a movie he was making called *Desperate Teenage Lovedolls*. I didn't see the movie when it was completed. But I appreciated the creative effort that clearly was still present in some corners of the punk rock scene at that time.

My prowess as a field scientist was driven as much by my enthusiasm to get out of town and eagerness to go camping as it was by my general curiosity about species and natural phenomena. I received a good reputation from instructors and other students as a faithful field companion and good observer. This afforded me no end of opportunities to go on field excursions. Club concerts still availed occasionally, but I was much happier escaping the city entirely, avoiding the banality of the monotonous, shallow nightlifers who populated our scene in 1985.

At home I spent time writing when I wasn't studying. Through some conversations with my old pal Brett, I learned that he was interested in recording another Bad Religion record. He said he was cool with not playing on it, but since he was building a new studio, maybe he could just be present as producer and engineer. I always was uplifted by his involvement, and at the same time, I wanted to support his work toward a career in producing, so I gladly accepted his offer to make a six-song EP called *Back to the Known*.

I had written a song that began with "When everybody dies around you from someone else's gun, it makes you stop and think about the time to come." I changed the tone of the song to reflect on the human race, but in reality I was commenting on the disappointments I harbored regarding my fellow punk rockers. The song was called "New Leaf" and it states simply, "You better turn over a new leaf, because the old one's turning on you." I was probably experimenting with a personal mantra at the time. It was, after all, a justification for my dedication to intellectual study and my continued search for less nihilism, drug abuse, and violence in my life, opposite of the typical punk scene. The EP also contains "Along the Way," a song about life's journey. It's as close to a religious song as I ever wrote, perhaps. The last line details a juvenile hope that somewhere along the path from molecules to man to death to dust I will again see my old pal Tommy from the old neighborhood in Racine, who had died unexpectedly while I was away doing fieldwork in Arizona. Tommy woke up one morning to take an exam at the University of Wisconsin, turned off his alarm clock, and his heart stopped. He never got out of bed. "My Tommy you are free and you will not follow me, but we'll see each other once more on the path along the way." Songs are so good at reflecting life's absurdities, ironies, and hardships that sometimes they overwhelm my abilities to perform or recite them without breaking down in tears. "Along the Way" would not be the last time I used songwriting to cope with personal tragedy.

Despite releasing the EP *Back to the Known*, Bad Religion's fans were few and far between. The gigs we played were still populated by mostly dudes, often drunk or wasted, usually on a weekday night, so only the professional drinkers and club-goers were in attendance.

Punk didn't come looking for me at this time. I'm sure that there were plenty of kids who were still clinging to some outdated notion of what punk "should be." But I wasn't it. I doubted that punk rock formed the core of any kind of vital music scene at this time. The punks around Hollywood were more into the nightlife, the debauchery, the idea of a punk lifestyle than they were into the songs or the creativity of punk rock. So, in a sense, my enjoyment of singing and writing new material was all that sustained the band. Bad Religion went looking for punk rather than the other way around. The only offers for Bad Religion shows came when Greg Hetson went looking for them at various dive bars and dingy clubs.

One of the last shows I remember during this "looking for punk" phase was a weird ad hoc gig thrown together by some hippie promoter up in the small ski resort community of Lake Tahoe, California, high in the Sierra

Nevada. Greg Hetson had been pals with Tony Alva, the famous skateboarder, who had a band, the Skoundrelz. Tony asked Greg if the Circle Jerks could play a show with them in Tahoe because a promoter up there was trying to bring in some SoCal credibility to the nightlife in that dull community. Greg Hetson and Tony Alva were big names at the time, and even though the punk scene was drab in Hollywood, it still had cachet in places that never experienced punk rock before. There was no way the Circle Jerks would play a show on spec; they were getting top billings in major cities all over the country at the time. But Greg suggested to Tony that Bad Religion could play the gig. Even though the promoter had heard of Bad Religion, he really knew nothing about the band, but he took the package of two bands from LA because his specific desire was to make connections between the LA punk / skateboard culture and his budding vision of a viable nightlife in the heart of Lake Tahoe ski country, all centered around his nightclub. Greg Hetson said the offer was five hundred bucks for a Saturday night gig in February.

I was up for a weekend jaunt up the Owens Valley, a place from which I had just returned during a geology field trip a few months prior. I always welcomed an opportunity to cruise Highway 395 to see the world-class geology and Mojave Desert biome up close. I drove the guys in a rental van and chose all my favorite rest stops, some on scenic dirt roads to take breaks, look at rocks, and take in the panoramic vistas. It was a majestic winter day with a dusting of snow covering the creosote bushes that stretched across the alluvial fans. The White Mountains to the east and the Sierra to the west were painted with a seam-straight horizontal snowline about halfway up to their crests, all draped with the wondrous, white, shimmering signature of the season. This five-thousand-foot marker line got lower as we got closer to our destination, and by the time we reached Lee Vining, California, the land was completely covered with a few feet of snow.

Lake Tahoe was about a seven- or eight-hour drive from West LA, so we had left early and arrived at the venue for a late sound check, around 7 p.m. The place was a wood-paneled mid-century modern building with a big fireplace in the foyer. It looked like a classic ski resort restaurant type place, perfect for warming up after a long day on the slopes but not appropriate at all for a punk concert. The promoter greeted us with the usual cheer: "Guys, it's great to see you! The doors open in a couple of hours so take your time setting up and then hang out in the backstage room. I'll order some pizzas and you can have a few beers at our cozy bar." Then he wasted no time in bumming us out: "The presale tickets are a little light, but I'm hoping for a big walk-up." We had heard that song so many times before that we already knew this place was a bust. No way did anyone in the vicinity care about punk rock, or knew of the Skoundrelz or Bad Religion. Maybe some skateboard insiders knew Tony Alva, and perhaps some weekend ski bums on vacation might have seen the Circle Jerks before, so that might bring in a few people (the flyers for the show mentioned "Greg Hetson from the Circle Jerks" in big letters).

As predicted, only a handful of people showed up. Punk rock was just not popular enough for outposts such as Lake Tahoe to attract a large enough audience to support a vibrant club scene. We were guinea pigs in this promoter's experiment. He thought he could bring in bands from LA and San Francisco for weekend gigs and pack the house. His vision was about ten years ahead of its time. The ski resorts had too few young kids into this kind of music. Snowboarding and X Games culture had not yet materialized. We were way ahead of that tide. The only people who showed up were the same down-and-outs who came to the Hollywood shows. Dark creatures, drunks, and speed freaks, into the idea of fast, aggressive music but not really interested in the songs. It seemed as though they wanted background music for their depression. Here in Tahoe, amid the majesty and winter spectacle of giant snow-clad forests and moonlit granite peaks, the dismal, dreary creatures of the night seemed even more out of place than in palm tree–lined streets of Hollywood. Like in the City of Angels, here they lurked too, but in smaller numbers, looking for a venue and a live soundtrack to fuck shit up and destroy themselves in the process.

Onstage, I gave a half-assed performance. They didn't care; they just wanted John to play faster beats on his drums and Greg Hetson to turn up his distorted guitar. The makeshift stage inside this multipurpose room that functioned as a restaurant during the day was not acoustically outfitted anyway. The monitor speakers were way too loud and too close together, so the lead vocal microphone was constantly in feedback mode. The on-site "soundman" corrected this by simply turning it down so far that the vocals got buried by the snare drum and guitar noise swirling around in the nearly empty hall. My mind began to wander: "Well, at least that was a hell of a scenery spectacle on our drive up the 395 today!"

When it came time to pack up and head home, I had to go "collect" (the euphemism for "get paid") from the promoter. I told the other guys to get their equipment into the van as soon as humanly possible because this was going to be a "take the money and run" situation. By this time the promoter had had one too many drinks and reported the dismal news from the ticket office: "We took in a lot less than I had hoped." ("No shit, Sherlock," I said to myself as I rolled my eyes.) He pulled out about $600 and showed me that this was all he received from the door ticket sales. "Can I pay you two hundred and make up the rest when you come back with another band from LA, like the Circle Jerks or something?" At this point I knew that he had made money selling drinks at the bar and wasn't sharing that info with me, so I asked him point-blank: "What does a guarantee mean to you?" We were guaranteed five hundred bucks, and he was offering to pay us less than half that amount. Even the "guarantee" was barely enough to pay our expenses for getting there in the first place, which included the rental van, gas, and a motel room. The guy was offering me his drunk sincerity, which was nothing more than righteous self-pity and self-centered logic. "I can't continue my quest to create a music scene up here if I keep losing money." I asked him another question that seemed to really make him despondent: "Why would I encourage any of my friends' bands to come play for you if your guarantees don't mean anything?" (In reality, Greg Hetson was my only friend in a famous band that meant something important outside of Hollywood, so this was kind of a bluff.) The promoter started to cry and said, "You can't cut me off like that! I need the connection, man!" (I guess he meant he needed contacts to meaningful bands from LA.) I took the opportunity to remove $500 from the pile of money and bolt out of his office just as Tony and the Skoundrelz were entering the room to collect their "guarantee." Whatever their fee was, I know that the guy had only about a hundred bucks left on the table, and the Skoundrelz were a lot less interested in asking him rhetorical or logical questions. Their methods were less cerebral than mine.

The guys were all waiting. The van was packed up and idling with the heater on. The tailpipe was billowing steam vapor. It was about twenty-two degrees outside, and the parking area was slushy and messy. I skipped across the parking lot from the backstage door, jumped in, and said, "Let's get the hell out of here. I got our guarantee. But I don't know how he's going to pay the Skoundrelz." "I'm sure they'll take the bar money!" said Greg Hetson. As we exited the parking lot, a vivid image in our rearview mirror was etched into my memory. The promoter was being chased out of his own venue by some of the Skoundrelz crew. We slowed to get a better view of the action, wondering what was to become of this hapless promoter. I could see him as he was surrounded by the assailants. He backed up with his palms facing forward, slurring and pleading with them: "Guys, you can't cut me off like this! I'm trying to build a scene here!" His words meant nothing. The Skoundrelz crew grabbed him like a sack of potatoes, held his legs to the sky as if to shake his pockets clean, and stuck him, head first, into a snowbank. We drove away down the dark corridor of Sierra forest highway with mirth and amusement, peering at the two-legged wiggly apparition casting moon shadows on the snow in our rearview mirror.

The debacle in Tahoe was by no means an uplifting prospect in terms of punk's growth and acceptance as a musical genre. Today, I look back and wish I could have been more magnanimous. But there was no scene, no community. Just a loose assemblage of opportunistic club owners trying to make ends meet.

The band went through various changes during this time. Jay had decided he wanted his position back, so he called up Tim, who had taken over on bass, and said, "Hey Tim, I think I'm going to play bass from now on." Tim said, "Okay dude, I was just saving the spot for you." Then we hired Lucky, Greg Hetson's old drummer from the Circle Jerks, to take over for

John on the skins for a while. Lucky was a freshly minted lawyer after leaving the Jerks to get his law degree. With this lineup we did a short tour in the dead of winter on the East Coast. Lucky was used to playing in a major headlining band, but this tour was nothing like the Circle Jerks. Small, dingy clubs with atrocious sound and lights were our fate at that time. Poorly attended and unhighlighted by any local music press, we withered on the road in cities such as Richmond, Virginia; Norwalk, Connecticut; Bethesda, Maryland; and even Boston, Massachusetts. We played to tiny crowds, only a handful of people, in each club. In fact, we missed the Boston show completely, arriving at 6 p.m. to find that the billing was for an afternoon matinee. The shows were so poorly organized that some of the clubs didn't even know we were coming. So-and-so got a call from so-and-so and said Greg Hetson of the Circle Jerks was coming to town with his other band, Bad Religion. It was not unusual for word-of-mouth bookings like this. No advertising, and very little fanfare (or staff) anticipated our arrival at these makeshift gigs. At one of the venues, Rocket's in Richmond, a glorified drinking establishment with a tiny stage at one end of the bar, Jay was answering the telephone, fielding questions from locals about whether there was going to be live music tonight. "RRRRRocket's! May I help you?" When they asked him who was playing tonight, he'd offer some comical name of a band and we'd all bust up. But jocularity aside, we weren't really having much fun on that trip. It was the end of the line for Lucky, who had lowered himself to play these shows, coming off of much more successful and uplifting shows all over the country with the Circle Jerks.

At a time when REM was headlining the Philadelphia Spectrum, one of the premier concert arenas in the country, there we were answering phones at a bar in Richmond, Virginia, a city that barely even knew who we were. REM was curious to me in that they had tapped into something called "college rock" that was to my ears, at that time, anyway, not too different from what we tried to do when we recorded *Into the Unknown*, an acknowledged failure. Their fame was puzzling because I *was* in college and had a band of my own, but I never thought of campus life as uniquely suited for only one style of music. There's too much diversity to form a coherent musical genre.

But I had the uplifting notion that maybe intelligence in music was in fact becoming a valued commodity again. This was perhaps the spark that made me long to rekindle a lost relationship with my co-writing partner, Brett.

But the live show was a different problem. What's the use of having good songs if you couldn't perform them in decent venues? The shitholes that were typical punk haunts at this time couldn't have cared less about presentation of the band. Greg Hetson used to say, "Just give me any stage and I will rock it!" That was his rationalization any time we showed up to a place with a makeshift stage and no PA. I wholeheartedly disagreed with that point of view. We weren't a jazz band where all the instruments can be heard regardless of whether the club had a good PA or not. We depended on our lyrics, and if I couldn't be heard, the ideas would go unshared, and the songs were as good as dead to me. At one of our shows in St. Louis, for instance, the bar ended at the stage. I could walk five feet and order a beer while performing! There was, however, no PA on site. When we asked how I could possibly be heard if there was no PA, the club owner claimed, "Look, all the bands do just fine here by using the house bass cabinet and turning around the stage monitors. We just had Gang Green in here last week, and they didn't complain. What? Are you guys special or something?" I didn't feel special. But if "special" meant taking exception to low standards, then yes, I was special. Punk audiences deserved as good production quality as any form of music, but too often there was this attitude that "it's JUST punk"; they don't need any decent equipment. Too many venues and promoters took this approach, and I felt powerless to change their attitudes.

What wasn't apparent to me at the time, and maybe none of us realized it, was that there was only one route to exit the dreary existence of dive bars and answering our own phones. We needed an agent who could establish and communicate our high standards with legitimate promoters who only dealt with venues that took production and presentation seriously. Lack of an agent was the main thing that separated us from our more successful touring peers like the Circle Jerks and Black Flag. We had to rely on word of mouth, which in those days of a dwindling punk scene didn't amount to much. If not for our friends at Goldenvoice and other regional promoters we wouldn't have ever gotten any offers, and even with friends in high places, the number of offers were still limited and somewhat arbitrary. Greg Hetson made friends with promoters in other regions of the USA during Circle Jerk's tours, often mentioning that his other band Bad Religion should be considered to come play. But those mentions more often than not got handed along to other less-well-established venues and promoters whose offers landed us in unadvertised beer joints far away from home. Only rarely did we end up playing in established venues where the Circle Jerks played, and when that did happen, such as at City Gardens in New Jersey, or, say the Living Room in Rhode Island, it turned out to be a dull thud rather than a spectacle. We weren't the Circle Jerks. And furthermore, the show flyers usually read: "Bad Religion featuring Greg Hetson of the Circle Jerks," which maybe was the key to our pitiful attendance. Fans wanted to see the Jerks but not their guitarist's side project.

Along we continued, agentless, into a long period of waiting for the phone to ring. For the next couple of years, whenever Goldenvoice needed a strong support band, a band that had a decent following, could sell a few tickets, were appropriate for the mishmash of thrash or metal or goth headliners that were touring at the time, they would call Bad Religion. Here began a steady stream of shows, every few months, at Fender's Ballroom in Long Beach or other Goldenvoice venues in the Southland. Slowly, over the next two years, the audiences began to change.

In the fall of 1987, Bad Religion got a couple random calls from promoters asking if we'd like to play as an opening band. Good old faithful, Fender's Ballroom, had a show with Shattered Faith where we showed up to open the show and we had more of a following than I anticipated. It was uplifting. Despite the Suicidal gang that frequented Fender's and caused havoc with many concertgoers, the violence actually subsided when we went on stage because so many of the Suicidal gang were Bad Religion fans. Uplifting too was the fact that we seemed to be attracting more females to these shows, despite the gang presence, which I found to be a sign of rejuvenation and broadening appeal.

How wide this appeal could extend, however, I never really gave much thought. If there were limits to Bad Religion's appeal, I was ever willing to test them. I really didn't care what bands we played with, so long as the stages were built with great sound equipment. Perhaps the best example of this scenario was an offer from Goldenvoice in November of 1987 to appear onstage with Dramarama, an early alternative rock band that had climbed the charts in LA thanks to the heavy airplay they received from radio station KROQ. Needing an opening band with some pull, Goldenvoice stuck us on the bill only about a week before the show was to take place. I can't recall a single advertisement that said we were added to the show, but to everyone's surprise, word of mouth spread quickly and we had a great turnout of our own fans. Even many of the Dramarama's thousands of followers took notice of our catchy, upbeat songs. This show left the promoters with a positive impression, and it reminded them of something Goldenvoice's founder, Gary Tovar, had said previously: "Never underestimate Bad Religion." This show proved that we not only could bring in fans of our own at clubs like Fender's, but we could also prove to be a draw on bigger stages at more established concert halls.

One day, shortly after my return from an expedition in Bolivia, Brett came over to my new apartment in Brentwood where Greta and I were living together. He had recently gotten clean and sober, and had rejoined the band for a gig in San Francisco. Brett had been doing a lot of recording and perfecting his sound engineering craft, so he had all the tools for making a new record at his studio, Westbeach Recorders.

That afternoon, while hanging out in Brentwood, we began discussing the possibility of recording again with the whole band. We were well aware that the radio station that used to play our songs, KROQ, didn't even have a punk show anymore. *Rodney on the ROQ* was playing a lot of retro garage band stuff from the 1960s, hosting bands like Redd Kross that were still making records that sounded like grungy surf music, and trying to get his listeners to believe that this stuff was "happening." But it wasn't. The popular music of the time on KROQ was pop-oriented club and dance music from bands such as Depeche Mode, Erasure, the

Smiths, and INXS, or early alternative rock bands like REM, U2, and
Dramarama. Our motivation was in no way shaped by the possibility of
having success at radio at that time.

But we felt that we could create something way better than our previous
recordings, and that was an attainable goal. We tinkered around a bit on
my acoustic guitar, but eventually I started to play some Neil Young cover
songs. When I strummed "Cowgirl in the Sand" Brett claimed, "That's a
killer chord change." And then we used that first guitar progression in the
song, a simple change of A minor to F suspended, to start what would become an album's worth of material that captured our worldviews and attitudes at the time. The song became the title track of our album, *Suffer*. Thus
began the most prolific period of songwriting in Bad Religion's history.

The Administrator. Mom, aka Marcella Graffin (*center*), with her staff, pictured at the height of her career as a dean of the learning skills department at the University of Wisconsin–Milwaukee in 1976. In August of that year, she accepted a deanship at UCLA, opening the California chapter of our family history.

The Professor. Dad, aka Walter Graffin (*with jacket and tie*), showing author Norman Mailer around the campus at the University of Wisconsin–Parkside in 1972. Dad acted as host to invited speakers in the English department, where he taught and served as chair for his entire academic career.

The man who would be step-Dad. Chuck, a highly talented multi-instrumentalist jazz performer: "Clubbin' it" with my mom at a Milwaukee nightclub around 1975.

Practicing sax around his apartment in Milwaukee around 1974.

In the role of step-Dad with me (*left*), my mom, and my brother, Grant (*right*), in Colorado during our cross-country emigration to California in 1976.

LAKE BLUFF SCHOOL
PARENT TEACHER ASSOCIATION
SHOREWOOD, WISCONSIN, 53211

May 14, 1976

Dear Mrs. Graffin,

The Lake Bluff PTA is pleased to inform you that
your son Greg has been granted $50.00 in
scholarship funds to be used toward attending
music camp this summer.

Mrs. Jane Perkins, Lake Bluff vocal music teacher,
made a recommendation to the PTA board based on
Greg's talent and potential in music, and the
PTA felt that they would like to help in furthering
his development through music camp.

We hope that Greg will enjoy his camp experience.

Very truly yours,

Joan Spector
Secretary, Lake Bluff PTA

First evidence of show-biz aptitude. A letter from my grade-school administrative office.

"The Fab Four" posing with friends Jeff (*standing left*), Frankie (*standing right*), and Danny (*kneeling left*) onstage at Lake Bluff Elementary in Shorewood (Milwaukee), Wisconsin.

In the act of performing a dance routine to "Boogie Fever" by the Sylvers, a no. 1 hit disco song of 1976.

Choir. Summer music clinic. My brother and me (*standing sixth and seventh to the left of the central music stand, with the "Prince Valiant" matching haircuts*) being instructed by the choirmaster during a rehearsal, preparing for a chorale concert at the University of Wisconsin–Madison in 1976.

Among the Profs, #1. The kids with their Gods/Fathers at a Greek restaurant in Racine, 1977. From left: Dad, Wryebo, Peter Martin, Tommy, Grant, Dan Zielinski, me.

Two homes, worlds apart. Our humble abode on Woodlake Avenue in Canoga Park, California, the place to which we moved with Mom in 1976.

Our humble abode on Saint Clair Street in Racine, Wisconsin, "Dad's house," that became our home in 1968 and still serves its original purpose as our family residence (depicted in this painting from artist Patrick King).

The Hell Hole. Behind the pleasant façades of the San Fernando Valley's neighborhood streets was a seemingly endless labyrinth of unfriendly alleyways lined with six-foot walls of fence-board and cinderblock stretching between countless two-car garages. Mom's garage, shown here on the left, became Bad Religion's rehearsal space. Affectionately known as the Hell Hole, it had no windows and no shade from the unrelenting California sunshine.

Punks in New York. Me (*left*) with my brother, Grant, (*center*) and pal Wryebo (*right*) on a trip to New York City with Dad in the summer of 1980. Before I was a singer, I had already established my understated "punk look" that I carried forward when Bad Religion was formed two months later in Los Angeles.

Punks in LA. Hanging out with singer Keith Morris (*holding beer can*) at a college frat party at USC, where the Circle Jerks and Bad Religion were invited to play, November 1980.

Photo by Gary Leonard

An impromptu photo session with the band (same event as in the previous photo): left to right, me, Jay Ziskrout, Brett Gurewitz, and Jay Bentley in a fraternity kitchen at USC.

Photo by Gary Leonard

Me (*lower right*) and Jay (*suspended in the act of tumbling, with back to camera in the striped shirt*) with our friends gathered in the Hell Hole during a Bad Religion rehearsal posing for a poster published by *Fer Youz* photographers Brian and Nikki Tucker in 1981.

Photo by Brian and Nikki Tucker of Fer Youz

Onstage at the Whisky a Go Go, 1982. While learning the craft of being a front man, my leather jacket served as a sort of security blanket and I wore a watch at all times, as seen in the photo on the next page. Barely visible over my right wrist is a brass pin from the National Honor Society, an academic adornment I stole from my dad (I had not yet achieved such a rank).

Getting away from it all. Keeping my distance from the "scene." Fieldwork, exploration, and research with fellow students informed my worldview and enriched my songwriting. Just after the release of our disastrous *Into the Unknown*, I headed to a remote field station at Estacion de Biologia, Chamela, Mexico in 1984: me (*back to the camera*) playing volleyball with biology pals Mark (*leaping*) and Jay (*behind him*).

Backpacking the eastern Sierra with artist Jerry Mahoney and my girlfriend Greta in 1986.

Hiking in Glacier National Park, a month prior to embarking on the "Suffer" tour, 1988.

Back home in Indiana. Well, not entirely. Whenever the Hoosier siblings got together, we sang good old-time tunes and I learned to pick along. Here we are in Mom's Virginia townhouse during a Thanksgiving family gathering, 1991. From left: Mom, Uncle Stanley, and me.

Tour buses, band, and family, Europe 1993. Our European tours were a mélange of punks, families, roadies, trucks, and buses. In this 1993 photo is a typical assemblage of roadworthy characters: Howard Menzies (*tour manager, fourth from left*), Greg Hetson (*next to him*), Graffin family with baby Graham (*center in light clothing*), Brett and Gina (*behind us*), and Bobby Schayer holding baby Max (*pointing at right*).

Soccer with band and crew, Hamburg, 1993. A day off from tour in 1994 for a friendly match of "footie" in Hamburg, Germany. The band's team (*in white*) was composed of me (*standing fifth from left*), Jay (*back row with cap and glasses*), Brett (*standing near middle with glasses*), Greg Hetson (*kneeling, with glasses*) and "coach" Howard Menzies (*far right, with striped shirt and glasses*). We were pitted against a fiercely competitive group of German roadies and musicians (*in dark jerseys*) including our friend and future agent, Jens Geiger (*standing at left*).

Among the profs, #2. Graduation for my master of science degree at UCLA, March 1990, with my advisory committee: Peter Vaughn, paleontologist (*far right*), Ted Reed, sedimentologist (*with handlebar mustache*), and Gerhard Oertel, petrologist (*far left*).

Me, Dad, and my PhD adviser, Will Provine, historian of science (*left*), at the celebration for my doctorate, Ithaca, 2002.

The guys at rehearsal, 2001. In the process of believing. Brett and I were writing together again and the band seemed recharged in 2001. Here we are at a rehearsal studio in Hollywood, before the addition of a new drummer, working on songs that would become *The Process of Belief*. From left: Jay, Brett, me, and Brian.

Photo by Lisa Johnson

The band and crew. The band and crew gather after shooting an online "live stream" concert at the Roxy Theater in Hollywood, California, April 2021. Pictured left to right (*front row*): Tess Herrera, Christina White, Jay Bentley, Dave Gibney, Mike Dimkich, me, Brian Baker, Gavin Caswell, Rick Marino; (*back row*): Ron Kimball, Greg Stocks, and Jamie Miller.

Photo by Caroline Jaecks

19
THE PATH TO
SUFFER

West LA is glamorous to outsiders, but living there can be rather monotonous, crowded, and uninspiring. Nonetheless, the seasonal pungent aroma of jasmine flowers in every apartment building foyer on the Westside stays with you for a lifetime. Geographic redolence at its utmost. The jasmine plant is from the East. West LA is filled with Eastern intrigue. In fact, it infects the thinking of many people who live within only a few miles of the Pacific strand line. In 1987, I was only 2.8 miles from the ocean. A short bike ride down San Vicente Boulevard from my apartment and I could be on the beach, though I usually just rode along it, never stopping to meditate or let the onshore breezes wash over me.

My girlfriend and future wife, Greta, along with our best friends from UCLA, Jerry and Inga, had never lived farther than a few miles from the beach for their entire lives. Even though they were raised in conventional

American Christian households, living by the beach, on the Pacific Rim, seemed to have a profound effect on their worldview. They, like so many others in SoCal, had their own blend of Christian values coupled with the popular notions of ancient Asian religions. Heaven meant happiness on Earth as well as eternity. It could be found by walking on the beach. Reincarnation was practicable, so respect for sea life was required since one day that might be you. "Health food" stands serving sprouts and protein shakes and all sorts of Asian herbs were highly respected. Meditation was preferred as a replacement for conventional Western prayers and rituals. In general, it was a pleasing blend of trying to live lightly on the Earth while disregarding the reality of overpopulation and urban sprawl for which LA was the poster child. All the makings of bad religion. Perfect fodder for songwriting!

I started graduate school in 1987 while living with Greta, who also served as the breadwinner. She had the best job for a beach bum: a waitress at an overpriced steak joint called the Chart House, in the heart of Westwood—our "college town" next to campus. It was one in a chain of six or eight restaurants, all within a stone's throw of a marina. One was in Malibu, one was in San Diego, one was in Sausalito, and this one, near UCLA, was the farthest one inland, about 4.5 miles from the beach. Despite its distance from the shore, however, it was THE place to hang out if you were dedicated to beach life. Surfers, volleyball players, fishermen, lifeguards, resort developers, yachtsmen, and all manners of lifestyles of the rich-and-famous made the Westwood Chart House their nightly stop for a quick surf-and-turf meal. The early-evening grill hours meant that there was plenty of time after the meal to go mingle in the wood-paneled warmth of the cocktail room where sexy servers in Hawaiian print dresses brought every concoction of tropical libation imaginable. The bar was the true attraction, and it stayed open into the wee hours of the night. The constant serenade of soft rock and New Wave ballads spilled from the bookshelf speakers. The soundtrack was *Breakfast Club* mixed with "Margaritaville." Cocktail waitresses made the most money because they could serve a steady flow of overpriced drinks for a consistent eight-hour workday. The food waitresses earned bigger tips, but the rush was only a few hours long, from about 5 to 9 p.m. In both cases, a waitress had no problem making hundreds of dollars every shift.

I was urged to "get a job" by my wife-to-be. I was content as a part-time audio engineer, but it brought in less than four hundred bucks a month. Greta could make that on a weekend. So she got me an entry-level position at the Chart House—the salad bar host. I enjoyed cheesing with the waitresses in the kitchen when there were breaks in the constant food and drink shuffle. But in general, this wasn't my scene. I didn't grow up on the beach. I didn't surf. I was studying the science of beaches—geology of the coasts, biology of the sea—but that wasn't lifestyle stuff. I just put on the Hawaiian shirt uniform, made the salad bar presentable, refilled the radishes, but mostly I chatted with people. I asked patrons how they were doing tonight. I met some famous personalities from Hollywood who frequented the joint. I met David Crosby at the salad bar. "How are you doing tonight, Mr. Crosby?" He had just gotten out of prison and responded, "Happiest guy this side of Texas!"

My manager at the restaurant would implore me to try harder. "Greg, you have to keep the copper on the salad bar shiny if someone spills some ranch dressing." "Greg, if you just show some initiative, we can move you up to busboy where you'll participate with the waitresses in earning some of the tips." Boy, did they misjudge me. I was only there to show the barest initiative possible, and that was to keep my relationship intact. Greta made having a job conditional with us living together. Fair enough. I valued our relationship more than "moving up" as a professional server. But one thing I valued greatly, and that was getting to know people who were not like me. All the waitresses, some of whom were Greta's best friends, were friendly and interesting. Many aspired to go on to careers in modeling and acting. Even if they were a bit "hippie-dippie," I enjoyed comparing worldviews with them. It was all in good fun, and yet I learned from talking to them that they were incredibly ignorant of what had transpired only a few miles inland over the last decade (the Hollywood punk scene). Beach types such as these never really spent much of their free time going to punk shows. At this stage in my life, however, that was just fine with me. As far as I could tell, very little intellectual stimulation was going on in Hollywood in 1987 anyway.

My friend from UCLA, Jerry, worked at the Chart House too, and his girlfriend Inga was a manager there. Jerry was a student of human behavior. An anthropologist of sorts, he knew the California beach lifestyle better than anyone, and yet he was equally critical and celebratory of all who practiced it. Jerry used to revel in the observation that most of these people were the shallowest minds of all. Most beach types, in his opinion, had not been privy to great enlightenment because they had spent their entire existence within one mile of the strand line. Del Mar and La Jolla—beach towns in California where Jerry was from—represented the ends of the Earth: true paradise where everyone on the planet dreamed of living. Those who lived there were acutely aware of their idyllic situation and therefore believed that there was nothing left to achieve or to long for. To them, life was just passing time, one more spectacular sunset, one more set of perfect waves, one more stiff drink before bed. Their reasoning had a dulling effect on their intellect, or so Jerry believed. "Why go anywhere else when everywhere else wishes it could be here?" This absurdism luckily never infected Jerry, who was always up for an adventure.

Jerry, the unwitting philosopher king of SoCal beach culture, was someone I looked up to and could pal around with, someone who shared my inquisitive search for meaning in a dissipated, frazzled society. Older than me by a few years, Jerry, like me, went to UCLA to search for more answers. Studying and practicing art, illustration, painting, and drawing, Jerry spent his time reflecting on the world's contradictions and displaying them in his artwork. Jerry had spent a lifetime as an early adopter of all things adventurous in California: new designs on surfboards, skateboards, and eventually even Segways. We bonded over mountain biking.

Living in West LA meant you could ride your bike anywhere. I lived about two miles from campus. I rode every day, and strapped my textbooks onto the rack. On weekends, Jerry and I might hit the trails for a day's outing or just cruise along the beach on commutes between our apartments. The fun and laughter never ceased when the girlfriends joined us. Whether working as a foursome at the Chart House on the same shift, having picnics at the beach, playing volleyball at Marina del Rey, or backpacking in the Sierra, life was becoming more and more domestic, routine, and stable. Nothing about this lifestyle was characteristically punk. But the burning desire to comment on life's absurdities did not dissipate in me.

When Jerry and Inga got married, for the ceremony they chose the place that all "alternative" spiritualists choose in Southern California: the Self-Realization Fellowship. Headquartered in Encinitas, not far from San Diego, the organization's ornate temple sits high on a cliff overlooking a beach known by local surfers as Swami's. A satellite temple located near Malibu provides easier access to God, in that it's closer to LA's publicity-craving spiritual-type celebrities. Jerry and Inga chose the Malibu location for their ceremony. The setting is typically New Age, with lots of lotus flowers and reflecting ponds. Jasmine scent is ever present while the roaring surf in the distance adds to the soothing auditory and visual sensations. Theirs were practical Western vows of matrimony despite the Eastern accoutrements.

It didn't escape my notice that there is something extremely attractive to many spiritual Southern Californians about the idea that you can create your own personal relationship to God, without all the doctrine and restrictions of conventional religions. Most of my friends in Wisconsin were completely secular. They didn't consider spirituality as something to pursue in life. But Jerry, Inga, and Greta, and even Brett to some degree, all smart Californians, found interest in blending a secular lifestyle with some aspects of Buddhism and Hinduism, such as Transcendental Meditation. Both Buddhism and Hinduism emphasized the importance of meditation, and these Eastern philosophies seeped into California culture.

My equally atheistic friends in Wisconsin never gave alternative spirituality any notice. Nonetheless, it served as an interesting philosophical topic that Jerry and I discussed at length from time to time, especially leading up to his marriage ceremony at the Self-Realization Fellowship temple.

"Permanent peace and happiness" is what the Self-Realization Fellowship was promoting, and it can be achieved through meditation, and God
can be found through self-discovery. This kind of New Age practice was
nonexistent in the Rust Belt. But in California it was everywhere. It came
in with the hippies as a popular way of thinking and flourished there.

If someone really wanted to find God, that's his business. But I always
thought it was a true luxury to think this way, a condition of someone with
a really privileged life. The kind of life you likely had if you lived within
a few miles of the California coast. The kids who grew up in Rust Belt
factory-working families didn't have the freedom to meditate or sit cross-
legged on the sand and watch the sunset. Their parents had to work the
long shifts. They learned how to find God in Sunday school doctrinal pam-
phlets and Bible lesson books. The lucky ones were kids like me who didn't
have to go to Sunday school. It was okay for us to believe that God didn't
really exist at all. So I never believed that an easy beach life was any closer
to God than a hard life on the frozen tundra.

Ironically, for a guy who never left a one-mile strip of land along the Pacific Coast, Jerry's art was always terrestrially themed. His philosophy was
too. There were never spirit animals from the sea nor myths of Poseidon
nor leviathan devils nor Polynesian magic in any of his work. But like so
many Southern Californians, he felt paralyzed by the thought of venturing
too far inland or living somewhere without a beach. Inland places were only
for short, inspirational visits, like to a national park, or perhaps a desert
palm oasis, but never for permanent habitation. It was natural, therefore,
for him to conceive of the torment and torture that must permeate the
youth who were bound to the inland neighborhoods, far from the beaches,
of Southern California. When it came to the topic of suffering, his worldview was inspired by Buddhism, and he spoke to me like a prophet.

One sunny afternoon, while hanging out on the porch of his and Inga's
Santa Monica apartment, Jerry said: "Life is really just a series of moments.
You remember only a few of them, but you extrapolate them into an entire childhood experience. If you have even just a few moments that are extremely traumatic, you forget all the good stuff." What he said made a lot of

sense. Closer to my interests, I suggested a nice parallel. "Yeah, you're right. I mean, there are songs that we remember for our entire lives. Not just the words, but the melodies they're associated with. There are parts of my brain that have locked words and melodies away despite decades of new songs, images, experiences, and emotions being added all the time. I may forget most of those new items, yet still that damn song remains intact!"

Jerry learned that Buddhists put a lot of emphasis on suffering. He told me: "Suffering is the result of psychic stress and actual painfulness caused by everyday mundane life. Everyone is suffering every day." I thought that this idea was consistent with an evolutionary worldview, and it was something I could get behind. We weren't geniuses concocting some doctrine to use as an opiate to attract a cult following, but our ideas would blossom and meld nicely with those heady thoughts that my bandmates and I had discussed over the years.

I told Jerry that Brett and I had recently written a song called "Suffer." Not specifically a song about Buddhism, Jerry nonetheless took an immediate liking to the religious innuendoes of the concept. We were going to be recording in Brett's studio every day for the next week, and I told Jerry that I could envision the concept of suffering as a good album cover. "Maybe you could illustrate an album cover for us, Jerry." As Jerry and I talked into the night, he came up with some ideas for album artwork.

In the spring of 1988, during these recording sessions for what would become our album *Suffer*, the band and I discussed ideas and themes of the songs. Full of our usual mirth and jocularity, we devolved into childlike goofing. "Picture this," I said. "What could be more emblematic of modern man's suffering than going to the dentist? We get an artist to draw the most realistic looking dental chair as the central image of human suffering." Dental realism began a series of absurdities that led to Brett's addition of lyrical couplets to Greg Hetson's comically imbecilic song title: "When Man First Hit Man":

> When Man first hit Man, he hit him with a rock,
> he hit him 'cuz another man was trying to touch his cock.

When Man first hit Man, he hit him with a stick,
he hit him 'cuz another man was trying to touch his dick.
When Man first hit Man, he hit him with a stone,
he hit him 'cuz another man was trying to touch his bone.

And on and on this went throughout the recording sessions, wasting time coming up with songs and lyrics that would never appear on any album. Through it all we failed to arrive at a visual concept for the album cover. In fact, other than the first EP cover art, which was Brett's logo idea, and our first album cover, which was my own idea, every subsequent album was created by outside artists who were inspired by song concepts that Brett and I presented to them. Jerry's "suffer-boy" image would become iconic.

After we were done recording, I couldn't wait to get Jerry and Brett together because they both were my friends, yet from different backgrounds, and they both shared deeply philosophical interests. The lyrical concepts on the album were a true reflection of Brett's and my take on a hodgepodge of philosophical topics from evolutionary biology, Marxist ideology, and capitalism to religious fanaticism. I was eager to see what illustrations Jerry could add to the mix with his Buddhist leanings and critical eye on society. Having heard some of the rough mixes without formally being hired as our artist, Jerry just started working on his own, creating sketches.

The song "Suffer" was one of the first that Jerry homed in on. He wasn't really into punk music per se, but he dug the words and appreciated the artistic integrity of the sound. He could tell, as we all could, that this was a serious album that could raise a lot of eyebrows if people would give it a close listen. Most of all, he loved how the concept of "Suffer" jibed with his Buddhist philosophy. He rendered a sketch of a kid, no more than twelve years old, stamping his feet in protest and shoving his fists down to his sides as if there were a fierce wind trying to blow him over. I wasn't sure where Jerry was going with this concept, but his sketches of the kid looked believable. Like some SoCal skateboarder who was getting booted out of a store's parking lot or something. A few days later, Jerry showed me the next rendering of the sketch. He had added a setting that resembled any of the thousands of nameless neighborhoods in the flat, inland basins of Southern California, just like ours in Canoga Park. Now I started to see what he was getting at. This kid is in the foreground, pissed off at his neighborhood.

But the clincher in the illustration came a few days later when Jerry married his Buddhist influences and philosophical leanings with what he perceived as the mundane reality of Southern California lifestyle. Jerry added a burning flame billowing from the kid's head. It represented the suffering that links the notorious Buddhist monk self-immolation image (in protest to the Catholic-led repression of South Vietnamese Buddhists in 1963) with the current trend of skateboarding and punk rock protest against the complacency of life in the suburbs. This absurdly interesting juxtaposition gave Jerry's image a deeper philosophical meaning and it very concisely summarized the fact that Bad Religion was more than an archetype of an outdated punk scene; we were continuing to pursue an enlightenment agenda as an alternative to traditional religious thinking. It was the perfect album cover for a rejuvenated Bad Religion. The allegorical flame of suffering became as meaningful an image as any concocted for a punk album throughout the history of the genre. The "suffer-boy" would become a popular tattoo for punk rockers the world over. When Brett saw the drawing, he commissioned Jerry to make a painting of it for the album cover. The image went on to countless reproductions, tattoos, skateboards, magazines, and fanzine covers. The album was set to be released in September of 1988.

For the first half of that year, we played every month in and around the Southern California region, coupled with a few shows in Arizona and San Francisco. Returning to familiar haunts such as Fender's Ballroom in Long Beach, it was clear that our audience in California was growing. We played the new music of *Suffer* even though none of the audience had the album yet. Thrash-metal kids and beach punks alike were showing up, and this blend of cultures was nicely complemented by an influx of female music fans who definitely helped to defuse the violence that had pervaded the punk shows during the previous few years. These were punk rock concerts with plenty of slam dancing, but the audiences seemed to be more about the music and less about hurting each other. Slower songs like "Drastic

Actions" from our earlier EP and "What Can You Do?" had great tempos
for dancing, and the melodies were infectious. We began to build our reputation as a melodic but heavy band with plenty of background "oohs and
ahhs" (aka "oozin' ahs").

By July of that year, the band had to take a break to accommodate my
academic work. I was off to Colorado to do some stratigraphy and fossil
collection in the Sangre de Cristo Mountains of Colorado, the location
I'd chosen for my master's degree in geology. Approved by my paleontology mentors, Peter Vaughn and Everett C. Olson, the locality was remote. I spent the month camping with my adviser, Ted Reed, collecting
fossils and mapping the stratigraphy high above tree line. This was a previously unpublished locality for some of Earth's oldest vertebrate fossils,
and Ted and I were there to find evidence of their environmental conditions. In keeping with my advisers' wishes, and appealing to my attitude
of challenging the "held view," my project sought to shed light on an unpopular, but difficult to ignore, hypothesis regarding the origin of the vertebrates. The conventional wisdom was that vertebrates had originated in
the ocean. Ted and I found the sedimentary rocks of the Sangre de Cristo
Mountains were deltaic and beach deposits that had small feeder chan-
nels with terrestrially derived clasts and sand grains. This is where the
vertebrate fossils were located, in the terrestrial sediments. They were
absent in the marine deposits. I concluded that the earliest vertebrates
were freshwater creatures. My published report was widely ignored. But
the evidence remains.

Being punk trained me not to get disheartened by the lack of enthusiasm surrounding my work. There was, and still is, a quasi-mythological
conviction in the paleontological community that vertebrate life must have
originated in the ocean since all other animal life-forms originated there.
This narrative colors all discoveries and is used as a starting point in the
unraveling of any aquatic vertebrate fossil find. Challenging this notion was
not popular and a sure path to ostracism within the field of paleontology.
Even though there was a precedent—one of the most celebrated paleontologists of the twentieth century, A. S. Romer of Harvard, advocated a

freshwater origin based on kidney physiology—my work became negatively scrutinized after it was published.

This bothered me little. In fact, lack of recognition can be a great motivator if you believe in the value of your work. I knew that the science was sound, and since all my advisers signed off on the thesis, my confidence in the conclusion was reinforced and remains strong to this day. The lack of recognition from other scientific peers seemed in concert with the lack of credit given to Bad Religion at that time. Not many people believed in us, but as punk rock slowly began its resurgence, many would come to recognize *Suffer* as a significant contribution to the genre.

20
MOVING

I entered "holy" matrimony in August 1988 at a church less than a stone's throw from where the surf meets the turf in Del Mar, California. Greta and I had been living together in a one bedroom Brentwood apartment near the UCLA campus and we did everything together. Our weekends were filled with unremarkable activities, going to movie theaters, hanging with our friends Jerry and Inga, working at the Chart House, sometimes puttering down to the beach on my Yamaha motorcycle. Typical young couple stuff. Bad Religion gigs took up occasional weekends, but since my graduate school work was demanding, the band didn't travel much that year. But our sedentary status was about to change.

The wedding chapel overlooked the ocean. All my bandmates were there. Some of my friends from Wisconsin made the journey too. It was the first time I had my childhood friends from back East hanging out with my friends from LA, a crew that they had only heard about in stories. The whole bunch gave Greta and me a nice send-off at the Del Mar train station for our honeymoon. We took the train up to Montana and stayed at the lodge in Glacier National Park. On one of our day hikes in the park I broke it to her: "Pretty soon, after we get home from this trip, the guys and I are going to tour the USA. We are really stoked about how *Suffer* sounds, and we've got about twenty-five shows lined up!" I can't really imagine what I was thinking, breaking this news on our honeymoon. I was definitely high from the magic of the moment—being in wilderness amidst world-class mountain scenery—and maybe I felt a tinge of altitude sickness. But let's just say my enthusiasm was quickly blunted by her protests. Greta did her best to voice her displeasure while restraining her outrage, and obviously, my inability to focus on just the two of us during our honeymoon must have been a drag. But even out there on the trail, I was swept up in my private thoughts about the burgeoning enthusiasm for Bad Religion. An argument ensued. We hiked back to the lodge, both disgruntled. I was leaving for tour right after the honeymoon. Only a few weeks after the wedding day, it should have been clear that the marriage was doomed, although we added a few happy chapters before that occurred.

Suffer was released in September, right after we returned from our honeymoon. We had played some successful small shows in Hollywood, including a headlining show at the Stardust Ballroom on Sunset Boulevard two nights before I took the vows, and they were packed. In 1988 our shows were getting bigger in Southern California, and more diverse as well. The influx of thrash-metal crossover fans was definitely having a positive effect. Here was a scene that cited punk bands as their influence but rejected most of the violence and nihilism of the punk scene. By rejecting the lifestyle components, thrash metal came to focus more on the music. Clothing choices and hairstyles were more pedestrian, an indication that thrash-metalers paid less attention to those outward fashion elements than the punks did. Or perhaps it was that the thrash-metal scene had less interest in leather and spikes, wristbands and bandanas, any accoutrements associated with the street-fighter aesthetic of the past. Music itself was the lifestyle, and punk or not, that suited me just fine.

People were responding favorably to this new album of ours. *Suffer* gave us all the spark we needed to believe in ourselves. We were sure the enthusiasm could translate to other cities. In LA it was no secret that we'd built up a new following over the previous couple years because of consistently playing those small shows at the Cathay de Grande, opening for various bands throughout the Southland, and being dependable enough that promoters came to us more frequently. It didn't hurt that we still had a sizable number of original fans from the older scene. They added to the influx of thrash-metal kids who were now taking an interest in us. And furthermore, now we had a sonic masterpiece (or so we believed at the time) to share with the world at large.

But perhaps the most important element for me was that Brett believed in the album enough that he was willing to support it fully. As soon as we got back from our honeymoon, Brett called me up and said, "Dude, we're going across the USA to play punk rock!" We didn't have a booking agent at the time. Nearly all the shows were put together by a loose network of acquaintances or friends of Greg Hetson who tried his best to field calls and book advance dates for our upcoming shows. Some club owners would call Brett because he had an office at his recording studio that simultaneously served as the headquarters for the band and record company. Brett didn't hesitate to send them promotional materials for the *Suffer* album and a band photo. But there was no concerted national advertising and no written agreements with any of the venues. We simply took off on a tour to hit a series of clubs that were holding spots for us. It was implicit that we would have to haggle with the promoters each night to get paid. As it turned out, some nights we wouldn't get a penny.

The genuine hype that we experienced at our shows in Southern California did not translate to other towns across the country. Our first stop was Houston, fourth largest city in the USA at the time, and there were less than fifty people in attendance. In Chicago, second largest city in America, we played a famous bar across from Wrigley Field, the Cubby Bear. Maybe twenty-five people showed up. Even fewer attended the night before in St. Louis. Despite the local club owners' flyers that stated "featuring Greg Hetson of the Circle Jerks," it was clear that the billing of Bad Religion "from Los Angeles" didn't mean much in these major metropolitan areas.

To make matters worse, the record was not in the stores yet. There was little to no coordination between the record distributor and the tour dates. Our shows preceded the availability of *Suffer* by a number of weeks in many cities, and we didn't carry any records with us for sale at that time. Brett's relationships with national record distributors was brand new. Even though Epitaph Records had been a label in name for a number of years, these were the early stages of his push to sign new bands and distribute more than just Bad Religion albums. There were assurances that by the time we got to New York we would see *Suffer* in record stores.

On September 18, 1988, we finally made it to the Big Apple. En route, we played a disco in Rochester, New York, and passed through the wooded wilderness of the Finger Lakes region. I was taken by the endless hills and verdant valleys, all synced together by winding roads and dotted with colonial villages. I thought, "This area has it all—wilderness, woods, and waterfalls, all within a short drive of numerous metropolitan areas." Little did I suspect that I would be moving there in a couple of years to make a home around Cornell University.

CBGB in New York City proved to be uplifting. Not only was it a legendary place, but it also had that "vibe" of importance to musicians and fans alike. It was a place that transcended time and persisted through all the changes in underground music throughout the decades. On the outside, it was a grimy shithole; inside was not much better, especially the holding tank, a back room where the bands were sequestered before they hit the tiny stage. The walls and ceiling were black but spattered with old flyers, old paint, new graffiti, or dried bits of last night's deli tray. Nonetheless, the aura of significance oozed through the scummy décor. This was the same club where the Ramones hung out and debuted along with Blondie, the Dead Boys, Talking Heads, Devo, and Johnny Thunders. This made it feel like a welcoming, even comforting, waypoint in an otherwise chaotic odyssey of grubbing for peanuts from promoters and club owners who couldn't have cared less who Bad Religion was. We joined a bill with some other local New York hardcore bands on a typical Sunday "matinee" show, and the place was packed. It was a familiar feeling to look out at a crowd of music fans similar to those in LA, one portion of punks mixed together with thrash-metal kids and a healthy smattering of females too. I was excited to see some Bad Religion "*Suffer* tour" T-shirts for sale at a makeshift merch table in the corner of the venue. With the proceeds, I hoped that we could afford to maybe increase our nightly motel budget to two rooms instead of us all piling into one.

All in all, the tour was a financial failure. My new wife was not stoked that I brought home with me a credit card bill of nearly $2,000 from various expenses I collected during the tour. Luckily, I earned a decent wage as a TA, teaching comparative anatomy to premed students so we could pay our bills. Further good fortune came from a flurry of offers to tour and play regional shows near SoCal. They never ceased, and 1989 and 1990 saw an increasing outpouring of interest in the band. Simultaneously, my academic career was taking a step forward.

For the next year I carefully balanced my bread-and-butter academic teaching job with an ever-increasing touring schedule. The tours were short and mostly regional. They provided some decent pocket cash, but I didn't want to sacrifice the predictable and steady income from teaching, so we continued to tour around the academic calendar. Our first tour in Europe was during summer vacation in 1989, and instead of a credit card bill, I came home with $3,000 in foreign currency. I started to believe that playing live shows could be just as reliable as an academic salary. Nonetheless, I applied for and was accepted into the PhD program at Cornell University across the continent in Ithaca, New York.

On July 23, 1990, Bad Religion wrapped up our second European tour in Berlin. With a few thousand dollars in the bank, I returned to LA, sold my motorcycle, wrapped up my personal belongings, loaded them into our Dodge Ramcharger, and within one week Greta and I said goodbye to our Brentwood apartment and set off on a cross-country trek to an unknown future.

Interstate 10 was the ribbon of highway that led me away from the Southland to my next chapter in life. It passes directly down the middle of the Coachella Valley, that geological wonderland where we students of the guild spent so many weekends and field trips trekking, hammering, and sampling the outcrops along the San Andreas Fault. I entered California for the first time exactly fourteen years prior, to the month. Here I was departing, saying "so long for now," ascending the gentle escarpment that rises from the floor of the desert along a superhighway etched straight as an arrow due east, over the Chiriaco Summit, and a beeline for the Arizona border and a horizon that opens wide to beckon all young men who defiantly reverse course and go against the grain of history, from west to east. On that day, Coachella Valley, with its groves of dates and citrus quaking from the pervasive wind-blown dust, along with the lonely California fan palms, waved a parting salute in my rearview mirror. Bad Religion had grown to international notoriety. That fact was slowly sinking in. I had the option to stay put, maybe get my PhD at UCLA, build on my local reputation as a singer-scientist. But instead, as we crossed over the Colorado River a sense of elation overwhelmed me. The sense of going somewhere unknown, and being unknown in that new land, felt far more life-affirming. I was to enter a zoology PhD program to study paleontology at Cornell. The Geology Department at UCLA, prestigious in its own right, was nonetheless geared more toward the oil industry and less toward my true interest, the history of life. The Southland itself, typified by its geology that I felt I had mastered, was emblematic of an identity I was eager to leave behind; to me the place had become old hat.

SECTION THREE

21
UPPING THE GAME

Anew life in New York, 1990. If this was punk, you wouldn't know it from the lifestyles I was about to enter. I was headed for a rural outpost called Ithaca, the most enlightened little town in America (if you believe the progressive digest *Utne Reader* that voted it so). Surrounding it are farms and forest, rocky gorges and lakes. Hundreds of square miles of verdant landscapes form a patchwork of wilderness pervaded by hiking trails in a dozen state parks and a national forest, creating a veritable paradise for any naturalist or outdoor enthusiast. The remoteness of the campus (the closest interstate is about twenty miles away) and the surrounding natural beauty were about as foreign to the aesthetic of punk as one could possibly get.

In some ways, it was the antithesis of the world I'd just left behind in LA. The right coast of the country as opposed to the left. I came to settle in the hinterlands of the most populous state in the East, its countless tiny villages, like Ithaca, little changed since the nineteenth century. How could anyone abandon the glitz and glamour of LA to end up here? Cornell

University was the reason for my treason. Having been accepted to their PhD program, I spent little time deliberating about emigrating from the land of my beloved punk scene. I assured the band that our schedule of recording and touring would not be affected. I committed myself to using air travel whenever necessary if they needed me. In that year, 1990, our touring was focused as much on Europe as it was on the East Coast and Midwest of the USA. As I saw it, my geographic location mattered little. In fact, it was more convenient to fly across the pond from New York to start a European tour than it was to depart from LAX. With our band headquarters at Epitaph in LA, I felt like I could pursue my academic work anywhere—in fact, my fieldwork was done in Colorado and Wyoming—while Brett and the guys carried on with their daily work in the Southland.

We had an album coming out soon, *Against the Grain*. Unlike in 1982 when we all pitched in to package, write label copy, and hand-deliver records to stores, I wasn't involved in anything having to do with record manufacturing or marketing. So I wasn't needed on-site for any of the work that was being done for subsequent album releases. My reach and impact would be felt wherever those records were heard, however, and this led me to the realization that my physical whereabouts were less significant in the grand scheme of things. This was rejuvenating.

Far from the glimmer and "grit" of the other New York—the five-borough metropolitan area, where Bad Religion had already made inroads playing concerts at CBGB—Ithaca was more of an escape from rather than a move toward any kind of new music scene. It's a town for serious young people, most of whom are attending Cornell or its cross-town little sibling, Ithaca College, made famous by one of its professors, Rod Serling, as a top-rated school for broadcasting and writing. Cornell had its famous personalities as well. Reassuring to me was knowing that the astronomer Carl Sagan had made cross country treks to Los Angeles part of his normal routine while filming his blockbuster TV series *Cosmos* in decades prior. His sojourns between California and Ithaca were par for the course even after I arrived, as Sagan balanced his Cornell lecture schedule with production meetings in Hollywood for his upcoming movie *Contact*. Here I was a nobody, just another graduate student teaching comparative anatomy and various classes in zoology. My university colleagues may have cared little for my worldly reputation as a singer and songwriter, but like Sagan, I still remained committed to touring far and wide in the interest of extracurricular creative endeavors. It never aroused the awareness of the local townsfolk, which was just fine with me.

The opportunities came increasingly. I had barely gotten started in my new research and teaching routine when the phone rang. "We've got some show opportunities out here, headliners at Iguanas and some theater in North Hollywood, followed by some shows up north. When can you be available?" It was Andy, a friend of Greg Hetson and a successful booking agent for the Circle Jerks. He often would call me with a condescending, cynical tone that went something like this: "I know you're busy trying to make it as a scientist or whatever, but we have real offers on the table." Luckily, the guys in the band were not like this. Outwardly, they always seemed to give wide berth to my academic pursuits. They often showed their support in humorous ways. For instance, whenever we played halls with a lectern, they would set it up in the middle of the stage as if their singer was preparing for a lecture. I just played along, and played it up. Or, on occasion, they might call me up in the middle of the afternoon and ask, "Hey, Greg, what's the difference between an insect and an arachnid?" or some other zoological or nomenclatural quiz. I'd shoot back, "You dummies, they're both arthropods! You're comparing a subphylum with a family!" We always had fun with the back-and-forth razzing.

But no such humor from Andy. He wanted total unwavering commitment to his pursuits which, to his credit, would have greatly increased Bad Religion's income. But with my outside interests always getting in the way, we were always going to be hampered, according to him. The only reason he agreed to book Bad Religion in the first place was because of his association with Greg Hetson, who was busy as ever with the Circle Jerks. So not only was Andy discontent that I couldn't devote full time to his touring plans, he also was malcontent that Greg Hetson couldn't play a Circle Jerks show if he booked a Bad Religion gig.

By this time, the only academic break I could devote to tours was between semesters. Immediately after Christmas that year, it was off to LA
to meet up with the band on December 27 for a quick brush-up rehearsal.
The next day we headed to Tijuana to play at the illustrious Iguanas venue.
This place, lawless and cold, was made warm each night by the body heat
from countless music fans and partygoers from both sides of the border.
Iguanas was an exciting nightlife destination rather than a genre-specific
showcase venue. It had an open-to-the-elements feel—not completely open
air, but there was always an outside breeze coming through. It had an excellent sounding PA, and a concrete ballroom floor that was surrounded
by low hanging balconies that were always overfilled with people trying to
jump onstage or plummet onto the frenzy of the slam dancing taking place
just below. Our shows there were always riotously fun. And with our new
songs being debuted on this particular night, everyone was full of anticipation. The show went off without a hitch.

Our next show was at the El Portal Theater in North Hollywood. This
venue was to be our US debut show for a highly anticipated album release, and the thousand-capacity theater was sold out in advance. I had
skipped the sound check and missed the opening band, Pennywise. Arriving late, I saw fire engines, police cars, and a throng of people outside the
venue. Were they actually streaming out of the building? Just as I passed
the marquee to turn left for the artist entrance, I saw the huge glass windows of a neighboring building being smashed by some members of the
crowd. "What's old is new again," I thought to myself. At the parking area
in back where a makeshift "loading dock" was located, one of our roadies informed me, "Pennywise played, but NOFX didn't get to go on. The
fire marshal shut down the show." I responded, "Well, then I guess I'm
not needed here." I immediately drove back to Del Mar, where I had left
my wife at her mother's house. I made it back in time to watch the eleven
o'clock news. Much to my surprise, the concert had been elevated to riot
status! I guess after I left the scene, things got really ugly and cars were
overturned and properties were damaged. All because they didn't get to
see Bad Religion play. Even more surprising, CNN decided to pick up the

story and reported that "heavy metal band Bad Religion" had a riot at one of their shows. Wow! Now we had become the stuff of sensationalism. I felt that these kind of news stories were really bad news for humanity. With the advent of the twenty-four-hour news cycle it was becoming easier than ever to fulfill Andy Warhol's prediction of fifteen minutes of fame for everyone. But it was diluting the public sense of what was important and what wasn't. This event, the riot in North Hollywood, was not important on a national scale, despite CNN's elevation of it to their prime-time headlines all the next day. It was more interesting as a local story that entailed a promoter who oversold a seated venue with no room to slam dance, and a venue owner who had no idea what a punk rock audience was capable of.

All the tickets that were sold were going to be honored by the promoter, Goldenvoice, who announced that another gig would be planned at the Whisky a Go Go. The problem is, they didn't check with Bad Religion to see if we could be available to make up the show. As it turned out, on the date they wanted to do the makeup gig I was going to be back at my other job at Cornell. This gave Brett an opportunity to exercise some business-savvy muscle and at the same time elevate Bad Religion's status to something more meaningful than merely darlings of the twenty-four-hour news cycle for a day. Since there were already a thousand tickets sold to see Bad Religion, the promoter as well as the band should work together, even though it was Goldenvoice not Bad Religion who ultimately had to refund the tickets. But why not work on this together? Since the show sold out in presale, and since we had a new album out that was proving to be very popular, Brett believed we could sell more than a thousand tickets because it was not merely a makeup concert for "the riot," but it was also a debut concert for *Against the Grain*. Brett established the band's position that we would play only if Goldenvoice secured the Hollywood Palladium for us. We weren't interested in playing any other venue in LA. We had previously helped out Goldenvoice when they needed a "local" opening band with a good draw to help sell some tickets for flagging shows by Dramarama. But what we really wanted was for Goldenvoice to believe in Bad Religion as a major headliner in our own hometown. This was our chance to prove it to the promoters and to ourselves. Goldenvoice reluctantly agreed. The show would be rescheduled for February 1, and we went public with the announcement by creating radio ads that were announced on KROQ all week long beginning on New Year's Eve. The Palladium show sold out in two days. In addition to the 1,000 tickets sold for the ill-fated show at the El Portal Theater in North Hollywood, we sold an additional 2,500 tickets to establish a sell-out capacity of 3,500 people at the Hollywood Palladium.

After a successful couple of shows in Seattle and Victoria, British Columbia, I flew back to Ithaca to begin my second semester in late January 1991. I was probably reeking of formaldehyde from teaching comparative anatomy when I stepped right back onto a plane a week later to head back to LA. It was time for the band's biggest and most satisfying concert achievement of our life: headlining the Hollywood Palladium.

22
EUROPE

Being on tour always had a semiprofessional feeling to it. I mean, sure, since 1982 we had been getting paid to perform, $250 here and there, maybe $500 or $1,000 for bigger shows, so in a literal sense we WERE a professional band. But I can't say we were ever very well organized to the extent that it felt like a "professional organization." We were a loose assemblage of pals and acquaintances who, mostly through personal references, got hired for concerts all over this land and even across the pond.

Our first tours in Europe were strategic gambles to say the least. Without a manager, or contracts with promoters, we purchased our own plane tickets and loaded up vans driven by local roadies (who "double dipped," as they got a salary and a rental fee for their vehicles). In some cases, we simply met these guys for the first time when they greeted us at the airport. The whole affair was often arranged by phone calls. Our trust stemmed only from the fact that the person on the other end of the line had been successful booking other punk bands in his region. We had no idea what the total income would be, but we nonetheless found ourselves following an itinerary provided by self-proclaimed booking agents; guys our age who were ambitious enough to travel with us and negotiate for us after each concert.

In the USA, by 1990, we had a booking agent named Andy. Now, instead of phone calls coming directly to band members from various friends of friends or promoters in this or that city, things were more organized. All calls from that point on would go through a representative (Andy) who had a real office and a roster of other bands. Punk concerts were still only a minor draw in comparison to metal shows. Andy, who also represented numerous metal acts, had a modest degree of clout, and like most agents' attitudes toward punk bands of the time, he made you feel like it was some sort of privilege to answer your calls or be on his roster. (In fact, Bad Religion was purposely kept off his published roster at the time.) His general attitude toward Bad Religion could be summed up as follows: "Look guys, I'm only doing this as a favor to Gingles" (his nickname for Greg Hetson).

Most of the local shows that Andy booked for us were no different than the shows we could have booked for ourselves. By 1990, we had become a solid, predictable draw throughout Southern California, Arizona, and Las Vegas. Most of the promoters knew us personally and could reach any of the band members by phone. These were our top-selling concert regions, and we were playing in theater-sized venues in each of them. By taking on a booking agent, we were committing 10 percent of our income to his commission, just for the formality of representation. But that expense was made up for by the fact that Andy had numerous relationships with promoters in other regions who might be willing to take a risk on booking Bad Religion in legitimate, established venues outside of our home region, where we had never played before. Some of these places, despite their "legitimacy," were still run by questionable promoters who gave low guaranteed fees for bands and had to be haggled with each night after the box-office counts were done.

Not only did Bad Religion function without an agent for most of the first decade, but even after we hired Andy we had no one but band members and a roadie–sound technician to "collect" cash after the shows. Dealing with promoters back then was nearly as dehumanizing as dealing with reluctant agents. They made you feel as though they just did you a favor, letting you play at their venue. Often, Andy would book a show at some place, let's say in the Northeast, where another one of his bands, say Testament, had just played the month before. The promoter of that venue made it clear: "Look, guys, I'm only doing this as a favor to Andy Somers (who in turn was only doing this for Gingles) because we had so much success last month with Testament." This was the normal spiel when it came time to pay the band. More often than not, this was the preamble to the next thing out of the promoter's mouth: "Guys, can you just give me a break? We didn't sell as many tickets as we thought. I'll pay you half of what we agreed on, but the NEXT time Andy calls me, I will significantly increase my offer." Ah, those were the days. We had to take whatever the promoters would give us because we had another show in a different city the next day.

I called Andy to complain about our treatment from some of these unscrupulous promoters. "Andy, they're paying us only half of what you said they agreed to pay!" He sided with the promoters every time. "Greg, I build in to every one of my deals a solid 15 percent profit for the venue. Why should my promoters take a loss on any concert?" MY PROMOTERS? I knew right then and there who Andy was favoring. In fairness, he was dealing with regional promoters with numerous other acts, most of whom were highly profitable, and indeed Bad Religion hadn't established themselves in these markets yet. So, had I been more worldly at the time, I would have had a better understanding of what Andy was intimating. But at the time, I took it personally. He was sending us into the jaws of the sharks, out on the road to deal with promoters who were used to having sold-out venues with Andy's other acts. Bad Religion was sometimes a disappointing draw outside of our home region, and these promoters weren't interested in helping to build our following in their region. Despite the mismatch, and with varying degrees of financial successes and losses, Andy's placement of Bad Religion with thrash-metal promoters and venues throughout the USA brought us to some new places and audiences.

The year 1989 marked the first time we toured in Europe, and over there we were truly on our own. The only link to our touring activity in the USA was a local scenester from New England with punk friends in Europe named Doug. He had seen us play the previous year at Anthrax, a thrash-metal club in Connecticut, and approached us after the show. A short-haired terrier of a man-child, accompanied by a trench-coated sidekick who was sipping Robitussin directly out of the bottle, Doug introduced himself. "Hey, I'm Doug and this is Johnny. We promote shows. Youz guys have a record out don't yehz?" he asked. "I'm going to call my friends in Yourope who do touahs over deyah. You'll be hearing from me." But we were already making our way back to California, one gig at a time, and he was a distant memory for many months thereafter.

There's something about seeing a printed itinerary that makes a pipe dream seem more reliable and worthy of commitment. After about a half year of silence, we heard from Doug again. He sent us a fax that showed nineteen different cities in Europe with venues, dates, and offers of guaranteed fees for Bad Religion concerts planned for August 1989. He followed up the fax with a phone call. "Are youz guys ready for the Bad Religion Youropean summah holiday?"

I had always wanted to go to Europe, so the mere idea of having an all-expenses-paid trip to visit romantic places like Pisa, Berlin, Amsterdam, and Vienna was very appealing to me. Still, we didn't have any professional touring administration, no road manager, no accountant or travel agent. Each of us looked to one another for answers. Whoever had the most experience on a given topic was consulted. Brett had the most business experience, but he had no interest in doing the tour books. He instructed me on how to track income and expenses for each day we were on the road. I had organizational skills and notebooks and was a proven travel journaler from my fieldwork in remote places. So, by default, I became the tour accountant. For each city I devoted a page to a journal. After the shows, I would enter income—from T-shirt sales, our percentage of the ticket sales, and any bonuses—and also detail our expenses in travel for the day (food, petrol, hotels, and so forth). Greg Hetson was the most experienced of the touring partners, so he kept the "float" cash in a duffel bag (money accumulated over the course of the tour that paid expenses). In those days, there was a different currency in every country we played, and sometimes we played four different countries in just that many days, so his money sack became like a big, kaleidoscopic jumble of loose bills.

Brett had other interests in going to Europe that year, in addition to performing. Our first tour in Europe marked the release of *Suffer* in that territory and he was motivated to get it heard by distributors and pick their brains about the quickly accumulating catalog of Epitaph recordings overseas. I too had interests alongside the performance part of the tour. Even though music was an important part of my life, I couldn't ignore the academic work on my plate. I went to Europe excited to visit some of the best natural history museums in the world. I sought to build a network of correspondence with some well-known European paleontologists. So, based solely on a faxed itinerary, we were off to Europe for our first international tour outside of North America.

There was hardly any precedent among our peers for what we were attempting to do. Black Flag had toured in Germany, as did the Dead Kennedys before us. But their tours were short, and regional, and they didn't consider us as their peers, so we learned nothing from them. NOFX reached Europe before us, but their tour organizers were different from ours and they didn't share much information. Other than some vague advice on international travel from Greg Hetson (who had visited on a high school trip), we didn't have any knowledge on how to go about a European tour. Sure, countless commercial and mainstream bands from the USA had toured Europe before us. But most of them were signed to major record labels or had affiliations with multinational booking agencies. We were "wingin' it."

We learned the logistics as we went along. In fact, all we had was that single piece of fax paper. Our itinerary included only one hotel, even though there were nineteen concerts in nineteen cities. Did anyone even consider where we might be sleeping each night? Such questions didn't dissuade us in our eager quest to see the Continent. Moreover, we had no idea what a European punk rock audience was going to be like. We had never even met a punk from Europe. We didn't know how they might think, what they might rebel against. How were we going to relate to them? These heady social conundrums were the primary concerns on my mind. I wanted to make a positive impression wherever we went.

The itinerary stated that after we land at Schiphol Airport in Amsterdam, we were to proceed to a pension (one-star hotel) near the Leidseplein (a youthful neighborhood in Amsterdam) where we would be met by our American booking agent–tour manager Doug, the guy who had introduced himself back in Connecticut.

Before Doug arrived we were let out of our airport shuttle van and greeted by the pension proprietor. "Hello, Bed Rrrreligion!" he said in nearly perfect English. "Wow, we must be famous here," I thought. In fact, it was not from fame, but from general hospitality. Whereas we were always met with scorn or mistrust at motels in the USA, our first brush with a European stranger was cordial and upbeat. "Sit down here in the courrrtyart while we prepare your rooms. Take some waterrr as a welcome trink." It was my first taste of Spa, the fizzy carbonated water drink so common in Holland, but unavailable elsewhere at that time.

Later that day, we had a sound check at our first venue, a famous club called the Melkweg. What was most shocking to me was that the venue had staff members who looked like they really enjoyed having you in their building. There were nice drinks in the backstage area; there were showers if you wanted to clean up before or after the show. More importantly, the sound system in the audience hall was incredible, and the onstage monitoring system was equally high tech. The quality of the musical experience was obviously placed very high on their list of values, and that was the most motivating factor as far as I was concerned. It made me want to put on a good show because I really believed that the venue was set up to showcase the band's music. This was the polar opposite of the countless dives that we had played in the USA, where the dancing experience of the concertgoers was tertiary, the sound quality was secondary, and the primary concern of the venue operators was simply the current stock of alcoholic offerings at the venue's bar.

Sound checks had become an important part of our daily routine. For me, it was purely to quell anxiety over whether or not the venue actually had a decent stage and some kind of sound system that would allow my voice to be heard over the drums and guitars. Sometimes, the club's stage manager would greet us with a question: "You mean you guys don't travel with your own PA?" Having no manager, and no one to "advance" the show (call ahead and go over technical details), we usually just used whatever the venue provided. Only rarely, at certain established music venues, did we arrive at a venue that had a "house sound tech" who was on staff and willing to help us out. In general, it's safe to say that during Bad Religion's early years of touring in the States, being a totally independent band with little organization and no management brought us face-to-face with skeptical, grumpy staffers at most venues. I often felt as if I was putting them out, disrupting their evening, or threatening their authority because I had the temerity to ask them if we could use the lighting system during our show. It was not at all uncommon for them to ask us to pay them a fee if we wanted someone to work the lighting system. Since we couldn't pay it, we played in the dark, with only a few overhead randomly colored lights. On numerous occasions the venues had a center spotlight, for the singer and guitar solos, but refused to turn it on unless another fee was paid (the spotlight fee, or some stupid designation like that).

This kind of nickel-and-dime, grumpy mentality is a kind of uniquely American disease. It's basically saying, "You're nobody if you can't pay for it." Or more analytically, "In order to be perceived as something important, you have to pay for it." This sickness devolved into another trend that I heard about around the late 1980s and all through the 1990s, although Bad Religion never participated in it: pay-to-play. Numerous acts were well funded by major record labels and using some of those deep pockets to pay club promoters or venue owners hefty fees in order to use their stages and productions for concerts. To them it was just dollars and cents—the staff had to be paid. Never mind that the venues made money hand over fist from their alcohol sales alone, and even a modestly popular band could sell enough tickets to cover most of the evening's operating costs. Pay-to-play put the venue in front of the band in order of importance. To me, this was a disrespectful treatment of artists and it shortchanged the patrons as well. Paying audiences should get the best production value possible at any venue.

Usually when you hear bands talk about touring in Europe, you hear the hardships—the language barriers, the adaptation to new and weird social expectations, the paucity of easy and cheap food, incomprehensible currency, the uncomfortable budget hotels, and so on. Add to these the usual drags of being on the road for weeks at a time—the road fatigue, strange bathrooms, no clean laundry—and it all sounds downright lonely and miserable. But a funny thing happened on that first tour in Europe: we discovered humanity in the entertainment industry.

Throughout Europe we experienced a repeating pattern of treatment that put the artist in the proper order of importance, as far as I was concerned. That is to say, FIRST. In Europe, a venue wouldn't be considered valid if it didn't have a good sound system. The audience was paying to hear a band, and therefore it simply would be unthinkable to call something a concert venue or club if it didn't sound good inside.

Sound checks became pleasurable because they were a welcoming expression of the venue's best assets—good sound systems, thoughtful accommodations backstage (like a clean shower and a common area for meals), and an English-speaking interpreter who acted as a stage manager, runner, or technical consultant. These things were commonplace in Europe, even though the venues were equally small as the ones we played in the States. In other words, the band was no more important in Europe than we were back home, but the venues made us feel as though we were. In reality, it reflected the attitude of the European mindset—that the guild of musical performers would always be placed above the venue in a hierarchy of importance. And that suited me just fine. In Europe, it didn't matter if you were playing at a no-name club or at a legendary concert hall, you could expect that you would be treated the same as any musician. So long as you were contracted to play on a given night, you could expect good sound, good lights, some sort of catering backstage, and a decent place to clean up after the show. And we thrived in that environment because our intentions matched those of the venue. We both wanted the same thing. In Bad Religion, the vocals need to be heard, and I felt that the venue cared about that and was willing to help me and the band achieve that.

To say that it was all roses, however, would be an overstatement. Although we were thrilled to get such good treatment, there were some preconceptions that we had to dispel. For instance, it was just assumed that every punk band was vegan. I'm not sure where this came from, but I assume that veganism was a sort of rebellion to European cuisine at the time. Meat was king to the European diet. Vegetarianism, in general, was practiced by many post-hippie-movement "outsiders" who still lingered in pop culture. Less of a cuisine, and more of an active symbol of protest, we were often fed rice and some sort of tomato mélange as our backstage catering meal throughout our tour in various countries. This came to be known as *Reis mit Scheisse* (translation: rice with shit), and it was difficult to let the caterers know that we weren't actually vegan without getting looks of true disappointment.

Many of the shows were miserably hot, despite the cool European climate. Even though the venues and their staffs seemed to care a great deal about the technical quality of the concert, and the catering details, these shows followed a common trend that pervades European touring to this day: a general disdain for air-conditioning. The sound was good, the lights were decent, the beer was plentiful, the audiences even sang along, but the heat and sweat inside the building at these concerts made the rafters start dripping with condensation. The microphones would become waterlogged and make my voice sound like I was shouting into a pillow. This scenario was replayed each night for an entire week when we played in Germany. The first foreign phrase I ever learned was *Öffnen die Fenster!* (Open the windows!), which I would chant to the audience over and over again until they all protested with me.

Those German audiences, with their unbridled excitement and recognition of our songs, made us realize our full potential. It was clear that Europe could become a focal point for our future rather than just a sideshow to our touring enterprise.

The humanity in our lyrics found resonance with the embodiment of the enlightenment quest that seems to be in the DNA of all Europeans, but particularly those who call themselves punks. In fact, it is not rebellious in Europe to accept many of the tenets of humanistic enlightenment such as atheism, contraception, scientific naturalism, and egalitarianism. These liberal tendencies have become lifestyle norms for most of western Europe's population since World War II. The fall of fascism, and, before that, the dissolution of monarchies and empires based on primogeniture—all of which cost Europe's citizens great strife and spilled blood for generations—resulted in a more "open" society where polite tolerance became normal. The citizens generally believed that tolerating opposing viewpoints is better than more bloodshed. This trend in thinking was matched by the formation of highly formalized governments with parliamentary debates acting as the theater of conflict to craft new legislation. Part of the legislation included strict and challenging academic rigor for all school-age children.

It was under this kind of heavy-handed social engineering that most of the western European punks of the 1980s were raised. They understood implicitly that posing the proper questions was the first step in making any kind of social change. Punk, to those in western Europe, was a freethinkers' musical celebration, a place to clash with the stodgy norms of fashion while also feeling free to have a philosophy of one's own. It was a tacit expectation that a punk should live his or her life in a way that was thoughtful, and with respect to bettering society for everyone, not just a privileged few. Bad Religion seemed preadapted to thrive in this kind of social environment.

It was commonplace in the early years of our European touring to play concerts at repurposed public buildings from a bygone era. Some were office buildings in the center of cities that somehow escaped damage from Allied bombing raids during World War II. Europe is full of cities that were essentially leveled and subsequently rebuilt. One of the most conspicuous attributes of these places—anyone with even a casual interest in architecture could readily observe them—is the preponderance of pedestrian, unremarkable, yet highly functional, buildings in the city centers. War destroyed so much of the original architecture in western Europe that it is uncommon to find an original city center intact. One example of a rebuilt city center is Brussels. Its entire downtown area is full of large three-story buildings with featureless facades that take up entire blocks. They were erected during the reconstruction period after the war. Shopping plazas and government administration buildings alike blend seamlessly together to form a generally blasé architectural environment. The Marshall Plan provided funds to rebuild these city centers, and most of them were quickly rebuilt with more efficient but less architecturally unique downtown areas. Today, based on the architecture alone, it's hard to discern if you're standing in an important city in Germany, such as Düsseldorf, or in parts of Berlin, or in a completely different cultural milieu such as Milan, Italy. All of these places, and hundreds of others like them, have an architectural continuity because the postwar buildings all look the same.

There are of course some remarkable exceptions. A hallmark of European culture is the city center, and most of the venues we played were located in them. Brussels took pains to reassemble the rubble from their bombed-out city-center plaza (known as Grand Place), and the original buildings were restored to instill a sense of municipal pride and re-create the old character of the city for all visitors to enjoy. Some of the most characteristic emblems of particular city centers were the cathedrals. Like the Grand Place of Brussels, many were leveled to the ground by bombs. The Catholic Church helped with funds of their own to assist municipalities that received money from the Marshall Plan, and slowly the squares of shops and surrounding commons began to take on their original Gothic flavor. This can be witnessed in cities such as Vienna, Munich, and Cologne, all of which we visited on that first tour. In a strange irony, I found an instant attraction to these magnificent edifices of religion during my first Bad Religion tour.

Hamburg also rebuilt their city center, which included a people's building, a rathskeller (also known as a "folks building" or city hall) that was a central gathering place for city festivals and public events. Our first show in Hamburg was just down the street from it, at a government-funded concert hall called Kulturfabrik (Culture Factory). It was here that I realized a central tenet of modern Europe: what the architecture lacked in frivolous detail was more than made up for by the investment in humanity.

It is a wonderful thing when your government is not saddled with having to build and pay for a global police force in the name of democracy. After World War II, most of the recipients of Marshall Plan money had to agree that their government would not create a military force for anything other than defensive purposes. Relieved of the billions of dollars it cost to maintain a military-industrial complex, the countries of western Europe could put tax dollars to work. In some cases that money was spent to rebuild and plan new city centers. In other cases, it was reinvested into the people, creating funds that could be used to enrich society and, in some cases, help young people pursue their interests.

I was so impressed with the merging of civic involvement in punk rock venues during that first tour of Europe. We had never experienced such support from any city in the USA. The Kulturfabrik, for instance, was created as a co-op of sorts between the city government and some enterprising local punks, artists, and aspiring promoters. Nearly every city in western Europe had money available for the arts. This included musical entertainment. Furthermore, funds were available for "youth activity centers" throughout Europe. In Hamburg, the well-organized punk rockers who promoted that first Bad Religion show had applied for funding from the city and used the funds to throw events in their newly created factory for culture.

Ours was the biggest show of the year at the Kulturfabrik. The stage looked out to an auditorium that held about eight hundred punks, all squashed in like sardines. Overhead was a narrow balcony on each side of the hall where another three hundred concertgoers could cram together, held in by a chest-high railing over which they could view the tops of their cohorts' heads slam dancing below. It was miserably hot, but it sounded good, and they even had a second microphone that I could swap with my waterlogged mic halfway through the concert.

After the show we were given keys to a pension where three rooms had been set aside for us to spend the night. All paid for by the city, the promoters assured us that the night attendants would let us enter after hours, and that no bills would be issued to us at checkout. We were so suspicious of this favorable treatment. Nothing like this ever happens in the states. After USA gigs, you're on your own to find a place to sleep, eat, shower, and get to the next city. But in Europe, concert personnel treated us with respect and kindness. All the bills were paid. The promoters cared and tried to be of service to the wary traveling minstrels. We made a hefty portion of the ticket sales too. What's going on here? Had we died and gone to Commie heaven? Exploitation and highway robbery—two American hallmarks of the entertainment industry—seemed to have no home here.

The logistics of touring, however, particularly with respect to getting around from town to town, were not well oiled for us. We were given an old VW passenger van, loaned by one of the bands that accompanied us on this first tour. The van had three benches, no heat, and it leaked water when it rained (which was nearly every other day of the tour). We were nine people all together—five band members, two crew members, and one tour manager in addition to the driver—plus equipment in the small cargo area behind the third bench. Each day the rain would spill into the leaking window gaskets and collect on the floor of the van. The floor was watertight, so pools of water, two inches deep, soaked our shoes and equipment.

We were kept in perpetual soggy, cramped, cold, misery throughout the long road journeys. Without any heat in the cabin there was no way to dry out or stay warm. In order to rid the van of the pooled-up water we came up with a technique. The driver would find an empty side street, accelerate just a bit and give us a signal: "Brace yourselves!" Here he would slam on the brakes with the doors open and give a slight turn to the steering wheel to make the van roll just a little. The pooled water would come splashing toward the front of the van, crash like ocean waves against the firewall, and spill out the side doors. This was fun for about two days, but the rainy weather, cool daytime temps, and van discomfort continued to plague us for the entire three-week tour.

The next night after Hamburg was a different town, Bremen, and a different repurposed building, but we were supported financially by the same kind of government program as in Hamburg. Paid for by a grant from the city's Youth Culture Bureau, the popular concert venue was called the

Schlachthof, the German word for slaughterhouse. Like in its slaughterhouse heyday, the place was funded by municipal taxes. The main room
in which the concerts took place was a sort of stock pavilion where the
animals had been gathered before they entered the killing and butchering
pens. The band performed on a stage where animals used to parade in front
of stock bidders before they were unceremoniously slaughtered. The backstage dressing areas were the carving rooms! This seemed like some sort of
dark German comedy, but hey, don't sweat the details, it's all paid for by
public funding! With a full staff of technicians there to run the PA, and operate a fancy lighting rig for our concert, Bremen's slaughterhouse proved
to be another great, sold-out show.

We heard that abandoned prewar buildings were called "squats," and
some punks who might be referred to as "street punks" (homeless runaways) chose such buildings as places to live. The romance of living and
working in a squat was put to its true test during these early tours. Some
abandoned halls were used as concert venues. Usually illegal, these unused
places in Europe that allowed punk shows to occur were not strictly squats.
City governments knew about the buildings and presumably had inspected
them. In order for local promoters to use a space, it had to pass muster with
respect to municipal building codes. Therefore, calling a venue a squat was
really punk hyperbole.

There were, however, abandoned buildings that met the criteria of a
squat in nearly every city we visited in western Europe. Left over from the
pre–World War II era, sometimes these were stone or brick office buildings, completely intact with durable old-world craftwork, massive, milled
hardwood doors and trim around the windows, baseboards and moldings
still straight as an arrow. Outside was beautiful masonry, perhaps a bit dirty
and unkempt, but nonetheless, it made for sturdy and erect facades that
towered skyward, supporting elaborate roofs, often in disrepair. Despite
the holes and missing tiles on the roofs and some broken windows in attic
dormers, these buildings in general were every bit as usable as they were
back in the day. Like tornadoes ripping through Midwestern cities back
in the USA, obliterating some rows of houses entirely while leaving some

standing, Allied bombs missed some of these structures. They remained standing through decades of deferred maintenance, seemingly forgotten. After seasons of slow decay, some bohemian citizen or punk rocker discovered their charms and used them for the limited benefits that they might provide. Free and illegal to inhabit, the building was now a true "squat."

In our case, the promoter punks often suggested we attend an "after party" at such a place nearby. Each night we were implored by some friendly but insistent scenester: "Vee make pahty ant relex. You might alzo en-choy sleeping zehr, it is a *schlaff haus* [sleeping quarters]." It might have been in Bielefeld, or Kassel, or Essen, or Hannover, or any of a number of cities in Germany that we played on those first tours. As a visiting punk band from Los Angeles without language skills or geographic bearings, we had no choice but to follow our local guides to wherever they led us. Usually dog-tired and hungry after the concerts, I took whatever guaranteed the closest promise of some grub and a bed and blanket.

Surrounded by nocturnal revelers, we entered these forgotten lodges. Some of our touring party found renewed energy for imbibing the local brew, smoke, or other happy libations in their dimly lit antechambers. The characters who claimed dominion over these party places were from various walks of life. Some were old hippies, dressed like some sort of wizard, fully bearded and robed in weathered lederhosen, suspenders, and gabardine work shirts. Complete with pointy hats, rucksacks, and walking sticks, they were the guild of wanderers, roaming throughout the land going from town to town, finding abandoned buildings to temporarily renovate with salvaged furniture, battery-powered lanterns, and kerosene camp stoves. Often decorated with official certifications from the trades, they were true craftsmen with skills they could put to use if need be. But more often, they loved the bohemian lifestyle, and punk concerts were the perfect place to exercise it. We called them "Gandalfs" and, in small numbers, they became a fixture of the punk scene throughout Europe.

We came across other types of eccentrics too. Martin and Kollek were film students, dedicated to the travel and adventure that a punk tour could promise. Nights of drinking and free accommodation in squats was film worthy, and they kept their handheld video recorders going throughout our first tour in 1989. They released a documentary, *Along the Way*, that exemplifies the high levels of artistic integrity expected of European students. It sounds and looks authentic and captivating. Even though they had no funds to create the movie, they asked us if they could follow the tour. We gave them full access to every privilege extended to us, whatever that might turn out to be. They came along with their own car and a creative drive to boot.

One night, the party continued until dawn at a squat in some small city, perhaps it was Leonberg. The house was just across the street from the venue, and it was less of a house and more like an abandoned two-story apartment building with single bedroom units on each floor. The rooms straddled a long central hallway that led away from a large lobby-like entrance foyer. There was only dim illumination in this place from what seemed like battery-powered emergency backup lighting. Our host pointed to the stairway. "Gice, up zayer you can find da bant rooms." He was friends with Thorsten and Kollek. It was exciting for them to host an international band. We felt like ambassadors of goodwill from the USA. No matter how coarse the accommodations, or how dreary the *Reis-mit-Scheisse* catering, we felt a strange obligation to honor their hospitality. I was growing tired, however, of our sound guy, Rudy, who violently smashed a full bottle in the parking lot. "Beeeeecks???!!! Goddam it, I can get this shit back in LA!!" But in general, we were polite and tried to be accepting of their offers.

As the party raged downstairs with lots of shouting, some boom box tunage, and breaking glass from beer bottles smashing against the walls of the reception hallway, I had no energy for social engagement, and I wasn't a drinker, so I didn't enjoy the local lukewarm beer. I really just needed some hydration, which unfortunately was nowhere to be found since these abandoned buildings had no running water. The band members and I scuttled through the reveling crowd and found the stairway to the second floor. Finding one of the rooms quiet when I peeked inside the blackness, I pulled out a little pocket flashlight from my backpack. The room had a couple of old leatherette sofas with a few holes in the upholstery, a cloth recliner chair and ottoman, and a couple of folded blankets and duvets on a shelf. Everything passed the smell test and there was even a large area rug on the floor. "This must be the band rooms," I said, and we went inside and lay down to sleep. When I shut off my pocket flashlight the room was pitch black. I recognized the snores of Jay sleeping nearby, and Brett across the way. We chatted a bit in the dark as one by one the others fell asleep, first Peter, then Greg Hetson.

I couldn't fall asleep. There we were experiencing the most successful string of sold-out shows in our eight-year tenure as a band, and yet, we were in a foreign land, sleeping in an illegal squat, somehow confident that we were expanding the mission of enlightenment punk, when in fact we were the recipients of adulation from a more enlightened punk scene than that of our own. This pleasant irony nearly made me fall off into slumber, but something told me to reach for my pocket flashlight again.

When I turned it on, I was horrified to see Kollek, with his greasy black hair, ghost-white Prussian face, rosy cheeks, and a dazed look in his eyes, like a pudgy Sid Vicious mad-dogging me from only two feet away. I shined the light directly in his face which, oddly, caused him no squinting whatsoever. He had a large twenty-ounce beer bottle in his hand, and he raised it to show me the label as if proudly declaring the cause of his deranged condition. He just stared back without saying a word. It was like the Catholic schoolkid game Bloody Mary, where you stand in the dark in front of a mirror and chant "bloody Mary, full of grace" over and over until an apparition of the Virgin appears as a ghostly, soft iridescence, staring back at you from the looking glass. I tried to play it cool and said, "Hey man, what's going on?" It woke the others, but no answer came from Kollek. He just slowly took another sip of his ale, and staggered drunk out into the hallway.

Within a few hours, having drifted off into deep sleep, we were woken by shouting from down the hall. German anger boiled up to frightful utterances from the punks while older officials seemed to be calmly reading them the riot act. Suddenly, there was a loud rap on our door. Bounding into the room, a uniformed officer said, "Morning, collectively." This really confused us because not only was it an awkward thing to say, but he sounded like John Cleese from *Monty Python* (many of the German schools taught English with British accents). At first I didn't remember what country I was in. "*Polizei,*" he announced, then, "passports please." We were so groggy from little sleep and from worry about being woken by other drunk, stumbling partygoers that we struggled to find our travel documents. We actually didn't have to explain much; the German policeman did most of the talking. "You are vehrking vit dis goy who says he's your promoter?" Yes, we nodded. "Did you know dis goy is sqvatting and it is illeeekal?" No, I responded. "Da konzert last night, iss okay, no poblems zehr, baaht you cannot stay heeeah any longer. Zoh, you must go!" And that was that. We had broken the law in a foreign land, but the penalty for doing so was less than a slap on the wrist.

Instead of busting heads and showing who is tougher, like the police in Los Angeles who confronted punk rockers outside concert venues, these cops were just doing their community maintenance. Sweeping through the potentially squattable buildings to ensure that no destitute junkies nor wayward criminals were taking up permanent residence there. Again, we were met by a gentler humanity in Europe than in our own land.

The morning had broken as we loaded the van, and a typical late summer rain made it feel like autumn. Cold and wet, we headed off to the next city to meet more colorful characters and continue our pace of playing in a different city every day of the tour.

One of the most interesting squatted buildings was in Berlin. It was occupied by an expat with dual citizenship named David, who was quick to become our friend. With a short, well-proportioned kickboxer-like frame, David had a head that he kept always erect, with tight-cropped hair, and a perpetual adventurer's gleam in his eye. Like so many German punks, he wore a leather jacket, but he had an outward appearance that was equal parts business and fashion.

Although he was a few years older than me, David and I hit it off. He grew up in San Francisco, and then came to Berlin in the late 1970s, constantly traveling between family members' houses in the Bay Area of

California and in Germany. He spoke fluent German as well as English. He was married to a Berliner, Petra, and together they inhabited this building, in Kreuzberg, the section of town that bordered East Germany, only a short walk from Checkpoint Charlie, the notorious gate that divided the Soviet world from the West.

David and Petra took an interest in my academic background. They entertained my curious questions about Berlin, the museums, the architecture, the differences between life in the DDR and the various neighborhoods of West Berlin. Both David and Petra were encyclopedias of information to a first-time visitor and they had answers to everything: where the best food was, where the cool bars were, and how to cross over into the East (which we did) and not be afraid of the soldiers guarding the Berlin Wall. These youthful Soviet soldiers looked mean, but they were just as eager as the kids in the West to see the Berlin Wall come down. Rumors of this happening were already in the air at the time of our visit in the summer of 1989.

David and Petra's squat apartment, on the third floor of a prewar building, resembled the industrial loft spaces of New York's SoHo district. With high ceilings, large open rooms with wide wood moldings and handcrafted details throughout, their multiroom apartment was spacious and inviting, even though the entrance stairway was a bit past its prime and the hallways in the main building were dark and cavernous. Upon entering their living space you noticed nice furnishings, comfortable accommodations, a new kitchen and all the electronic appliances of any modern household. "David, I thought you lived in a squat building," I said. He replied, "Yacht, so I am able to make a deal with the city, okay? And if I improve on this space and live here for a certain amount of time then I become the owner of it." I was impressed by his and Petra's determination to build upon a discarded but usable resource. It showed vision and I admired that. It was clear to me that they were enterprising and forward thinking. This was made even clearer when, near the end of our visit, David mentioned that we should partner with him and his touring company, Destiny Tourbooking, to make an even longer tour in Europe the next year.

David became our agent and tour manager in Europe for the next two years. Europe was turning into an annual touring event for Bad Religion. A summer tour fit in perfectly with my academic calendar. I could always find six or eight weeks in a row to devote to a concert tour each summer, and the band was getting better offers from European promoters than we were getting in the USA. So it was across the pond we ventured every year, as predictable as the annual bird migrations.

David's first tour was another van tour, like our initial one in 1989. The driver was named Kuxer, and he was generally ornery but knowledgeable. His favorite words in English were "I don't give a FUCK!" Expressing a German form of sarcasm, we never got offended by his humorous rants, and he turned out to be a hearty, able member of the team. His vehicle was a large, yellowish diesel cargo van with no windows, a six-foot-high box-on-frame cargo bay, barn doors in the rear, and a single-bench cab. The driver and two others could sit in front, but that left three band members and two crew members having to find space in the cargo bay. I enjoyed navigating up front as much as possible, and I collected maps from gas stations along the autobahn. Jay most often enjoyed finding a long, flat area near the speaker cabinets in back to stretch out his long frame. Brett and our new drummer Bobby often found clever ways of propping the suitcases or power amps to create makeshift seats where they and the others could sit for the long hauls. Exceedingly unsafe as this arrangement was, we didn't care. Whatever method allowed us to get our equipment and bodies to the next venue was fine with us.

The discomfort, however, grew tiresome. We decided to rotate often so that everyone had some time to sit on the front bench, but in reality, as Jay demonstrated, it was actually more comfortable to lie down like a piece of equipment on the bed of the cargo bay. This was a work truck, designed to carry furniture or boxes across town. It was not meant to carry human beings across the country on the autobahn, nor was it equipped to provide any sort of refuge from the bumps and hardships of long journeys.

Safety of the equipment was always in the back of our minds. There were no seatbelts, of course, and there were no proper tie-downs for the heavy musical equipment. If Kuxer had to swerve, for any reason, it caused a panicked scramble among those of us in the cargo bay to immediately brace the towering speaker cabinets with our outstretched arms lest they tumble down on top of us.

One day, we were stuck in autobahn traffic, creeping along, perpetually starting and stopping for over an hour. Each time Kuxer hit the brakes or accelerated, the people in the back had to snap to attention to secure the equipment. It was tedious, uncomfortable, and ridiculous! Then, out of nowhere came a loud bang on the rear barn doors. I was sitting up front and my head was jolted a bit. "Oh shit!" Kuxer said. "Someone hit us!" Immediately I heard Brett shouting, "Owww, my wrist, oh fuck!" and Jay was in back too, saying, "What the fuck is going on up there?" Kuxer pulled the van over and jumped out and was inspecting the situation. A semi-trailer truck had plowed into the back of the van. Even though the semi wasn't traveling very fast, just creeping along in stop-and-go traffic, it struck the back of our van with such force that it caused a violent but short-lived collision. Jay was shaken, but his legs were stretched out along the bed and the impact just made him slide toward the back a bit. Bobby and Greg Hetson were sitting upright and the speaker cabinets toppled on them.

The van was dented, but drivable, and the guys had bruises and bumps, but nothing serious. Brett's wrist was injured and swollen, but it was on his right side, not his fretting fingers, so he wrapped it up and dealt with the pain for the remainder of the tour. After that experience, we were done with van tours.

By 1991, David said, "Hey, I have a friend named Martin who is a bus driver. Maybe he can get us a bus!" In those days you had to be careful with making such a prudent decision for your safety and well-being. In the USA, a van was the accepted mode of transportation for punk bands. For whatever reason, anything larger or safer, or more technologically advanced, was seen as appropriate for only commercial bands or celebrities, or for those poseurs who wanted to appear important. At all costs, punks were tacitly urged to avoid such trappings. But we had had two years of poor experiences and dodging potential catastrophes in vans on the autobahn, so we were ready for a change. What better place to make this practical switch than in Europe? Punks in Europe didn't seem to judge us for any practical decisions we made, even if the trappings appeared more ostentatious.

Sure enough, when we landed at the airport in Berlin for the start of our 1991 tour, Martin and David met us with a sixty-seat tour bus. We were excited to step onto the massive vehicle and find plush cloth reclining seats, a bathroom, and plenty of room for our nine-member traveling party to spread out. Furthermore, the luggage and cargo was out of sight, tucked securely away in compartments below the seating deck. Still far from luxurious, this was a tourist bus, repurposed in its summer off-season for Martin's side gig. His normal day job was taking retirees on skiing vacations up into the Alps during the winter months. In the summer, we were making use of his idle resource and giving Martin a chance to earn some money. It was a practical and mutually beneficial decision for us to migrate to buses. And we never toured in a van again.

Soon our traveling party grew. We had so much extra space on the bus that we brought along two super-fans from the UK, Mark and Dylan, who met us in Germany and told us they were planning to follow the entire tour. We said "hop on!"—we'll drive you and give you backstage passes to boot! Also, my chum Wryebo—who had just graduated from the University of Wisconsin film school—came along for the entire tour. He brought his video camera and filmed every show. Various friends, groupies, and other musicians joined us throughout our 1991 bus tour of Europe. Even my brother Grant came along for a portion of it. Each night we had sold-out shows, and even though we still didn't have a manager, we ran a pretty tight ship.

But it was clear that the ship was entering tumultuous waters. We were starting to play venues that many bigger bands played and the offers were nonstop. We could easily play every night of the year in cities throughout Europe and the USA if we wanted to. I started to worry about the balance of my academic and musical careers. I had to find a way to keep a foot in both. This would not be a quick transition nor would it be an easy task. It became a lifelong dance.

23
FROM DIY TO COLLABORATIVE ENTERPRISE

After that 1991 summer tour, I headed back to the USA with a lot on my mind. Jumping right back in to my academic research and teaching, I spent my evenings writing songs and living the life of a married graduate student. Greta gave birth to our baby boy, Graham, in January of 1992. I spent the days on campus, and at night I enjoyed my domestic tranquility. My earnings from touring had become sufficient to support our modest lifestyle. No real extravagances, but we had enough money in the bank and Greta decided to quit her job as a teacher to be a full-time mom, which suited me just fine because I could only ever be a part-time at-home Dad with all the touring that we planned to do. Teaching and research took up much of my day-to-day productivity during the school year. I wanted to have a somewhat "normal" life for the family, if you consider an academic upbringing like the one I had "normal."

But to many outside the university, I was becoming a tad bit notorious to music writers and others in the entertainment industry: an oddball punk rock singer-songwriter, noteworthy for Bad Religion's interesting melodies and harmonies, but also a scholar pursuing his PhD. Music came so naturally to me that I didn't really have to work too hard at it. At the time, I considered my academic work to be my main concerted effort. It took more concentration, and it required more challenging thinking.

To provide an at-home musical distraction from my studies, I purchased my first grand piano around this time. A local voice professor named Ed had a piano shop where he restored antique instruments. On his annual trips to Europe, he found Mozart-era pianos and other items in disrepair and brought them home to rejuvenate. His shop was full of other vintage instruments as well. Ed sold me a refurbished American parlor grand piano from around my birth year. Not yet an antique, but a solid instrument nonetheless. It was a Knabe, made of walnut. I played it when I wrote "Struck a Nerve," celebrating the birth of my first boy. I could dillydally for hours playing chord progressions and melodies on it.

Back on campus, I spent many hours in the teaching lab with specimens and dissections. But I couldn't ignore what I had experienced during the last European tour: that the audiences were getting much larger and that there was no end in sight to the potential growth of the band.

I came to a conclusion, privately, that in order to accelerate the growth of the band we needed help. Even though we relished the idea of DIY, we could still cling to that ideal and call the shots ourselves and enlist other professionals to help us in our cause. Brett felt that way too. He sensed our larger potential in additional ways, too, because he, and Jay as well, were at ground zero in Los Angeles while I was away across the continent at Cornell. Brett's label, Epitaph, was growing rapidly, and with him at the helm, and Jay working in the shipping department, they saw Bad Religion's growing importance firsthand because so many records were leaving the warehouse. They were getting ready to ship a hundred thousand units of our new album, *Generator*. Even many major-label rock bands weren't able to achieve those numbers. When it came time to begin thinking about our next European tour, we all agreed that we should enlist a booking agency to handle our tours rather than continue on a DIY path with our friend David. We had done quite a lot on our own, and David was a good booking agent and tour manager, but his operation was small. Furthermore, we felt that it was really important to make a splash in the UK, and David had few connections there.

Almost every professional we consulted suggested the same thing: "You should look to the UK for a booking agency." "But we're not that big in the UK; we are much more of an important act in Germany," we countered. "Still, the most important entertainers and bands from the USA use British companies to book their tours all over the European continent." Andy, our on-again, off-again booking agent in the USA, made some phone calls for us and soon we were connected to Prestige International, an agency from London who booked the band the Police, among other important international acts. They assigned us an agent named Rob, who sounded really smooth on the phone and promised us that he would get us good shows in the UK and make sure we continued our upward trajectory on the Continent.

Equally important to the booking arrangements, the agency also supplied us with a tour manager. I began receiving phone calls from the agency soon after we hired them. A man with a strong North London accent named Howard was on the other line. "Hello, is that Greg, yah? This is Howard Menzies, your new tour manager. Wonderful to make your acquaintance by tele." Wow, I thought. Very formal, very professional! Howard treated me with respect, which really shocked me. I wasn't used to talking about punk tours with any sense of formality. Howard was the first music industry professional who seemed to be concerned with doing the job right. Instead of self-importance, he seemed to really care about collaboration and mutual effort to bring about a successful tour.

There would be no more one-sheet faxes that simply listed cities and dates. Howard followed the custom of the booking agency and issued tour booklets with every detail noted. Each tour city had a page of its own with prebooked hotel information, addresses of venues we were playing, and capacities of those venues. Travel distances and departure times were also noted. The preceding pages read like a table of contents with a summary page of all the dates and cities of the tour, personnel lists that included staff members at the talent agency and their phone numbers, in addition to the representatives from the promoters that were set to greet us in various cities. Howard even included a list of rules, or in essence a code of conduct, that he expected everyone in the tour party to obey. It read as follows:

"A Guide to a Good Stabbing!"

or

"A Little Consideration and Common Sense
Makes Everyone's Life Enjoyable"

1. Each person is responsible for the payment of their own hotel extras. Repeated non-payment of extras could result in a good stabbing!

2. There are 9 people in the crew and 5 people in the band. If one person is late it is inconsiderate to everyone else. If you are late you will be given 5 minutes grace and fined 50 pence per minute thereafter.

3. Please ensure that you are in position well in advance of the set time so that the show can start on time. If not, you will be stabbed.

4. Please always keep your laminated pass on your person at all times. Never give it away, not even to Dodgy Boilers! If you show up without it you will be stabbed.

5. The band and crew are reminded that continuous moaning or whinging about anything and everything is uncalled for and lowers morale. If it is a clerical or administrative problem, the tour manager will dispose of it. If it is a person that is causing the problem, they will be stabbed.

6. Remember if anything goes wrong, it's not my fault!

Despite all his organizational skills and wisdom in tour management, Howard had a good sense of British humor to boot. None of us in the band took the "Guide" too seriously. But it was a lighthearted way to get people alerted that there are a lot of pieces to making a successful tour, and I felt good having a set of expectations clearly written down in these handy tour booklets.

For weeks ahead of the first show in London, we spoke on the phone regularly. Howard got to know the band by spending a lot of time talking and asking questions. This was the beginning, for me, where the intrusion of professional obligations began. A man with an English accent was calling me at my house to request my attention to details that were being put in place for events far away and for later in the year. Contracts were being drawn up with expectations, demands, and points of consideration. It was a bit daunting, since I thought of myself as a student and academic. An artist maybe, but not the kind who is at all concerned with business in any way. But it was also very exciting.

I was convinced that we needed to surround ourselves with professionals who weren't punks, necessarily, because punks were just our peers, learning as they go, just as we were learning the ropes and developing our chops as we navigated the music industry. If we wanted to advance our station and be taken more seriously than "just another punk band," then we needed to show that we were worthy of wider consideration in the sphere of popular music and the music industry. Whether I was right or wrong about my hunch, my bias in thinking is perfectly in keeping with my experience in the universities. In the universities, a student is guided through life by a series of relationships with experienced advisers. It begins in the freshman year of undergraduate learning. All students are assigned some sort of adviser for their major course of study, and usually they meet with their advisers throughout their years until they graduate. If the goal is to get an undergraduate diploma, the relationship with the adviser usually ends at graduation. But there are higher academic achievements: master's degree,

PhD, postdoc, lecturer, assistant professor, associate professor, full professor, Nobel laureate (well, you get the picture). Every step of the way students must surround themselves with good, like-minded people who will interact and collaborate to mutually encourage their students' intellectual development. That's the only kind of advancement I ever knew. My views, naturally, were influenced by my own academic experience and were an outgrowth of my family's structuring of Graffin U. But at this stage, I was concerned that there were no mentors, no professionals with more experience than us to guide the band to "the next level."

It should be clear, from this confession, why I was so eager to have outside professionals help guide the great ship HMS *Bad Religion* to our next port of call. We band members all agreed that we wanted to be taken seriously as a musical force, but we didn't actually discuss how to make that happen. Our meetings were casual and usually undertaken to address a particular question about a tour, such as, "Should we bring along this band or that band as an opening act?" or "Should we use this artwork or that image for our stage backdrop?" Brett and I were still committed to a unified intellectual approach to our songwriting. Even though I knew Brett was thinking a lot about marketing and selling records, to me he was a writing partner, an intellectual equal, and I appreciated that our relationship seemed focused on that. I began to feel like the band had a life of its own and was developing like a growing organism. I was a part of the brain, but the organism had its own ontogeny. It was going to grow as fast and large as its environment would allow. My job was to keep the ideas coming, and make them as interesting as possible. I believed that surrounding the band with a more professional support team would only help to bring them to fruition. People who had more experience, rather than our peers and friends from the punk scene, were like trusted advisers to me.

Unfortunately, not everyone in the entertainment industry is such a good fit. Sometimes it works out well, and you might get good advice. But the problem in the music industry is that no one can say how your band or your next song will be received by a constantly changing environment of public preference or taste. Just because an agent has had success in the past with a different band, for instance, there is no guarantee that he can deliver the same success for your band.

Around the time Howard came on board he had to interact with Rob, our newly assigned agent in the UK. A tall Englishman with a Richard Branson–like accent, Rob wore sporty clothing and had great success booking some of Prestige's biggest acts. His claim to fame was discovering Duran Duran and booking them at the Marquee Club in London. When we heard that Rob was coming to work with us we thought, "Wow! He's handled Duran Duran, so he must know a thing or two about helping a band grow in popularity."

But the music industry didn't turn out to be like my experience in academia. What works for Duran Duran is not easy to replicate for every band. Rob's expertise, at that time, extended only as far as another similar band in the same genre as Duran Duran. Bad Religion was like taking a physics student and placing them under the tutelage of a cultural anthropology professor. Sure the student might be smart, but they would not have the training to excel in cultural anthropology, so they would have to do a lot of remedial training to get up to speed in a different field of study.

Rob's first attempt to get Bad Religion playing in front of larger audiences backfired. He got us on a metal festival in Denmark, but none of the bands were compatible with us. In those days, festivals were much more xenophobic than they are today. Metal festivals only wanted metal bands. Bad Religion was not welcomed, and we didn't go over very well. Our sizeable fan base in Denmark stayed away from this festival and consequently we missed a great opportunity to debut our new album, *Generator*, to our Danish fans. Needless to say, this relationship with Rob—a music industry bigwig who nonetheless didn't understand our audience—ended quickly.

Howard stayed on and wisely recognized that he was a bit out of touch with the culture of European punk. Always eager to listen to smart scenesters who showed interest in Bad Religion, Howard met a guy from Germany named Jens. Jens followed Bad Religion's progress while he finished his degree in economics at one of Germany's most important schools for accounting. Jens was unique in that he seemed eager to observe and learn about rock 'n' roll touring. Howard was married to a German woman from rock royalty, the sister of the Schenker brothers (from Scorpions and UFO), and he understood German culture, so the two of them made a great pair. Jens instructed Howard about the German punk scene and Howard showed Jens the nuances of tour managing.

Jens was great at accounting and budget details. He offered to come along on tour with us for no salary, just to gain experience on tour. Howard appreciated his enthusiasm and loved the idea of not having to tend to the details of a spreadsheet (Howard didn't even carry a computer). It was agreed that Jens could join us for the entire tour. Howard and Jens made a great team and we became fast friends. Jens could negotiate with promoters in Germany for Howard, and order from restaurants in his native tongue.

With Jens doing financials and tour accounting, Howard doing the management, advancing shows, reading budgets, and the rest of it, Brett doing recording and making distribution deals, and me doing academic work in graduate school, one might assume that we were on some sort of evangelical mission to form a traveling academy or a new religion. In fact, we were all part of a growing punk enterprise, but all of us were doing very unpunk things when we weren't on stage. Was this some sort of identity crisis? Were we betraying our philosophical purpose? Giving in to, instead of resisting, the expectations of "society"? No. As individuals, we were answering our "calling" and following the dictates of our personal conscience, the same things that made us punk in the first place. Personally, I felt like I was pushing the boundaries of what was expected of me, and that flowed consistently upward and outward, through the spirit of Bad Religion.

24

THE BIG SELLOUT

Sellout. The betrayal of "the cause." By 1993, I had been associated with punk for nearly fifteen years and, although an active participant, I still couldn't discern exactly what traits were unique to the genre. Still in the process of evolving, Bad Religion exhibited a consistent musical and ideological theme. Never focused on commercialism, we nonetheless ran headlong into a climate of judgment and scrutiny not seen previously.

"Sellout" had become a word thrown around by punk rock fans, music writers, and fellow musicians. It was the ultimate criticism, suggesting discord between the spirit of the fan base and the secret intentions of the band members. On one hand, I deemed it a good thing that the audience was engaged, a hopeful indication that maybe punk rock helped listeners use their brains and question society. Unfortunately, on the other hand, the sellout accusations were slung about so readily and haphazardly that it soon led to the revelation that most fans of punk were no different than average citizens, hypercritical of the people who they themselves had placed on a pedestal for some arbitrary ideal or perceived virtue. It was an insight about human behavior I've witnessed over and over again. The most vociferous critics are actually projecting their own self-doubt, revealing secret transgressions of their own behavior. If you want to understand the person pointing the finger, just imagine their finger turned around, somehow aimed at their own subconsciousness.

The world had become so commercialized. Shopping malls were in their heyday. Everyone but the most hardened stalwarts bought goods manufactured in sweatshops, sourced in far-off locations, by people totally disconnected from those who would consume them. Music-lifestyle goods and band merchandise was also for sale in the same malls that offered designer clothing, luxury jewelry, hair salons, and home furnishings. Even though most music fans shopped at malls, they still wanted to retain an exception for their favorite bands as existing somewhere outside all the crass commercialism. At home they watched MTV and idealized their favorite singers. The ethical purity of the bands became highly scrutinized.

The perceptions, so often ill informed, could easily become tarnished by reputation and hearsay, often published in fanzines or by word of mouth. A common complaint might read, "So-and-so's band played at a commercial club, therefore they have secret intentions to be more famous and charge higher ticket prices so they can make more money!" which ultimately meant the band was a "sellout." Any time a hero or a band broke away from their narrowly defined roles, they were no longer seen as fulfilling their pure intentions of old.

Many of the fans in the mid-1990s had entirely missed the previous incarnations of the scene. They were informed by a romantic, but inaccurate, narrative of punk in the late 1970s and early 1980s: fighting against the government, protesting police brutality, unified battalions of socially conscious, street-smart, do-it-yourselfers. All in the interest of an ill-defined "cause" without concern for sustenance or a roof overhead.

But the tendrils of punk's reach were extending to the realm of mainstream, corporate entertainment. Our involvement in that process stemmed from our personal relationships with other bands and individuals. Green

Day opened for us on their first national tour. Already they were shipping hundreds of thousands of copies of their album that would launch them into the stratosphere. One of the most commercially successful bands of the entire decade, they would soon be fixtures on commercial radio and television across the land. Gore Verbinski of the Epitaph Records band Little Kings directed our first videos that were seen on MTV, specifically "American Jesus," which debuted on MTV's *120 Minutes* program in October of 1993. We never discussed the commercial aspirations of our friend Gore. His ideas matched ours and we collaborated as artists. Who could have predicted that he would go on to become one of the most commercially successful Hollywood directors of all time? Eddie Vedder, who sang with me on 1993's *Recipe for Hate* album, was already becoming rock 'n' roll royalty, enjoying huge commercial sales with his band Pearl Jam. The Offspring, also Epitaph labelmates, became one of the most commercially successful indie bands of all time. We were surrounded on all sides by success stories of musicians, raised on punk music, who were quickly crossing over to mainstream notoriety.

Even bands that were perceived to be strictly "DIY," such as Fugazi, were publicly associating with commercially motivated stars like Michael Stipe from REM. Fugazi retained their mystique by shunning all associations with making videos (save for a self-released "documentary" explaining what they were all about). But such measures did nothing to slow down the obvious, rapidly expanding perception of punk as a valid commercial form of music in the USA. More records were being sold, more viewers were tuning in to music television, and more tickets for live shows were being sold than ever before. Every popular music genre experienced growth in the 1990s and punk rock was swept up in the fray.

Dealing with this increase in eyeballs was awkward for me. My interviews from that time period revealed an average-looking graduate student suddenly thrust in front of a camera being asked about the state of the scene, or how I felt about punk's commercial success. I wanted to say, "Look, when I'm not on stage, I'm busy writing, studying, or taking care of my kids. I have no idea what's going on in the clubs." But instead I tried to play along. MTV and other television outlets were giving fans more access than they ever had to see their favorite singers and songwriters in interviews. Everyone putting on airs, hiding their true selves, appearing self-confident, over-compensating for their fears that anything they might say could be used against them in the court of public opinion. I had somehow silently, seamlessly, transformed—from a music fan in the slam pit into the focus of attention itself. Oh, how I wished that we could just perform our music and not have to answer any questions from some ill-informed interviewer. But we were entering a new world where hundreds of thousands of dollars and millions of fans were now at stake.

An entire generation of music fans had missed out on Minor Threat, Rites of Spring, Black Flag, Dead Kennedys, Circle Jerks, Fear, Misfits, and the like in the 1980s. None of these politically charged bands were making punk records anymore in 1993. Bad Religion had been there all along, releasing album after album. The burgeoning music scene of new fans expected that anyone tied to the punk scene of 1980 must have seasoned their hardcore views into full-blown social philosophies by now. The expectations were high.

But I had no conventional hardcore views to offer. I wasn't committed to any kind of special narrative to maintain punk credibility. In their second rounds, Ian MacKaye had his five dollar ticket; Johnny Rotten had his diatribes against censorship, while his band, PIL, was making pop music that contained nothing to censor; and Henry Rollins, like Glenn Danzig, both with new bands, had their overtly aggressive, double-down-as-a-punk badass image with whom no one would dare fuck. All of these were newsworthy tidbits seized upon by the watchers of MTV. It was as if punk rock was finally getting recognized by major media as a genre with something important to say, but the spokespeople they chose to highlight only represented the most superficial qualities from the early punk scene. It was modern-day Ecclesiastes. Nothing new under the sun. The heightened publicity, more often than not, dealt with some inane accoutrement like ticket prices or costs involved in stage productions, or it was about aggression, that old, recurring stereotype, stemming from some loosely defined social ill. All the richness of the punk experience, stemming from the song-book of the early 1980s, seemed irrelevant to this new MTV generation.

There was little intellectual merit to what they were prepared to believe. Self-proclaimed "artists" would go on record saying, "Rather than get too popular, we broke up the band." So, poof! No more Operation Ivy. Why? They would have been too good? Too widely appreciated? Was this some sort of radical new musical protest? "We broke up because it was clear that we were going to be too popular." No one with half a brain should ever accept such a low bar for a protest. You cannot know how popular you "would have" become if you didn't stick around to experience it! The fans, nonetheless, seemed to accept it, and the music writers applauded and validated it as a legitimate strategy to maintain punk credibility. "Look!" I found myself arguing with a magazine article, "if you don't want to be popular, then why go on stage in the first place? It's super easy to be unpopular!" It all seemed to me a shallow, ad hoc explanation for a music genre in the midst of a midlife crisis. The music writers and fans needed to know what punk's renewed purpose was!

I had little to offer on such topics. The proximate purpose in my life was to continue my education, help my family, and continue with Bad Religion—a full plate! Ultimately, I was in the throes of fulfilling the subconscious dictates of Graffin U. In none of these areas did a stereotypic punk lifestyle play a role. Yet, if you define punk as living on the fringe of the mainstream, then as punk became mainstream, I still fit the definition. My atypical lifestyle suited me just fine because it satisfied my belief that punk was never supposed to be hemmed in by some litmus test for inclusion, but rather it was hallmarked by the idea that one cannot judge by appearances alone. I fully embraced the atypical. I was pretty sure that that dictum made me too cryptic for easy marketing, too elusive for music writers to use as a subject for a fluff piece, and too difficult for many punk fans to embrace as a messiah. But I was convinced that my and Brett's songwriting and Bad Religion's music spoke for itself, so I didn't care if the newly emerging music press viewed me as a spokesperson for punk or not.

24A. WITHDRAWAL

My desire to withdraw from punk's growing publicity began to take hold around this time. I craved the solitude of nature, hiking trails, studying outcrops and ecosystems, taking notes and photographs without anyone around, just flooding my senses with the stimuli of the natural surroundings. Far from the bustle and dysfunction of the metropolis is where I increasingly found myself wanting to be. This desire was, from what I've read, akin to a religious experience, where daydreaming can become trancelike and borderline obsessive. Based on my experiences on prior expeditions, I had a longing to go back and collect more data in wilderness areas I had visited before. Sometimes, I would dream up expedition plans, consult my growing map collection, and plan weeks-long adventures in the mountains of the western USA, Alaska, or the Amazon basin. While the band's popularity continued to grow, I felt more and more like escaping from the pressure of having to front it. Music writers and fans alike wanted to make sense of us. Why did it take so long for Bad Religion to become this popular? What is the meaning of punk nowadays? Is your indie lifestyle consistent with getting an overprivileged graduate school education? All of these unanswerable questions made me feel constantly on defense. I couldn't satisfy the writers or the punk fans with sufficient answers.

Not long after moving to Ithaca, I was on NPR's *Fresh Air* with Terry Gross. All of my graduate school friends and academic advisers listened to that show. It was a big deal for them. But none of my punk friends could have cared less about it. The only unique thing about my story that the interviewer cared to focus on was that I was a punk rocker in graduate school studying the origin of vertebrates. Interesting to biologists maybe, but head scratchingly off-putting to most. The punk stories that were coming out in the major press in the 1990s, reinforced on television shows that interviewed former punks, were really no different than the stereotypes established in the middle to late 1980s. If you were streetwise, hard-edged, disadvantaged, lived in your car, drug addicted, mean-spirited—all things I was not—then you could be painted as a worthy poster boy for punk. Gone was the notion that musical ability or songwriting prowess might be a more worthy thing to publicize. It's as if none of the music writers could appreciate the music, so they just wrote about the peripherals, the fashion, the politics, the stereotypes. I wasn't going to be a public face for the genre, and that was okay by me. It meant two things: (1) I could focus more on the music and let it do the talking for me; and (2) I could live a lifestyle that suited me, felt natural, and not constantly obsess over my public persona.

Brett used to joke that I only felt comfortable dressing like a graduate student doing fieldwork. Actually, there was more truth in that than he knew. My "style" was unpretentious, involved lightweight hiking boots, cargo shorts, and pocketed shirts. Functional clothing that soon was adopted by many in the grunge rock world as their preferred fashion. I'm not suggesting that I invented their style. But I appreciated "blending in" rather than "sticking out" with a leather jacket, dyed hair, and combat boots. Those things were fun to provoke stares and confrontations as a high schooler in LA. But now, I was more content to avoid the pitfalls of fashion, preferring instead to announce my presence through songwriting.

———

24B. THE TWO CULTURES

The mere idea of righteous prognosticators with visions of what was good and bad for punk was ridiculous to me. If ever a genre of music defied conventional definition it was punk. Brett was put on the hot seat by punk writers from fanzines who expected to grill him, rake him over the coals for being a hypocrite. "How could you write songs about the evils of capitalism and then make money off of them? How could you create a record label that itself serves as a corporation? That's not punk!" But similar absurdities emanated from other punk moguls, themselves trying to protect their own enterprises by decrying the evils of "corporate music" (whatever that was supposed to mean) as inherently detrimental to the "punk way" of thinking (whatever that was supposed to mean). "We're not here to entertain you" was a common attitude among the "thinking men" of the post-punk generation.* My attitude

---

* See the *Washington Post* article by Eric Brace, "Punk Lives! Washington's Fugazi Claims It's Just a Band. So Why Do So Many Kids Think It's God?" August 1, 1993.

was just the opposite: I was ONLY there to entertain the audience. If not for them, why would I go on tour?

There was a noticeable separation of cultures at play. On the one hand, there were the punks from the early '80s, call them the second wave punks, who now had a hardened worldview that punk should be about anger and disillusionment with society; and on the other hand, there were punks like us who had outgrown that hardcore mentality. While the former believed in rigid prescriptions for the punk lifestyle, we urged a more expansive, inclusive spirit to the genre.

Outside, after a 1993 concert in Chicago, Jay and I were accosted by an angry punk. "Nice van, assholes!" Stupidly, I engaged in the conversation and said, "That's not a van, it's a tour bus, you idiot!" The dude was ready to throw down with me and Jay, for playing at a "commercial venue" (The Vic Theater) and getting chauffeured around the country in a tour bus. He was accusing us of betraying punk culture!

Now that I was a graduate student, steeped in intellectual debate, as I departed the scene I was reminded of C. P. Snow's "The Two Cultures" of science and literature. C. P. Snow wrote:[*] "Not to have read *War and Peace* . . . is not to be educated, but so is not to have a glimmer of the Second Law of Thermodynamics." In other words, just because a scientist is totally engaged with scientific literature does not give him primacy over those who engage in social studies or literary fiction. Ethnocentrism prevents us from judging any culture as inferior, because our values are derived only from within our own culture. According to Snow, "There are benefits to be gained from listening to intelligent men, utterly removed from the literary scene and unconcerned as to who's in and who's out."

The deep divide between punk culture and all others was man-made and arbitrary. Some punks were deeply invested in keeping those divisions unbridgeable. I always believed, like C. P. Snow suggested, that much gain could come from bridging the gaps and eliminating the litmus-test mentality from the genre. Punk culture, from my perspective, always depended

* See "The Two Cultures" by C. P. Snow in the *New Statesman*, reprinted January 2, 2013.

on a breaking of the expected rules, so I always found it odd to hear from critics that we somehow failed them in not being predictably punk enough. Still, it was unavoidable. If your concerts were full and albums were popular, or even if you made practical but expensive decisions about touring, you were subject to the accusations of being sellouts!

Avoiding the pitfalls of being labeled a sellout was not that difficult for me. I was in a small town in upstate New York. Back in LA, Brett and Jay had to endure more daily scrutiny. They were in the heat of the battle. The fanzine writers had easy access, for Brett and Jay could be found every day at Epitaph's headquarters, a new office and adjacent warehouse on Santa Monica Boulevard. If you called Epitaph, Brett or Jay would answer the phone. Jay would welcome the questions and talk the caller's ear off. Even punk fans could stop by at Epitaph any time to visit with their favorite band members, and bands could drop off their latest demo tapes with Brett himself. Not only was Brett actively signing bands, but he, Jay, and other punk rockers could be found hanging out in the office and adjacent warehouse. The scene was always very informal.

The scarlet letter "S" (sellout label) could mar the reputation of Brett and Epitaph irreparably. If bands thought he was ungenuine or noncommittal, it could possibly detract from his ability to sign new bands. He was as committed to building Epitaph as I was to my own pursuits, so integrity was very important to us. For me, it revolved around singing and songwriting. I believed that music is for everyone, and that there is no limit on who is allowed to listen to what and who isn't. I didn't care to debate about who the "target" audience was supposed to be. I honestly didn't even care if some people protested that my songs weren't punk enough. Brett was a bit more guarded in interviews around this time. He began to get as many requests to talk about Epitaph as he did for Bad Religion. His two-hat approach—one as a songwriter-guitarist and the other as a record mogul—had been cultivated for a number of years, but now it started to reach a fever pitch. Eventually, we reached a point where Brett's two hats could not be juggled successfully.

24C. SELLING OUT

In the summer of 1993, Bad Religion reached an agreement with Atlantic Records to record four albums over the coming years. Signing the execution copies of the new recording contract meant no longer having an ongoing professional relationship with Epitaph Records. We were now officially sellouts to many in the punk community, and this was the icing on the cake. But I didn't feel that way. Selling out could not have been further from my mind in the first half of 1993. I was busy buying into my new lifestyle, having just purchased a lovely brick colonial, not far from campus, with a large TV room, formal living room for the new piano, a two-car garage with a studio over it, and a large basement with enough room for a drum kit and a thirty-two-channel recording console. I was as excited as ever about making music.

The growing family had plenty of room to mill about while I could escape to the basement or piano room to write new songs. I had long dreamed about having a "compound" where I was able to have a family as well as a factory for music production à la Frank Zappa and his famous studio-home complex, the Utility Muffin Research Kitchen, in Los Angeles. The problem was, in LA the real estate values were too steep for me to accomplish such a vision. But in upstate New York, it was feasible. From the money I saved over the years of touring and the royalty cash from Epitaph it was possible for me to buy a house and have a home studio too.

Brett probably thought various things about Bad Religion at this time, privately, but he did not share them all with me. We, in fact, didn't communicate about most business decisions during this period of time. But we had a very close relationship as artists. He didn't trust anyone else to sing his songs, or to consult with about concepts, and I felt the same way toward him when it came to proposing new song ideas of my own. We would consult closely during the demo phases, record ideas on our Portastudios, share tapes with each other, and work out an album's contents before we played them to other band members. So it was the artist-hat-wearing Brett who talked with me, and who respected my opinions when it came to songwriting and arranging. But partly because of my lack of interest in PR, and even more, my disinterest in the music business (selling and marketing), Brett did a lot more talking AT me rather than discussing business strategy. I appreciated this. He was from a business family. I was from an academic family. He had the experience, and it was because of this that I respected his decisions.

If Brett said to sign something, like all the recording contracts he is-sued for our Epitaph albums, I just signed. I didn't seek "outside counsel" or question his honesty. I don't even know that I ever read them. If Brett said, "This is the way we're going to do it," I just said okay. I trusted him on such matters. Just like he trusted me on matters of melody, harmony, and arranging. Usually, if I said "This is the way I'm gonna sing it," he just said okay. We grew up together, and this had always been our style of mutual trust. There was no concept in my mind, nor precedent in my experience, to suggest a variance on the way we always worked together.

Therefore, in matters of business formalities, I never argued or disagreed with the Epitaph contracts Brett set down for us all to sign. In fact, for the years prior to 1993, we didn't even have a band lawyer. There were no nego-tiations at all. So, when it came time to sign on the dotted line with Atlantic Records, I never would have signed it without the tacit approval of Brett, who in fact had signed also. Later, he expressed regret and even went on record to claim that he did it just "for the money," which I knew was bullshit because it wasn't as much money as we were making on Epitaph. But he had to say something because the punk police, music writers, and fanzine readers all wanted to know how the author of some of the best punk rock songs and owner of the best punk label could sell out to a corporation just like that.

My own conflicts were mounting. For the first time in my life I had to think about supporting other people: a wife, a child, and another one on the way, and keeping a roof over our heads and food on the table. I was starting to fear the worst of academia: work your ass off with your head in the books, digging for some lost nugget of overlooked truth to write up in some arcane journal, read by only a handful of similar sociopathic re-cluses who make up "the field," only to ascend a measly rung on the ladder of underappreciation in service to the university. You can come up for air occasionally to glad-hand all the senior faculty and administrators at their socially awkward gatherings and weekly committee meetings, ruffling no feathers as you modify your research interests to suit the administrative needs of the university—the tacit signal that you're willing to "play ball"— and if you succeed at it long enough, fail upward high enough, they'll name a building after you where your portrait may hang on the wall, ignored and dusty for generations until some renovation contractor takes notice and sticks you in the archive forever. All the while, you enjoy the privilege of being coddled financially with a just-sufficient, guaranteed paycheck, fighting for scraps of rewards, and receiving a nice pension, while saddled with society's most derisive adjectives of modern life: ninny, book smart, liberal, teacher of useless information, ivory tower intellectual.

With such pessimistic thoughts as these circling in my brain, I was also privately fretting about the music business. The achievements in entertainment could be every bit as modest as those in academia. You could spend months, or years, obsessing over content and context for your next album, writing entire songs with melodies and chord progressions, playing it through hundreds of times, only to scrap the entire project to start again from scratch for no other reason than a self-loathing lack of confidence. You can do everything right with a new album: write excellent songs, make compelling and captivating sonic results in the studio, enjoy expert marketing and "placement" of the "product," and go on successful world tours and still come home to modest sales, professional disappointments, and scrutiny from the marketplace and the critics. All the while, the personal costs are high: long absences from family while touring the world, bringing with it exhaustion, poor nutrition, poor sleeping, poor health, and nightly extremes of psychic stress on stage.

On balance, the entertainment world seemed more overtly honest than the academic world. It's a spoken truth that in the music industry there are no guarantees. If you dedicate your life to music, the rewards can be astronomical—money, fame, respect—but only if you get lucky. So at least you know that you are gambling, and if you're good, you can game the system and increase your chances of success by creating good work.

Meanwhile, in academia, you experience dishonesty. It is all set up to give the illusion that there ARE guarantees. As long as you perfectly execute all the tasks, jump through the right hoops, you will graduate to some new level of expertise, respect, and modest monetary reward. But after graduate school, matriculation is much more sluggish. You can complete all those aforementioned prerequisites and still stagnate, never reaching the heights that formerly seemed like guarantees. If some vindictive colleague or adviser judges your work substandard, you will forever wallow in the basement of your chosen field, always hunting around for some better-paying lecturing gig or research lab.

I discovered a way to be true to myself, which is the only antidote to selling out. Rather than abandon academics entirely I would, instead, continue my studies. I simply could not give up academia lest I reject whole parts of myself, my intellectual development, my family tradition. But I also could not remain there full-time. Music was demanding more and more of my time. Keeping up an active schedule in each enterprise was a daunting prospect, but I was willing to attempt the feat. It would be an adventurous journey. Whether it could be sustained only time would tell.

It was increasingly clear that I was not going to be able to give my band anything in the.way of newsworthy fashion or cutting-edge coolness. I felt awkward even trying. The *Washington Post* wrote a high-profile review in their Arts & Entertainment section that referred to me as "too good natured to front such an angry band." Anger, angst, disaffection. These were the words of the day used to characterize punk rock, words that had been there from the start in the 1970s. But now, in 1993, the faces of punk had changed. Instead of spiked and wild-colored hair, or safety pins through the cheek à la Sid and Johnny, you had a more diverse array of singers. Some, like Tim Armstrong of Rancid, were still flying the flag of 1979 and sporting liberty spikes. Fat Mike of NOFX looked a little like me, but his bleached or colored cropped hair and dark eyebrows and sleeveless T-shirt look was something I would have worn onstage at the Country Club or Starwood ten years prior. I wasn't going to venture back to those days of shabby clothes just for fashion's sake. Another style was Bryan "Dexter" Holland from the Offspring, and Billie Joe Armstrong from Green Day. These guys both had the youth and charm of the teenage kid on your suburban block who skateboards on your driveway. You wanna be pissed at him, but he's just too darn cute and innocent. So you let him skate and hope he finds greener pastures elsewhere. I knew I was already an "old man" in this world of new faces. Plus I never skated or surfed, so I really didn't fit in. The front man images of the new music at the time, the looks that got the most coverage, were either these youthful punk styles or the alternative look—the brooding, pensive, questionably deranged singer, hiding perhaps a serious mental condition, so seething with anger that he sings to you beneath a permanently furrowed brow. This type of front man was typified by Kurt Cobain of Nirvana, who claimed that year, "I'm a much happier guy than a lot of people think I am."[*] Rolling Stone featured him on the cover and spoke of how "the roots of his angst, public and personal, go much deeper." It was all there on the page written out before me, the music writer in tandem with the rock icon crystallizing a new narrative, new horizons for a singer's appeal thanks to "Nirvana's mass punk-wanna-be flock." Ian MacKaye of Fugazi also had this appeal, so perpetually displeased and disappointed in society that flashing a smile to the audience was as unlikely as seeing a colored lighting gel onstage at one of their shows. And then there was the style of Trent Reznor of Nine Inch Nails, who was depicted on the cover of *Alternative Press* with the old punk words "Anger Is an Energy." Calm and "normal" looking, but deeply mysterious, Reznor's music was a psychological puzzle for the audience to figure out from whence came this psychic tempest.

No, I wasn't going to fit neatly into any of the roles that were materializing for my contemporaries. I felt that I was already a has-been, unwilling to participate in the frenzy of new stereotypes these singers were now fulfilling, all of them destined for huge commercial success, the embodiment of a punk narrative that writers had been honing for a generation now. Being

---

[*] David Fricke, "Kurt Cobain, The Rolling Stone Interview: Success Doesn't Suck. Our man in Nirvana rages on (and on) about stardom, fatherhood, his feud with Pearl Jam, the . . ." *Rolling Stone*, January 27, 1994.

"unique," a poor fit for the mainstream pegboard, wasn't going to cut it in this world where the journalists, record companies, and media outlets were intent on bringing punk and its offspring out of the closet and illuminating it fully for mass consumption. Now they wanted psychic pain or anger or incessant irritation at society's dumbness, or even more palatable, light-hearted, youthful pabulum as some kind of commentary on the blandness of consumer culture in the USA. How ironic!

That's what the lead singers who were getting all the press were selling. I, however, wasn't angry, and I couldn't pretend to be when I performed onstage. I was now a dad and an academic, just like my parents were before me. How would that truth ever translate? I was beginning to worry that I didn't matter.

Privately, I worried that we were losing some sort of competition, that Bad Religion wasn't up to the task of being in the limelight of all this new-found adoration of punk culture. Bad Religion's music was not an exercise in anger or disaffection, as so many writers incorrectly assumed. It was a reflection of a belief system. A system in which truth can only be found in observations, explorations, and verifications. The media was making gods out of former punks, so I had no confidence that the punk ethos was echoing anything that I had to say. Despite my worries, I focused on what I could control: delivering the message in our words in the most musical way that the genre would allow. The main goal: reach as many people as possible. I felt that this was an unassailable position, worthy of consideration in all of the band's business decisions.

25

MUSIC BUSINESS FORMAL LEGITIMACY

I f one had to describe the business structure of Bad Religion before 1992, it would not be inappropriate to say "amorphous
blob." In the 1958 feature film *The Blob*, an amoeboid organism grows
larger and larger without any centralized purpose or direction. The blob
merely follows opportunities, growing larger as it encounters more and
more humans along the way. Even though we were now growing rapidly,
Bad Religion had no administrative professional help for our first decade as
a band. We played concerts, recorded albums, and went on tour simply by
the efforts and agreements of individual band members. Brett and I wrote
songs constantly, and we became a great songwriting team. Greg Hetson
and Jay Bentley had wide-ranging friendships throughout the punk scenes
in Orange County and Los Angeles, and they continued as scenesters while
I went to college and Brett went to sound engineering school. Most of our

early concerts were opportunities to join other bands we knew and to get to know the regional promoters. We followed the opportunities that presented themselves to us, with no clear objective of where these opportunities were headed. The first "professional" administrative position we hired was a booking agent in 1988.

By 1992, Brett suggested that we would benefit from hiring a business manager. We were starting to amass sizeable record royalties and the band didn't even have any articles of incorporation or a bank account! Our search for a business manager took longer than expected, and in early 1993 we hired an accountant named Steven who helped shape us into a more legitimate financial entity. Greg Hetson's other band, the Circle Jerks, were represented by a management company, had signed with I.R.S. Records, and most significantly, had hired an entertainment law firm to negotiate all contracts. On Greg Hetson's tip we went to meet with a lawyer named Eric whose firm also represented the Circle Jerks and Red Hot Chili Peppers at that time. Eric and I got along well, as did the other guys, and Brett liked the idea of having the band represented by someone other than the person issuing the recording contracts. We all were satisfied when Eric agreed to look over our contracts, but the most important aspect of our association was not the previous contracts, but the one for our next album.

Eric discussed with us individually his opinions of the pros and cons about leaving Epitaph. Brett, being equal parts band member and label owner, had his own ideas about the topic, but he kept them pretty much to himself. I thought that all of us were on the same page, and ultimately would agree on what was best for the band. The discussions, however, never reached a conclusion—just a lot of loose ends and things to think about as we all packed our bags and left for our tour of Europe.

We were on the road in June 1993, starting our summer tour in Finland and spending two months touring in ten countries. Somehow, while Brett was performing at the Paradiso in Amsterdam on June 4 of that year, with me and all the other guys next to him onstage, he oversaw the release on Epitaph of our album *Recipe for Hate* back in the USA.

Epitaph Records had a handful of employees at that time, but their boss was often on tour when street dates for new albums came up. I would visit his hotel room and find his laptop attached awkwardly to a handheld phone receiver squealing data across the earpiece. He would call me over. "Dude, check this out! Here's my home screen." It was before cell phones, and most of the mid-priced and low-end rock 'n' roll hotels we stayed at had dial-up telephones with no data lines at all. Brett kept tabs on schedules, sales, marketing, and all the necessary items of business going on back in LA, even when we were thousands of miles away and performing concerts every night.

The label had grown steadily since 1991, when it first reached a notable milestone few other independent labels could boast: producing one hundred thousand "units," which means copies of an album. In that year, Bad Religion released *Against the Grain* and it shipped a hundred thousand units. The next year, we recorded *Generator*, which also shipped a hundred thousand units. By the time *Recipe for Hate* was released in 1993, Epitaph was busy releasing other successful bands that Brett had signed, such as NOFX, the Offspring, Rancid, and Pennywise. In fact, in 1993, the little operation that started out with us four band members stuffing three thousand Bad Religion records into sleeves with custom-made plastic coverings donated by PolyPac (Brett's dad's plastic company) now had grown into a serious label that shipped over one million units that year. Brett had captained a home-grown project into a serious indie powerhouse.

Through it all, I remained unconcerned with the inner workings of the business side of things. I trusted that Brett was doing what was best for the band, but I also recognized that other bands that he signed were demanding more of his attention too. The only concern that wouldn't go away was the notion that other bands on the label seemed to be attracting attention away from Bad Religion. I knew that Brett had begun expanding his Epitaph Records empire, opened an office in Europe, and hired marketing, distribution, radio, and PR personnel for the label. They were all eager and competent people, as far as I could tell. But I also was skeptical of what might happen if another band that Brett signed became the dominant best seller of the label's roster. I feared that we would no longer be the primary focus of the label we founded. To counter this fear, I found it an alluring daydream to think that a major media company, such as Warner Brothers or RCA or Sony, might have such deep pockets that they could assign an almost unlimited supply of personnel exclusively to a new record by Bad Religion.

As the tour of Europe went on, *Recipe for Hate* continued to raise eyebrows back in the States. I called my old friend from college, Mark, who had just finished his PhD and was moving on to a career in environmental science. "What's up, Mark? Congratulations on finishing! Or should I call you doctor now? Hahaahaha." Mark started working at Santa Monica's Heal the Bay, an environmental nonprofit, and his brother, Jonathan (who became famous later as the only food writer to earn a Pulitzer Prize) was a staff writer at the *LA Times*. "Deeud," Mark said, "Jon is writing a review of your new album." I couldn't believe it. The *LA Times* had finally agreed to feature us. This was a big surprise to me because up until that time we had been featured in just about every weekly publication and monthly music magazine in the Southland, but never hardly mentioned in the *LA Times*, our hometown's most respected paper.

Jonathan's article was titled "PC Punkers Take Opposite Tacks."* In it, he featured the two bands he considered the "alpha and omega" of underground rock 'n' roll, Bad Religion and Fugazi. I appreciated how Jonathan understood the differences between our bands. He knew me from my college years, hanging out with Mark, but I don't feel like that biased his high-profile assessment of our bands' uniqueness. Whereas Fugazi represented "what pops into every rock kid's head when the initials *PC* are mentioned," he saw Bad Religion as something different. We had, after all, in 1992 recorded a spoken-word seven-inch with the foremost intellectual in the USA, Noam Chomsky, which Jonathan made note of in the article. As I saw it, in other words, political correctness was not as important to

---

* Jonathan Gold, "PC Punkers Take Opposite Tacks," *Los Angeles Times*, July 25, 1993.

Bad Religion as was academic intellectualism. The article went on further to note the dissimilarity in our music.

The Washington, DC, sound of Fugazi, with vocal wails that twisted into "Rollins-esque barks," was distinct from my "catchy folk melodies" that "sounds commercial whether it means to or not." I was totally content with sounding commercial, and I was greatly satisfied that Jonathan took the time to contrast what he saw as the differences between what the DC punk scene had become and what I hoped we could establish as the maturation of the LA punk scene. He gave both albums the rating of "good," three stars, just shy of the highest rating, four stars, for "excellent."

Nearly all the important music magazines had taken notice of our new album, but the *LA Times* article created renewed interest in it and rejuvenated discussions with our lawyer, Eric, who was keeping abreast of our progress from afar. "Hey, Greg," he said on the phone one day in August 1993, "I'd like you to meet someone at Atlantic Records in New York. Danny Goldberg just took over as the president there and he'd like to meet you next week. This week he's out here in LA and he'll be meeting the other guys."

It was easy for me to "pop" down to the Big Apple. In fact, that was one of the strong reasons for deciding to live in New York State. Never being far away from the world's premier city has its perks. On any given morning, we could wake up, decide we wanted to go see a Broadway show that night, or head to any of the world-class museums for an afternoon of high culture. And yet, we lived far away enough that all the chaos, dysfunction, filth, and anger that typifies life in the city seemed out of sight and out of mind. In central New York, it's easy to find peace and quiet, but it's also easy to do business in the world's financial capital if you don't mind the four hours of driving into New York City.

On a Friday in August 1993 I did just that: woke up, headed down to NYC, and arrived in Midtown Manhattan around ten-thirty in the morning. After stashing my Pontiac in a Midtown parking garage, I walked over, amidst the glittering skyscrapers and iconic theaters, to ground zero of corporate entertainment in America: Rockefeller Center. I spent a few minutes taking in the bustle at its central plaza, catching the power-lunch meetings of suited execs and watching stressed-out professionals everywhere as they marched like drone ant soldiers to their offices in the sky. The whole scene seemed to emit a buzzing atmosphere, perhaps from the billions of overactive synapses in the frenzied brains of Midtowners racing between offices, jumping trains, and dodging cars. Amidst the flurry of humanity I was by myself. No friends or family by my side. The dreamlike choreography of all these people too busy to stop and say hi, offer a warm smile, or care about who they were sidestepping reinforced a feeling of disconnection. Here we all were in the world's most densely crowded place, and yet so many like me were just floating on by, heading to separate destinies.

Lost in my reverie, my thoughts went to familiar ground, old soundtracks from Mom and Dad days. Wistfully I hummed to myself "The Boxer" and "The Only Living Boy in New York" from the Simon and Garfunkel album *Bridge Over Troubled Water*. The first one was about a boy out on his own having "left my home and my family," while the other was about a best pal, songwriting partner, off in a faraway place. My "Tom" (Brett) was in LA, and it really dawned on me that our distance, like our ever-increasing division of labor (him running the label, me going to school) had come full circle. More wistfully still, my other "Tom" (Tommy from the old neighborhood), the namesake in the third verse of my song "Along the Way," had already been dead nearly a decade, making me feel somewhat less childlike amidst the fantastic dreamscape of the Big Apple.

Dad taught me everything that was noteworthy about this city. He had brought me here as a kid, and as a preteen. He had every book imaginable on architecture, culture, and literature that featured New York. But now I had business of my own, and the torch of NY-o-philia passed to me. If Bad Religion signed to Atlantic Records, I would be the band's East Coast ambassador and friendly face to the label. After all, now I lived in the shadow of this metropolis. Its name was emblazoned on my driver's license.

I thought back to the urban sprawl of LA and considered New York somehow more manageable. As a city, it's easier to escape. LA just goes on and on. "LA is a great big freeway" was already a veritable truth when

Dionne Warwick sang it in 1968. It took hours to escape the place and truly get out of town. In LA, you're always surrounded by a sea of humanity. In New York, one can be in the middle of a quiet forest within an hour or two drive from Midtown Manhattan. The density of people is overwhelming, but it tapers off quickly with every mile of road you put behind you. This feeling of easy escape was reassuring. It's always kept me at ease in the chaos of Manhattan. If I felt trapped in the city, without easy access to the relief valve that is the George Washington Bridge, I'd be ruined. I thought back to the sense of peace and calm I felt when I drove away from the urban jungle of LA to settle in New York's "middle landscape." The sense of peace and calmness of natural surroundings, forests, lakes, creeks, and trails became a remedial salve that spurred my creativity, assisted my meditative studies, and balanced my loud exertions as a punk singer.

Watching the scene in Rockefeller Plaza gave me a sense of gratitude, in that I was glad I didn't have to endure it every day. But I also felt a great sense of excitement from all the buzz. Being able to participate in it, at a distance even, felt like a prospect that could suit me just fine. I crossed the plaza surrounded by a cluster of art deco skyscrapers and came upon a wide glass wall with two turnstile doors in the center. The transom overhead read "Time Warner Building." This was the entryway to entertainment history!

It doesn't require too much imagination to understand why I would be seduced by all this. The greatest musical influences of my life before punk passed through these hallways. The building blocks of my creative personality all revolved around music that was created and distributed from here. Atlantic bands such as Yes; Emerson, Lake & Palmer; Genesis; and King Crimson all were on heavy rotation back in Jeff's basement when we dreamed of being rock stars. I could sing every word on those albums. Furthermore, Mom's endless playlist of Roberta Flack and Donny Hathaway made the divorce seem more palatable. All of it came from this label. The distinctive Atlantic Records logo on its bright red label spinning clockwise on the turntable while reassuring, familiar music filled the room was a mysterious, formative, deeply significant figment of my self-image, and there it was, etched into the glass doors of the elevator lobby in front of me.

I was standing in the same entry foyer as the artists who made so much of my life's soundtrack. They walked these halls just like I was doing now, heading to meetings about creative visions and new projects with people in suits who could pull strings to bring those dreams to fruition. I was dressed like the graduate student I was. Collared shirt, but no tie, tucked into a pair of 501 jeans with a belt and a pair of leather Red Wing shoes.

I approached a wide desk and was greeted abruptly by a well-dressed woman in business attire who said sternly, "Who are you here to see?" "I'm Greg Graffin, here to see Danny Goldberg," I responded without mirth or my usual charm. "Please have a seat and someone will be with you in a moment." After a few minutes an assistant came and escorted me to his office.

When I met him, he came across as casual and easygoing as could be. If not for his corporate uniform, I imagined that Danny would have been just as comfortable wearing jeans, just like me. We talked about songwriting. "You know, the only thing that civilizations are built upon is the foundation of words and ideas," he said. I really appreciated his offhanded analysis. It showed that he viewed entertainment as a foundation of society—very apropos to Graffin U. Singing was something that came naturally to me. But writing and coming up with new song ideas was something that both Brett and I took very seriously. Danny had taken on this corporate job after building his management empire, Gold Mountain. He was Nirvana's manager, and he talked a lot about Kurt Cobain, what a genius he was, and so on. I told him that our paths had never crossed except that we played most of the same venues that Nirvana played over in Europe. I found this chitchat interesting enough, but I was mostly interested in what the current number one record label in the world could do for Bad Religion.

Soon joining us in Danny's office were two newly hired associates, Kim and Mike. Mike was a former fanzine writer now embarking on a new career as an artist and repertoire (A&R) specialist. These were people of my own age and dressed like me: uncorporate, unpretentious, just friendly and peerlike. Kim was quick to point out that she graduated from Ithaca College, so we had some laughs about the townsfolk and the farmers market, and that helped to break the ice. Mike just spoke about seeing us at the New Jersey venue called City Gardens and dropped names of obscure punk bands. In my mind I really hoped that Mike understood that I was interested in getting far away from those dingy punk venues and obscure punk bands. I thought that Bad Religion was primed to play in theaters and larger places, and that was one reason I believed that being on a major label with their almost unlimited resources of marketing and distribution could be a logical next step.

After about a half hour of hanging out, eating some lunch sandwiches in Danny's office, and meeting some other people from the floors below, we concluded our meeting. Everyone was friendly and feeling enthusiastic about Bad Religion. Danny got up to walk with me to the elevator lobby, and he saw the chairman in the hallway. "Mr. Ertegun, this is Greg Graffin. He's the singer of the band Bad Religion, a band that we are very excited about." I was quite confident that Ahmet Ertegun had never heard of me or the band, but his "Oh, how do you do?" as he was quickly whisked away to more important business, remains as one of those memorable sidebars to important events in my life. Danny also had more pressing business being the president of the label, so I left the premises feeling unsure that anything would come from the interest shown to me and the band.

I exited the Time Warner Building and hightailed it back home. During the drive home, I wondered if Danny Goldberg had a positive effect on the other guys when he met them back in LA. I knew that Brett really admired the success of Nirvana, so he might trust that Danny Goldberg could pilot our ship in the precarious waters of commercial success. He would likely understand that our strongest asset was our credibility as a punk band, and he surely would help us retain it if we signed to Atlantic. Whatever the case, I couldn't get too excited about anything until I got home to talk with the guys on the telephone.

But that talk never happened. Instead, later that same day, in the early evening, I got a call from our lawyer Eric who had heard back from Danny Goldberg. Eric said, "Well, the meeting went great, I hear." "Uhhh, I guess so," I said. "Eric, did you hear from the other guys?" "Yeah, they're in." "Really?" I couldn't believe it happened so fast. Before I could even talk with the other guys, a contract had been faxed over with Brett's, Jay's, Bobby's, and Greg Hetson's names on it waiting to be signed. I called them each, one by one, and said, "We doin' dis?" and each one said, "Sure!"

Maybe there was a lot of private soul searching, closed-door meetings, and phone calls back and forth on the West Coast to which I was not privy. But I doubt it. The situation of our band's growth and the surge of interest industrywide created a void of communication in the band. One might think that as a band gets more and more famous, they would tend to have more and more scheduled conference calls. But that wasn't the case. Now there were just more and more individual calls to one or the other band member, and we weren't that good at following up those calls with summaries to each other. I can't recall a single phone call or strategy session with my bandmates regarding the pros and cons of signing with Atlantic Records. All I remember is telling Eric that if Brett signs, then I too will sign the contract.

Sure enough, within a week of the trip to New York, with still barely a month to go before embarking on our US tour for *Recipe for Hate*, the entire band had signed the contract. Our next four albums would be made under the direction of Atlantic Records. We, of course, had no desire to be directed artistically, and it was clear, from the discussions before we signed, that we would not settle for any constraints on our artistic freedom. We just wanted a fair deal and a strong effort from them to get our records on the radio and distributed far and wide. In return, Eric negotiated a modest recording advance (an amount that was roughly equal to what we were earning on Epitaph) and one of the highest royalty rates Atlantic ever paid (again, roughly equal to what Brett was paying us/himself/his own band).

My life was about to change in a drastic fashion. Ironically, it had nothing directly to do with signing to a major label. I felt like I was on the precipice of the life I always wanted. A life worthy of my aspirations. An Ivy League doctorate, a stable family life, a nice house to come home to, and a band that was taken seriously in the world of professional music. It turned out, however, that every one of these items would become an "almost-but-not-quite" within the next twelve months.

26
ADJUSTMENTS AND STRAINS

Difficult professional decisions were to be the norm for the next phase of my life. I say "difficult" to give you an idea that the choices required deep reflection. They weren't particularly painful decisions at first, but rather just practical choices that led to alterations of life's path that forked occasionally and took some unexpected turns.

Some decisions were easy. Could we afford a bigger house? Yes, purely from my touring income alone we could afford to buy a nice big brick house with four bedrooms in a quiet neighborhood not far from campus. This seemed like a no-brainer because Greta and I had little Graham running around and Ella on the way. No quibbling, just a quick signature on the mortgage application and boom, we were moving on up.

Other decisions were more difficult. Could I continue to work full time on my academic obligations? I had not even applied for a teaching assistantship in the fall of 1993 because I knew that my tour was going to overlap significantly with the semester's calendar. But something else had to be broached. As a professional musician under contract with a major label, I had to recognize that my new obligation was going to demand a change of priorities. For years I was balancing my work in academia and being a performer. I had a certain gift for music, it came easy to me, but I had to work harder to be a scholar. The talents I developed in doing research and fieldwork and my general skills at observing nature had been honed gradually in college and graduate school. Suddenly, the demands of a growing family combined with a more serious professional obligation to Atlantic Records meant that something had to give. I had to consider giving up academia, a decision with worrisome, profound implications.

Academia is sometimes accused of being an "old boy's network." That term is outdated. Now it's more apt to call it a "network of favoritism" regardless of gender affiliation. The criticism is founded on the idea that your merits and accomplishments in academia are bestowed upon you from those in your field. If you get to know the most powerful people in that area of expertise, then you are more likely to rise through the ranks and achieve a higher status yourself. In other words, it's a system that's criticized for being inherently unfair.

The music industry can be similarly criticized. It is often said that in entertainment "it's all who you know." The legend of "Hollywood and Vine," two thoroughfares in LA that intersect at Tinseltown's ground zero, is ever present in people's minds because of the "discoveries" that were made at a lunch counter inside Schwab's Pharmacy, a drugstore on Sunset Boulevard. Movie moguls and aspiring actors used to frequent the place. The most famous discovery is of course from a bygone era, when Lana Turner ditched school to go there and order a snack. She was noticed by a publicist named Wilkerson who introduced her to an agent named Marx (Zeppo), and the rest is Hollywood history. She became an international star. The notion that the entertainment industry depends on a network of friends and acquaintances is still intact. If you are talented, or good looking, or special in any way, your opportunities for reaching a receptive audience are increased dramatically if you associate with the right people. If you decide not to associate with anyone, you are a "nobody."

These ideas were never far from my consciousness. Little cracks of doubt began to enter my mind. I worried that I might be a "nobody" in music and a "nobody" in academia. For reassurance, I took a personal inventory. I knew that I was in good company for my academic work. I was at a top university, with scholars who were well respected in the field, and my work was unique and favorably praised. In fact, I had applied for, and received, funding from the National Academy of Sciences for the next three years to pay for some of the expensive microscopy supplies required for my project. All the pieces of my academic life seemed to be in place, solid and functioning.

I also had a satisfying network of musical affiliations. Talented and dedicated bandmates, an agent in Europe and one in the USA, a new business manager and entertainment attorney in the USA. All seemed prepared and willing to use their skills and connections to put my talent to work. It was satisfying to feel like they depended on me so that we all could reach our next objectives, a global tour and an album in the charts perhaps. It seemed like both sides of my life were equally complementary. Ditching one for the other might take a drastic toll by throwing off the balance.

I set up my life to be a constant philosophical meander, like a river coursing over a wide mud plain whose mouth spit out into the ocean of knowledge. Its delta has its source in an imaginative landscape where the grains of truth from music and science blend equally from the river's creative force. Despite this quasi-religious envisioning of my life's objective, more practical concerns crept in to force my hand.

For the first time in the band's existence, I could not successfully partition the months of the year to accommodate the academic and touring calendars equally. The Recipe for Hate Tour, in support of that album, spanned the entire fall semester. It was with a heavy heart that I had to meet with my academic committee and let them know that I was going to take a leave of absence. The fall semester and entire next calendar year were already committed to music.

The committee adjourned, granted my "leave," and wished me well. Even though I would eventually come back to finish my PhD, I would never convene this same group of advisers again. These were specialists in anatomy and physiology. I was putting my study of early vertebrate bones on the shelf. I had been able to make progress on it over the last four years by heading out to Colorado and Wyoming for fossil collecting whenever the band wasn't on tour. On campus I studied the microscopic structure of my fossil collection, grinding them into thin sections, making photomicrographs, and comparing them with other tissues under the electron microscope. I got high praise for my electron microscopy, which was rewarding. But for now, I had to consider whether this reward would in the long run provide any of the practical necessities of my increasingly complicated life.

I had a personal reckoning and decided that change in the music industry happened much more rapidly than change in science. When we're talking about music, entire new genres or subcultures can come and go in a matter of a few years. Science, however, changes slowly. Becoming an expert in it is a lifetime's effort. The area in which I focused my study, the early vertebrates, was riddled with controversies that had not received any clarity for over half a century. My contributions could wait. What couldn't wait, however, was the rapidly increasing interest in Bad Religion. There was only one person who could satisfy that interest as the lead singer, and that was me.

Now instead of juggling months on the calendar, I would have to perhaps devote years to music before I could get back to working on my PhD. This was my resolution.

Choosing to focus on music came with some worries of its own, mostly concerning my relationship with Brett, who was producing bands that he signed, many of which had singers more overtly punk than me. I wasn't sure where Brett was headed creatively. I was worried that he favored a more overtly punk singer like Tim Armstrong from Rancid or Fat Mike from NOFX or Jim Lindberg from Pennywise, all bands that he worked closely with and had signed to Epitaph. I wanted all of Brett's focus to be on our songs. This is only logical, and it explains why I felt some relief when we signed to Atlantic Records. To me it meant that Brett and I could be songwriters, and even co-producers of our work, and yet have no conflicts of interest in the marketing and selling of our work. We would let a third party do that. I projected my hopes onto Brett and assumed that he, too, felt some relief that his own band could "get out of the way" of the younger bands on his label. We never discussed any of this in all the fracas that was going on, and it might just have been wishful thinking on my part. But it explains my state of mind at the time.

There was another order of business before we headed out on tour. Under the suggestion of our lawyer, Eric, it was decided that we would be better served by hiring a band manager. Neither Brett nor I had dealt with managers for our own band before. We developed a sense of artistic direction from years of songwriting. Trial and error. Some ideas were better than others, and some songs became fan favorites, which in turn pointed us toward refinement of those ideas. Never did we consult third parties about songs. We kept our writing close to our chests. Yet, despite this independence, we both agreed with the other guys in the band that it would serve us well to have a "go-to" person for negotiating and communicating all aspects of a band's business. Coordination among our agents, lawyer, business manager, and tour manager was crucial and had become a full-time job.

Eric narrowed it down to a handful of prospective managers, each one of whom had shown interest in the possibility of working with Bad Religion. All in all, there were really only two that appealed to us. One of them was Nirvana's new manager, John Silva. John worked for Danny Goldberg's management company, Gold Mountain. Nirvana was big at the time, and about to get even bigger within the year. This roster association seemed like a decent fit for the kind of high-profile reputation we were looking for. Although this got John "in the door" to meet with us, privately we all were thinking the same thing that was, ironically, a strike against him: "How could this guy possibly have enough time to tend to all our busy affairs if he's swamped with Nirvana business?"

The other guy who appealed to us was Danny Heaps. He didn't seem as busy as John Silva. He seemed more matter-of-fact, and he leveled with us. He used the phrase "in all candor" quite a bit. Candor was good, it impressed us to be spoken to like we weren't idiots. Plus, Danny had an interesting roster, having worked with Johnny Rotten (as Lydon) in PIL and also managing Robbie Robertson of the band the Band. In addition, Danny impressed us because he was one of the founders of the New Music Seminar, a festival of sorts that brought together music industry moguls and artists. This achievement demonstrated that he understood and cared about maintaining artistic credibility in the industry, which we felt was crucial to our success. So we decided on Danny Heaps there and then. I left the meeting happy to have a new manager. For the first time, we would be receiving professional advice. Not that we had to take it, but it still felt better to have it rather than rely on the guesswork and speculation of the past.

I was entering into a period of associating with professionals in the music industry, something totally new to me. Despite the newness, however, it had the feeling of familiarity. The music industry seemed to be loosely structured like the university, a hierarchy and social milieu that had been a part of my life from the get-go. It felt like a surrogate institution.

At every level of the music industry, there seemed to be an analogous position in academia. The manager, Danny Heaps, was like a new kind of academic adviser to me. The label president, Danny Goldberg, was like a dean or vice chancellor who only needed to be consulted occasionally and who oversaw progress from afar. The numerous executives assigned to Bad Religion's various activities—the project manager, Kim Kaiman, the marketing exec, Vicki Germaise, and others—were like department chairs at the university. The structure of this new professional journey felt very comfortable, and all the individuals were welcoming and open to meeting whenever I felt the urge.

The first thing I noticed, however, was that going to meet with music execs had a different vibe to it. Both academics and music industry professionals had similar rules of formality, similar courtesies. For instance, you wouldn't show up to eithers' offices looking like a slob or showing aloofness to the topic on the table. The meetings were always purposeful, to discuss "matters at hand," be they Bad Religion's touring success in the Pacific

Northwest on the one hand, or in the case of the scientists, perhaps field observations when you last visited the fossil beds of Colorado. Both academics and music industry professionals met with me in an easy conversational style. But there was a bit more tension in the conference rooms at the major labels than I felt at the universities. I chalked this up to the fact that jobs come and go quite frequently in entertainment companies, so being guarded around the "artists" is a way to preserve your good status. Imagine all the touchy, egotistical, megalomaniacal singers, songwriters, and band leaders who get offended because they don't like what someone says about their music or ideas. Now put them in a marketing meeting with the people who are responsible for selling their records. Anyone who speaks a word of skepticism might be singled out and taken off the project in the presence of the sensitive artist. Therefore, a culture of polite agreement and reserved judgment seemed to be the norm whenever I visited the people at Atlantic Records. One thing that seemed to be a genuine consensus, however, was the overt enthusiasm surrounding our upcoming tour.

The 1993 Recipe for Hate Tour was a remarkable run of shows, nearly all sold out in advance. Not only Bad Religion but also our "special guests" on the tour, Green Day, were making headlines and turning heads. Both of us had signed major label record deals that year, and their first album on Warner Brothers, *Dookie*, was already beginning to explode. Green Day's touring vehicle was a converted shuttle bus driven by one of their dads. We had fun on that tour. There was great camaraderie among band members. We often played football at truck stops or during bathroom breaks out on the interstates. Once I threw a bullet pass, a bit out of reach of our roadie, and it smashed the passenger window of the van driven by the opening band, Seaweed. I felt bad, but they felt worse. They couldn't roll up their window, and it was a cold October! I agreed to pay for it, and the tour rolled on.

After passing through thirty major cities in the USA (plus three in Canada), at iconic venues such as the Roseland Ballroom in New York City, the Hollywood Palladium, the Riviera Theater in Chicago, and the Warfield in San Francisco, we ended up at the infamous Iguanas nightclub in Tijuana, Mexico, playing two nights of sold-out mayhem. Finally, it was time to wrap the tour. And what better place than Hawaii to end it? We played two nights at a club in Honolulu called Pink's Garage, and we all flew the families out for some fun on the beach as we lingered for a few days after the gigs. Having no regrets that I put my academic work on hold for a while, the fringe benefits of touring began to settle in. I considered it the greatest privilege in the world to be able to support my family with my touring income and, in addition, afford to pay for them to come visit me in fantastic destinations like Hawaii. I was, however, in a world of my own: the strain of traveling with little kids, coordinating their preschool schedules, playdates with other kids, and providing the family with a sense of routine never really dawned on me. As romantic as it may seem, touring almost always turned out to be more of a strain on our familial relationships than it appeared to be in our picture books.

The tour didn't actually end there. We still had a few shows to play in the Southland, but not for another month or so. The first one was an important milestone for us, the KROQ acoustic Christmas show. This annual event, put on at the Universal Amphitheater, one of LA's most important concert venues at the time, was sponsored by the same radio station that gave us our first airplay over a decade prior. KROQ was the home of *Rodney on the ROQ*, our favorite radio show from back in the day. KROQ had become one of the most important stations in the country. Its playlist was referenced by other rock stations around the country and was considered the bellwether of up-and-coming bands emerging from their niche genres in their crossover to mainstream status. Being asked to play their annual Christmas event was like being baptized. It announced to the national radio market: "Here's a band that has our blessing, sounds good on the radio, and will be considered an important band from now on." Sure enough, our song "Struck a Nerve" was on regular rotation by that time, and us being a punk band, we asked if we could perform that song, and our entire set, plugged in instead of acoustic. We just didn't have a good arrangement for that song with only acoustic instruments. Much to our surprise, they said okay. Thus began a tradition where every band now plays electrified, and the annual event is now called Almost Acoustic Christmas.

About a month after the KROQ show we had a string of January 1994 shows that took us across the country from SoCal to New Jersey. The first couple of shows took place on college campus auditoriums in California, Fresno State and UC Irvine.

That's when we met Michele, who would become our day-to-day managerial contact. Friendly and enthusiastic, I asked her my usual first question, "Where did you go to college?" When she said "UC San Diego" I thought, "Great! She's going to understand my peculiarities and sentimental attachment to the university." She knew about my attending Cornell, but I didn't tell her right away that I was taking a leave of absence. "So, I saw you guys play at Iguanas a couple of years ago while I was still in school," she said. "Great!" I thought. Another plus. She's been to our shows and understands our audience and probably knows a good deal about the scene we came from. Michele was a great asset because she was sensitive to the needs of retaining our indie credibility, and she had a great sense of humor, which was crucial to all of us.

Now with Michele and Danny working as a team to manage the band, Eric working as our legal expert, and Steven working the financials, there seemed to be a perfect synergy with Jens and Howard organizing the tours. It seemed like we had a team that could lead us to bigger and better things. The band, crew, record company, and professional advisers seemed like a well-oiled V-8 that was set on cruise control.

Despite this, however, each band member had their own private feelings about what we were going through, how the situation was panning out, and what factors were most important to our success. Without talking to each other, we simply assumed, as a family does, that we were all equally motivated to reach the same goals. Brett, Jay, Greg Hetson, and I were in the same boat. We all had families with little kids at home that we prioritized as important in our lives, so there was a tacit understanding that Bad Religion couldn't be on tour all year long. This gave me optimism that I could be very present for my family. There was no reason to believe that this optimistic feeling of sustainable balance in my life couldn't continue for a long time into the future.

It was the first time in twelve solid years that my daily activities didn't revolve around the semester calendar of the university. I spent my time as a homebody, enjoying the pulse of family life on a winter's day in 1994. It was a tranquil time, with no pressing schedule except the anticipation of a second child coming in March. Graham was already two years old and his sister Ella was due any day now. She was born during a record snowfall at a hospital that was about ten miles away. The roads were closed by the highway department due to such a ferocious storm.

Recently, however, I had purchased a new Chevy Suburban with the royalty and tour money I'd earned. Putting that Suburban into four-wheel drive, and with snow coming down sideways, I made it to the hospital and picked up my wife and child and brought them both home. A great feeling of satisfaction came over me that night, not only to be safe and cozy with my new little girl, but also to be able to provide for her and her brother and their mom. It was moments like that where all the sacrifices of being away on tour so much and all the distractions of a public life away from home seemed to repay their costs. It seemed like I had achieved something I once believed to be unobtainable: a newly constructed house paid for with my own money from the most unconventional source. The house that punk built was a dream to many, a colonial four-bedroom job cased entirely in Watsontown red brick. Surrounded on three sides by hardwood forest—white pines, oaks, and hickory—that sang the song of winter on blustery nights like these. With a cozy fire crackling in the living room, Ella asleep in her mama's arms, Graham curled up next to me watching *Jurassic Park* on our VCR, we were the picture of homey security. My own mom was there too, cooking up some of her renowned Indiana country fare in the brand-new kitchen. This was a moment to savor. A moment of confidence that only the frigid winds of doubt could undermine.

27

THE CRUMBLING

27A. STRANGER THAN FICTION

It was time to write a new chapter. The cost of education at Graffin U. would eventually begin to creep higher. The student body was expanding. Two new little kids now had to become indoctrinated into our unique family milieu. What did we know about raising kids in an entertainment family? We had generations of teachers before us, leaders in the church, academics, machinists, farmers, all of able body and twentieth-century spirit. Before that, enlisted men in the Union Army. All lost wisdom due to broken families, rejection of religion and grandparents' ancient ways. Now, the millennial generation upon us, I would have to know something about raising the kids with a set of skills, a livelihood, never before experienced in our family. De novo parenting. Nowhere in our family's ancestry portfolio are entertainers, artists, or public persons such as I was becoming. No one told me of the toll it might take on the household relationships. In fact, within weeks of Ella's birth, I was already leaving home.

Brett and I agreed that we had written some of the best music of our careers. It was a good thing, too, because we were slated to begin recording in Los Angeles in April 1994. After numerous discussions with Brett and the other band members, we agreed that Andy Wallace was our top choice for producing the album that was to be our big major label debut. I was particularly fond of Andy's work with Slayer on the album *Seasons in the Abyss,* but Brett favored his work on *Rage Against the Machine* by the band of the same name, which he considered some of the best rock music ever mixed. Never far from our thoughts was the enormous success of Nirvana, the notoriety of which we would have loved to achieve. Having two of their key team members now on our team, Danny Goldberg (their manager) as our record company president and Andy Wallace (their mixing engineer) as our studio guru, seemed like an auspicious combination.

It didn't take a genius of logic to recognize that Brett was stretched thin. Epitaph was a sensation, a major success in the music industry. The talk of the town. Tinseltown, that is. A town in which I no longer chose to live. Brett was presiding over a budding empire that would soon prevail as the best indie label on the planet. I applauded, encouraged, and was proud of all his achievements. But I also knew that eventually something had to give. He couldn't continue touring at the pace that we were touring and run the label successfully if he continued to sign, produce, and direct the careers of other bands as well as try to be in Bad Religion full time.

Even though I worried that these things might take a personal toll on him, I didn't ever talk to Brett about his private struggles. We never had that kind of intimacy in our relationship. None of the guys in the band did. We all had personal issues, but the band business always seemed to get done in spite of them, ever since high school. So, even though the guys were all battling addictions at this time, I was not under any suspicion that such struggles would impact the band's business.

So it may sound ironic, but personal issues weren't the issue. What did seem to be a dark cloud waiting to burst over me was the professional activity of Brett, in that he was being stretched too thin to be a full-time member of the band. And yet, what was the band without him? His attention to the details of Epitaph and its growing roster made me feel insecure about my own importance to his future success.

Bad Religion didn't have to ask me what my commitments were; it was obvious because I chose to put my academic work on hold. I would never make him choose, but at the same time I knew that Brett would eventually reach a point where he'd have to commit to one or the other, band or label. So I had reservations about where our enterprise was headed as we prepared to enter the studio in 1994 to record *Stranger than Fiction*.

Andy Wallace liked the demos that Brett and I had recorded. Our new A&R man at Atlantic, Mike, organized a dinner in New Jersey where we could meet Andy months ahead of our own recording sessions. Andy was the top mixer in the business at the time and his schedule was booked solid, but he carved out six weeks to record with us in the spring of 1994. Our dinner was a "getting to know you" kind of formality. Andy could have been forty or seventy years old, impossible to tell. Wisdom has no age, and that's what mattered most to me. He was clearly a master and I was excited to have his ear. I explained how Brett and I always had an understanding that whoever wrote the song would have final say on an arrangement. But now, with Andy, we would have to relinquish that condition and let our new respected producer make the final assessment. Turned out, however, that Andy was not so forceful nor forthright to ever badger us in any way. It seemed like he respected our opinions as much as we did his.

In April 1994, we entered Rumbo Recorders in our old stomping grounds of Canoga Park, California. The bland-looking exterior was par for the course in studioville. Most places in LA that house expensive, technologically sophisticated production equipment look kind of dumpy from the outside. Rumbo was one such place, a single-story, ten-thousand-square-foot warehouse building on Saticoy Street, one of the San Fernando Valley's most unassuming east-west thoroughfares. Running right down the center of this urban basin, at its western extension, Saticoy was unremarkable as an address. It was one of countless residential corridors in the Valley, an alcove of over a million houses set on quarter-acre lots equally spaced on perfect square blocks laid out like an endless checkerboard interrupted by occasional strip malls, corner gas stations, or city parks. Unless you knew the address, you'd drive right past Rumbo. Looking for it, you'd barely remember that someone on the phone said to look for a dark-colored, spray-stucco facade with glass panels and a glass office door welcoming you to Rumbo Recorders. First, you'd have to be let into the small parking lot in front of the building, because the chain-link fence surrounding the whole compound had a sliding gate that was automated. The fencing gave the place a highly utilitarian feel but nonetheless a sense of importance in the humdrum heartland of blue-collar Los Angeles. For us, however, it was a very familiar vibe. It was only about six miles from the Hell Hole where we spent so much of our youth rehearsing in my mom's garage.

Rumbo was special for two reasons. One, because it had the equipment that Andy preferred. He had recorded there before and knew the rooms well, which meant that he had gained valuable experience by working with other bands using the Rumbo SSL 4000 series consoles. These would become the go-to choice for future Bad Religion albums as well, although at different studios and with different engineers and mixers. The other notable thing about Rumbo was that it was built and designed by the least punk person one could ever imagine, Daryl Dragon, also known as the Captain of the duo Captain & Tennille, who had their own weekly variety show on TV when I was a kid. Daryl was often in his office during our sessions. Tending to business, staying busy, figuring payroll for his employees—whatever the activity, he seemed nonplussed by the cadre of characters who passed by his open office door. I stopped by once and introduced myself. He had dark glasses on (the office work lights weren't that bright, were they?) and looked just like I remembered him on TV. He saw me as just another paying client, said, "Nice to meet you, Greg," and went on with his paperwork. Over the years he must have had similar exchanges with his other clients who recorded there, from Ozzy Osbourne, Axl Rose, David Lee Roth, Ronnie James Dio, and Gene Simmons to Tom Petty. Even though the Captain built a studio to record himself and Toni Tennille's middle-of-the-road soft pop, slow rock music, he sure had the right equipment to make some kick-ass hard rock records. We all hoped that ours was going to be one of them.

The place was comfortable, with a large open billiards area where band members could hang out with their guests. Just off this room was a full kitchen and a smaller TV area with a couch and overstuffed chair for a more solitary escape or quiet discussions. We spent a lot of time watching hockey on television and playing it on roller blades in the parking lot almost every day. It was a fairly predictable, productive work environment with a good daily routine.

Andy and I stayed at the same hotel, the Westwood Marquis, right across the street from my old alma mater, UCLA. Being only a stone's throw from the labs where I used to teach comparative anatomy made me feel at home. On days off I'd wander the campus, strolling the Westwood streets, thinking back to the countless, life-changing events that had happened there. Meeting Greta, who forced me to get a job at the Chart House where I met Jerry and Inga. On campus, conversing endlessly with my mentors, Peter Vaughn, Ted Reed, Everett C. Olson, and Clem Nelson, and meeting my friends, Jay and Mark, on the loading dock of the geology building to take the university Suburbans out into the wilds of California for weeks-long field trips. My life was so different now.

One day, I took a detour. Instead of going directly to the studio, I had lunch with the band's new management team, Michele and Danny, at their office in Beverly Hills, where their firm Addis Wechsler was located. The short drive from UCLA, along Wilshire Boulevard, first passes the financial district of the entertainment industry, Century City. With its high-rise glass buildings filled with accountants and money managers in business suits, one can instantly discern a quasi Wall Street meets United Nations vibe here, such as the famous Avenue of the Stars. This was exciting to me, because I used to ride my bike past these buildings on weekends when I was a student, but I never thought I'd have any reason to enter any of those cathedrals of material wealth. I was convinced that academics had their campuses and Hollywood stars had theirs and never did the twain mix. But today, where I was headed, to visit the offices of my new managers, I disproved my own theory.

Addis Wechsler wasn't too big or elaborate, but it had all the flair of a Hollywood media empire. The three-story building adorned with palms had a huge foyer that I entered through large glass doors. Sleek furniture and salmon-colored walls looked like leftovers from the 1980s. Posters and promo materials were on display. A recent hit movie was produced there, *The Player*, directed by Robert Altman, one of my favorite directors.

Altman's film was a satire, a send-up of the disgusting money-grab that the movie industry had become. It criticized Hollywood filmmaking for its tendency to settle for profit over artistic integrity or ambition. Easy, risk-free smash hits based on previous works were becoming the gold standard, rather than artistically driven masterpieces with intelligent scripts such as the box-office smashes of the 1970s. Hollywood was in an interesting place too, just like the music industry, where DIY had been replaced by corporate meddling. Martin Scorsese claimed that an era had passed around this time, the era where directors had a free hand in personally overseeing all the artistic elements of the film. Robert Altman—who had taken a decade off from filmmaking—resurrected this hands-on tradition when he made *The Player* for Addis Wechsler, restoring artistic integrity to filmmaking by satirizing the industry's corporate greed. As writer Alex Simon put it, Altman was an "eclectic maverick," which was an apt description of what I was feeling about myself at the time. I felt right at home having trusted my music career to managers of the same firm that bet on Robert Altman. *The Player* resonated with what I perceived to be going on in the smaller, but more personally relevant, industry of punk music. There were plenty of derivative bands making lots of money in punk. But I wanted to push the envelope of what was acceptable, expand the boundaries of the genre. I felt reassured that my new managers were on the same page.

Later that day, I headed over to the studio where Andy Wallace was busy recording overdubs on some of Brett's songs. I arrived around five o'clock to find our drummer, Bobby, pacing around nervously in the front lounge. He had placed a certain kind of percussion cymbal on the pool table and said, "Well, there it is!" "What is IT, Bobby?" I asked. "It's the reason I'm standing around here pacing back and forth even though I finished tracking my drums two days ago." Bobby had recorded all his drum parts for the entire album and was essentially excused from having to hang around the studio. None of us really enjoyed watching overdubs be recorded, but we had to be on call and available to perform if needed. Bobby usually enjoyed hanging out, but on this evening he had to cancel a dinner engagement because he was told by Andy Wallace and Brett that there was this one last overdub to record. "Brett wants me to add a little flourish on 'Infected,' but they are busy recording something else now," he said forlornly.

Another guest was also "on hold" that afternoon and was watching TV in the little room off the lounge. It was Lint from Operation Ivy. Bobby said, "Lint's here," as he pointed me toward the mohawked singer. Lint, also known as Tim Armstrong, introduced himself to me in a very cordial manner and said out of the blue, "You're my favorite singer." "Really?" I asked. "Thanks a lot." I didn't confess it, but I had not heard him sing a word up to that point. He was there to do the overdub vocal on "Television," a song Brett wrote about the electron-beamed cathode-ray tube. Andy Wallace and Brett both produced his vocal as Bobby and I waited out in the lounge. It ended up taking about four hours, and then Bobby finally got to record his part at around 10 p.m.

Lint, in his words of kind appreciation, made me feel good. I always felt honored that other punk rockers admired my voice. I never tried to sound "punk," it just came out that way. Dave Markey, the filmmaker, once said, "Graffin has the 'classic' hardcore voice." I couldn't really understand what that meant because a "sound" is usually created by the vocalist or producer to be something greater than the mere speaking voice. Divas speak of their voices as instruments, which implies that they use it in musical ways that are not apt for mere mortals. I always tried to deliver the words as a clear message, and singing always came as natural to me as speaking. Based on the attention Andy Wallace gave to my lead vocal tracks, and the number of takes I performed on each song, it was clear that my natural delivery and the reedy quality of my voice was still going to be the featured sound of Bad Religion on this album.

The final product, composed of fifteen songs and three "extra tracks," were mixed and mastered within weeks of the recording. The release date for *Stranger than Fiction* wasn't until September 6, 1994, which meant that I could have something that was a rare pleasure: summer vacation with the family.

—

27B. DOMESTIC LIFE, ARTISTIC STRIFE

Being at home in the summer, as opposed to being on tour, was a rare treat. Nonetheless, there were plenty of interviews, phoners from the home office, and faxes to write and respond to, in between trips to the farmers market, playdates with other couples who had kids, and hosting grandparents and friends who came to experience our young growing family. Occasional trips to New York City were part of the routine. At the drop of a hat, I would drive down to the City to appear on MTV's *120 Minutes* for an interview, or to meet with publicists, product managers, or marketing people from Atlantic Records to chat about the upcoming release of our record. Usually, it was just for fun, to get out of the house for the day, to have a "power lunch" in New York City and revel in the enthusiasm surrounding the album. It was a highly anticipated release, and there was much fanfare in the press and in the industry at large.

Back at the house, there was very little discussion about my professional life. Greta and I didn't talk about the future. She was busy with the day-to-day rearing of the kids. I could stroll in and play with them for a while, maybe watch a Disney flick on VHS with them, make popcorn and whatnot, but then I could always retreat to the music room when that stuff became too tedious. I'm easily bored, and music is a great friend because it seems like I'm doing hard work, writing a new song perhaps, when in fact I'm just killing boredom.

The dream life I thought I was creating for my family was always on the forefront of my mind. In fact, all the band members were committed to their families. It's almost as if the one unifying thing we all had in common was that we were trying to make happy families, as if that was the most important business affair in our lives. The problem is, being a professional musician has some inherent difficulties that require unconventional family arrangements. We had to learn that the hard way. We didn't know it at the time, but all of what we were trying to build was on a shaky foundation that in time would crumble.

The romantic notion of an artist relentlessly pursuing his own passion, his obsessive madness, his lonely and dedicated pursuit to root out the evil in his life at the cost of all those around him was not an apt account of my life. Still, I couldn't escape the truth: I had an unconscious mission to uphold. Like many Americans, I felt quietly desperate for some ideal that had been instilled in my subconscious mind. The attractiveness of punk, as an art form, had to jibe with this ideal or I would feel like a phony. From whence came this constitutional, intellectual, artistic inspiration? In part, it was due to the unspoken expectations of Graffin U.

As an undergraduate at UCLA I took a course called Intellectual History of the United States. It changed my life. It's where I met Greta, my first wife. But moreover, it crystallized my self-awareness as an artist. It taught me that aesthetics are the result of lifestyle traditions, some of which have surprisingly deep histories.

The concept of the "middle landscape" was introduced in this class, which centered on source material by Nathaniel Hawthorne, Ralph Waldo Emerson, Henry David Thoreau, and Thomas Jefferson. All of it was nicely woven into narrative by our main textbook for the course, a thesis by Leo Marx called *The Machine in the Garden*. I was drawn to the *Notes on the State of Virginia* by Thomas Jefferson, and I also enjoyed Henry David Thoreau whose evocative descriptions of the Eastern forests reminded me of those great vacations we took in Wisconsin's Door County in my youth.

The pulse of the course was exceedingly relevant to me because Bad Religion had become a major intellectual pursuit of mine by the time I was in college. What made Americans tick? This was a topic rife for criticism and deconstruction and parody. It was grist for the punk songbook. Endless fodder for songwriting. But I also couldn't shake the emotional connection that I drew from the readings in the class. In other words, it wasn't just a pragmatic course for me; it had emotional resonance that was aided by the excellent lectures given by the visiting professor, John King. There was something about the middle landscape that connected me with something larger than myself.

According to Leo Marx (a professor at MIT and no relation, by the way, to the Communist Karl Marx), the American experience can best be understood as a long train of thought first introduced by the early American writers of literature. You might think of yourself as a "city person" or maybe a "country boy" or something like that. But those perceptions are not unique. They were created by narratives and myths that are indelible parts of our culture.

The concept of "rural" as an ideal landscape goes back even further to classical literature, far, far away in the Roman Empire before the time of our Christian calendar. Virgil was a poet in those days and described a blissful experience in nature as "pastoral." Pastoral descriptions in literature and music through the ages came to form cultural ideals that have persisted and hardened over time.

Hawthorne describes the ideal plot of nature in "Sleepy Hollow," a passage from his *American Notebooks* of 1844, which describe in detail each event such as gentle winds, sunshine glimmering, and the contents of the forest floor. But suddenly, out of nowhere comes the shriek of a locomotive whistle—it is the rude entering of the machine in the garden. The locomotive is an evocative image that has been depicted tirelessly in Americana, songs, literature, movies, you name it. Leo Marx suggested that the reason for this sentimental feeling of what it is to be American comes from a simultaneous tension between two emotional poles: (1) the strong urge to romanticize the rural setting—part of our deep cultural connection with storytelling that goes all the way back to Virgil and the Roman civilization, and (2) an almost religious dedication to the belief in technology and industrialization—the necessary evil to enhance and "tame" the wild, pastoral setting.

The small, family-owned farmstead is the highest attainment of human life according to Thomas Jefferson, but it requires technological intrusion in order to function. Up until the twentieth century that was exemplified by the locomotive bringing cargo or the "dark satanic mills" producing goods (as written by William Blake in 1808). Today it is the pickup truck. These tools of humankind allowed all the manufactures of the city to be utilized in the rural setting as well. The machine, then, was seen as an essential part of American progress. As early as 1831 this view was the pervasive attitude in American thought.* In that year, a widely read essay made modern-sounding claims that are still believed today: "Intellectual progress can only come from leisure time when man is relieved of drudgery" and "Nations in which the greatest number of labor-saving machines are built will make the most progress intellectually." Furthermore, "machines are to perform all the drudgery of man . . . "† This shows that a cultural narrative of industrial intrusion has been part of American life from the get-go.

The tension has never abated. Americans are still puzzled as to how technology can interface peaceably with our other obsession, nature.

It's not a stretch to suggest that the same forces are at play in the conceptualizations of the suburb. Suburbs are engineered outgrowths of the middle landscape ideal. As Leo Marx put it, a timeless human impulse is depicted in the main characters of literature to effect a "reconciliation between the forces of civilization and nature."‡ Finally, with American punk rock, we reached a point where that ideal was rejected. As punk became a fixture in American suburbia, for the first time in history the middle landscape was identified as bogus and rejected in lieu of an as-yet-to-be-created new ideal for American identity. Punk was at the forefront of this movement, and possibly, with imagery such as the "suffer-boy," helped shape its aesthetic. Most punks gravitated toward the urban, just like any average American citizen tended to do in the twentieth century. But I consciously avoided the allure of urban life and embraced the technological intrusion

---

* See Leo Marx's *The Machine in the Garden: Technology and the Pastoral Ideal in America*, (New York: Oxford University Press, 2000), 182–185.
† See Timothy Walker's "Defense of Mechanical Philosophy (1831)," *North American Review*, 33 (June 1831): 122.
‡ See Leo Marx's *Machine in the Garden*, 35.

into the pastoral setting. Nature became my focal point, as opposed to social unrest or urban strife or any of the more typical punk themes.

Thus were the stubborn, pervasive intellectual motivations that drove
my songwriting, guided my analytical perspectives, and persuaded my lifestyle choices.

So much of my work was committed to exploring the false narrative of the middle landscape—having been brought to Los Angeles as a
passenger—and the longing to be away from it.

27C. THE PHONE CALL

In June of 1994, I got a devastating phone call that would be the first of three
knockdowns over the course of the next fourteen months that almost did
me in. It was Brett on the other end of the landline phone in my living room.
"Hey, Greg, I just quit the band." "What?" I said in disbelief, as I exited with
the handheld to a more private place. "Why would you quit the band now?"
I asked. "Jay and I just got in a fight and I'm sick of his bullshit. I can't take it
anymore," he said. Now, that seemed odd to me because we all got in fights
over the years—creative fights, intellectual debates, and even seething re-
sentments. Hell, I even remember slapping Jay at a gas station once on tour
because he thought he could pump the fuel better than me! So we've all had
little tiffs over the decades, but this time it was different. I had to process
the brief phone call, but I was distracted. In fact, the parents were visiting,
seeing their new granddaughter for the first time. The house was in a celebratory mood, and I had to maintain that cheer. But this news was hard to
take. The phone call continued for about fifteen minutes with me asking
what could be done to fix the problem. But Brett didn't even say, "It's him or
me," which indicated that he really had no intention of being in Bad Religion
anymore. "Brett, I'll have to call you back later, but do me a favor and think
about it, okay?"

As soon as I hung up and headed back down to the living room where
everyone was gathered, the phone rang again. I ascended back to the private

place. "Hello?" It was our manager, Danny. "Goddamn it," he said, as if a house of cards had been carefully erected on a kitchen table and someone just opened the sliding glass door, bringing blustery wind across the room. His voice and intonation seemed to say, "All is lost . . . " This gave me very little optimism. The guy we brought on board as manager, the guy who so skillfully was guiding the communication wing of our organization, who, along with Michele, added such an upbeat tone to the spirit of the band, now sounded like the reporter of the Hindenburg disaster. "I tried to talk Brett out of it, but he seems intent on leaving," he said. "Well, you're going to have to handle this, Danny." "Okay, go back and enjoy the family and we will be in touch."

After dinner, the family all retreated to their bedrooms. I told Greta about the phone call and she just looked at me with a glance of disappointment. I interpreted it as "I have no faith in you. This is another fine mess this band has gotten us into." Basically, I felt a heaping load of guilt and added responsibility to make the whole situation work out. I felt responsible, even though the predicament was clearly not my doing.

Late at night, when everyone was sleeping, I stole away to the studio over the garage. I had time to think about the gravity and profundity of the phone call. It was a turning point for sure. I reflected back to another long-distance phone call with Brett from years before, in 1983. At that time, I was in Wisconsin, attending college at UW-Madison, and Epitaph was a label only in name. Brett made another break during that call, but it had a more upbeat, hopeful feeling to it. "Dude, since we sort of started this label in your mom's living room and in the Hell Hole as well as in my parent's house, I just wanted to establish what my goals were and hope you don't mind. Since you're going off to college now I'd like to run the label as I see fit. Is that cool with you?" In essence, Brett was letting me know that he was going to set out on a constructive mission, building a label based on our band. I said, "Of course, go for it!" I wanted to have Bad Religion remain viable even if I was away at college. I thought as long as Brett was interested in pursuing a course of improving the label, Bad Religion would always benefit. So I stayed busy with school, and he stayed busy with the label. It felt good.

But now his phone call was more ominous. Leaving the band meant a deconstruction of our partnership. There was a sadness I felt because our friendship would no longer revolve around its most rewarding facet: writing, producing, and performing Bad Religion songs together. Furthermore, this time around, Brett was not only out of the band, but we had already signed with Atlantic Records, so we were also not even on his label either. It was like he wiped his slate clean. No more Bad Religion, which I took as no more "me" either.

Brett said something during this latest call that was an attempt at encouragement. "Dude, don't worry, just keep doing what you're doing. Remember, Van Halen got MORE popular when David Lee Roth left the band. And HE was their singer!" Those words struck me when he said them, and I could tell that he tacitly approved of me going on without him. This meant that I would have to redouble my efforts at being the front man and, now, principle songwriter. The voice of Bad Religion, my voice, was what people came to expect on records and on stage. For the immediate future, we had to find a guitarist to play Brett's parts for the upcoming tour. We already had an album in the bag, the release date was coming up soon, and within about two months we were going to begin a world tour to promote it.

Brett, Danny Heaps, and the entire band agreed that we would not announce or make a big publicity campaign around Brett's departure. In fact, most of the publicity at that time focused on a mutual effort to bolster the sales of tickets for a summer festival at which Bad Religion was a featured performer. The festival was to take place on July 29 at the Hollywood Palladium, and Brett was going to be on stage with us. The reason for this awkward occurrence, Brett quitting the band but playing this one last show, is because it was a celebration of the label's success: the Epitaph Summer Nationals.

This festival, in front of 3,500 punk fans, was one of the summer's premier events for our genre. It highlighted numerous bands from the Epitaph label: Pennywise, Rancid, NOFX, and, of course, Bad Religion. I thought it was kind of pointless to be playing the show since the founder of the label had decided to quit the founding band's roster. After all, my greatest support for the label was always solidly due to the friendship I had with Brett. But take Brett out of the equation, and my motivation was decidedly diminished. I was a champion of the band. And since the band had sold out the Palladium on our own, without the fanfare of the label, without the support of the other bands on Epitaph, I believed that our inclusion was doing more for other bands than it was doing for us. It certainly didn't feel like a celebration.

My snooty attitude didn't affect my performance. All of us remained professional and we played the show with aplomb. Brett hardly spoke to any of us, and I remember leaving the venue shortly after our set was finished without saying goodbye to him. This was the beginning of my effort to avoid confronting the uncomfortable interpersonal relations between band members, all in the interest of pushing forward and taking on the mounting challenges ahead.

The main challenge was going to be public perception. Live on stage, we could still impress, so long as we found a great guitarist to replace him. But we'd have to also weather the storm from the more critical punk fans and music writers all too eager to sensationalize Brett's departure as fallout from the band's recent migration from an indie label (owned by Brett himself, which they knew) to a "sellout" major label. For that, there was nothing we could do but clam up about the interpersonal "private" matters—the infighting—and focus on more constructive things such as the upcoming tour and the quick announcement of a superstar replacement for our very successful, but recently departed, label chief and guitarist.

This worked as a PR angle. But privately I had deeper fears. Brett and I had become a bona fide songwriting team by that time. By this, I mean a musical duo who contributes equal portions of written ideas, melodies, arrangements, and production concepts to an album's contents. Songwriting teams are a rarity in music, and even rarer in punk. There were many examples of "a guitarist and a singer" duos in punk, but usually both did not contribute equally as a songwriting team. It was more of a division of labor. The stereotype of great success in rock 'n' roll music usually revolves around one being the writing "genius" (guitarist) and one being the melodic "genius" (a lead singer). From Johnny Thunders and David Johansen (New York Dolls) to Ron Asheton and Iggy Pop (the Stooges) to Johnny Marr and Morrissey (the Smiths) to John Doe and Exene Cervenka (X) to Chris Stein and Debbie Harry (Blondie) to Cheetah Chrome and Stiv Bators (Dead Boys). Even among our own peers, Rikk Agnew and Tony Cadena (Adolescents) or Lucky Lehrer and Greg Hetson with Keith Morris as their singer (Circle Jerks) proved that divisions of labor rather than songwriting duos were the norm in punk rock. There were also plenty of examples of individual "geniuses" in punk and grunge who were not thought of principally as guitarists but rather singer-songwriters who also tinkered with the guitar. Think of Elvis Costello, Kurt Cobain, or David Byrne, for example. But Bad Religion was unique in having two principal songwriters each contributing roughly half of the songs. I had to shake off the fear of losing fifty percent of my songwriting team, double my efforts at writing new songs, and hope to find a suitable replacement for his guitar playing.

The best thing we could do to combat this perception and put a positive spin on a bad situation was to find a legendary guitarist to fill Brett's absence. Jay and Greg Hetson went to work immediately, calling their vast network of friends from other bands to see if any of them might be interested in replacing Brett. Bad Religion was about to enter the most labor-intensive period in its existence. We were going to be spending more time together than ever before. Even though we had grown apart to some degree, the band members had pretty much grown up together, so we knew each other's quirks and we knew where we could bond over shared interests. This new replacement member would have to be a chameleon, intelligent enough to easily engage in discussions as wide ranging as Jay's interests in motorcycles and bass guitars to Greg Hetson's interests in Asian cuisine in European cities to my own interests in human nature and American history. All the while, he would have to be witty, hilarious, and a kick-ass guitar player. That's a hell of a demanding list of attributes to check off to fill a job opening. But somehow, the one person who could accomplish all of these things and add plenty of his own content to round out the list was known to be working at a rehearsal studio in Hollywood at the time. His name was Brian Baker.

27D. BRIAN THE SOLUTION

The guys knew Brian because of his legendary tenure as a founding member of Minor Threat, who played gigs with the Circle Jerks, and who, as a founding member of Dag Nasty, knew Brett as their producer on their album for Epitaph, *Four on the Floor*. I had no knowledge of, nor acquaintance with, Brian until a conference call with the bandmates. "He's a bit of a rock slut," said Greg Hetson, which meant that he played in a lot of different bands. In fact, Brian had been playing in his rock band Junkyard up until the time he went to work at the rehearsal studio. But I trusted Greg and Jay's assessment of his incredible guitar skills. They were, after all, the ones more connected to scenester musicians in LA. Greg Hetson often hobnobbed with Brian at clubs and bars in Hollywood. Jay, a guitarist himself, told me, "He can do way more on guitar than Brett."

So, based on nothing more than my bandmates' enthusiasm, having no personal connection with him, nor familiarity with his skills, I joined Greg Hetson on a conference call to welcome Brian into the band. "When can you come visit?" I asked, knowing that there was much to be done in getting Brian up to speed. He had agreed to sing background parts that Brett used to sing on stage. Little did I know at the time that he was not as skilled at singing as he intimated to the other guys. Brian replied, "After we rehearse a bit here in LA and I get familiar with the tunes, I will head to your place in upstate New York for singing camp."

July was a month that I had planned to spend quietly at home, playing with Ella and Graham, and enjoying the garden and planting new trees. Our house was always buzzing with kids, playgroups with parents, and the usual trappings of young families. Brian, an unmarried urban bachelor, came to visit and was immediately thrust into the pulse of a different lifestyle. Early mornings, outdoor chores, trips to the farmers market, gardening, and nature walks were anathema to an LA nightlife scenester such as Brian. But it was the norm at our house. He was a good sport about it all, nonetheless, and the kids enjoyed having company.

Brian and I spent about two weeks together, going over songs and practicing singing. His parts weren't difficult, mostly oohs and aahs. He bought into the commitment that we had to be better than ever because we knew that some skeptical punks, many who called us sellouts, were just hoping for us to fail. Some came up with their own little fan club whose motto was "No Brett, no set." With Brett out of the band, they were dubious that we could maintain our credibility. Of course, this was a minority opinion. But if we could convince the most hardened skeptics, then the others would obviously be pleased as well. Once those naysayers realized "That's Brian Baker up there," the credibility portion of their criticism would be canceled immediately. But his sound, which is one of the most signature sounds in all of punk, and his virtuosity would do the rest of the talking. It complemented our songs, and blended perfectly with our style, and the audience would soon be treated to hearing a greatly enhanced live set from Bad Religion.

While we were running through our daily drills of learning songs, practicing singing, and listening to Bad Religion records, Brian and I watched an important television broadcast. Woodstock '94, the twenty-fifth anniversary concert, was happening only about 150 miles from my living room. We were too busy and distracted to make the drive to the chaotic festival, but we watched with interest because so many of our contemporaries and friends were playing on that festival stage. It was on our television for two days straight. Brian and I would take breaks and go downstairs and check out the TV whenever a band of interest was performing. We saw Trent Reznor and Green Day covered in mud, Jackyl covered in blood, and none of what we saw was particularly good. But we were both highly impressed by the massive crowd that gathered. It was nothing like the hippie culture that gathered for the 1969 event. This audience was full of grunge, thrash, and punk rockers who could just as easily have been at a Bad Religion concert. We watched with a sense of great possibility that Bad Religion could

grow and expand our status. There was nothing intimidating about any of
the bands we watched. We knew that we were as good as, or better than,
any of them. Many of the performers had already by that time acknowledged Bad Religion or Brian's former band, Minor Threat, as influential.
This made us jovial as we both agreed, "We belong on that goddamn stage!"
Watching punk rock played in front of a festival audience gave Brian a good
idea of what it was going to be like with Bad Religion because Brian's first
gig with the band, only five weeks away, was to be in front of thirty thousand people at a festival in Cologne, Germany, called the Bizarre Festival.

The kick-off and launch of our new tour to promote the high-profile,
major-label release of *Stranger than Fiction* took place in Europe, not America. Even though the album was still weeks away from its official release
date, the Bizarre Festival was a showcase of some new songs from that album. Brian performed without a flaw and proved that big stages or small,
he was the right guy to fill Brett's absence. Little did I know that, prior to us
taking the stage, someone had whispered in Brian's ear that Brett himself
would be watching the show from the sound booth out there among the
thirty thousand music fans. Even this didn't seem to shake Brian's confidence during the performance; it went off without a hitch.

The Stranger than Fiction Tour launched successfully and would go on to
be our biggest grossing tour up to that time. Due to some legal craftiness
by our lawyer, Eric, Atlantic Records handled North America only, but for
the rest of the world we would be on the Sony Music label. Sony had offices
and regional teams in every country of the world, and everywhere we went
we got used to seeing our albums promoted heavily in storefront windows
in the major shopping areas of cities as diverse as Stockholm and Berlin to
Milan and Barcelona. Thanks to Sony we had financial and marketing support that finally allowed us to tour in Japan and Australia, and they greatly
expanded our marketing and publicity that paved the way to expand our
efforts in Brazil, Argentina, and Chile.

27E. DIVORCE AVERSION

Despite the global success of the band, other parts of my life were crumbling. After putting my academic work on ice, I took my family for granted. Whenever I came home from a tour, I expected a hero's welcome from my wife. But to her, it was more like an adjustment to another person around the house. While I was away, a routine without me had to be implemented, so coming home was an abrupt change for both of us. I didn't take into account that while I was away she had to keep the family ticking with kids' routines, playdates, groceries, and so on. Even though we could afford one, she didn't want a full-time nanny, and I respected her wishes. In such a scenario, me with my head in the sky, brimming with the rigors and rewards of being a touring musician, her at home, mother of two kids and a life of toddler chaos, a playground monitor, parent host to other kids who came over, and all-around fixer of perpetual preschool dramas, it is not hard to understand the fracturing stresses pulling the family in opposite directions.

I wanted to include the family in my touring lifestyle. We had tried that in the past. On a tour of Europe in 1993, Brett and I rented our own tour bus and brought out the families and brought along friends as "nannies." I thought we all were having a great time. But it turned out that the fun was fleeting. For our family, the joy of seeing Europe's most romantic cities while living on a tour bus had its cost in the constant vigilance of taking care of kids in a foreign land and in unfamiliar surroundings. Sure, it was great to be in Paris and Frankfurt, but finding diapers, baby food, and all the routine necessities of childcare became tedious after about a week. Six weeks of this was just torture.

So we weren't going to become the Partridge Family. The studio projects in Hollywood or New York, the countless trips to London, Berlin, Frankfurt, Los Angeles, or Chicago, for press junkets, concerts, or festivals, were always on the calendar. But still, I believed that maybe we could balance the grueling demand of constant traveling by having a nanny and building in plenty of vacation time between tour legs. But it didn't work out that way.

When I returned from Europe in the summer of 1994, I began to recognize a distance developing in our household. Not between me and the kids—they were always stuck to me like glue whenever I came home from a tour. But more of a rift between me and my wife. It got more noticeable when mutual friends understood more about what daily life was like around my house than I did because I was away so much. I felt like a stranger in my own family to some degree, and this caused me no small amount of stress. Disagreements turned into unresolved fights that festered undiscussed. Too soon, I would have to depart for my next leg of the tour. So I wanted to enjoy every second that I could with the kids at home, have cookouts every night, watch lots of Disney movies, and go get ice cream. Where was the time to have serious marital discussions in all this?

The American leg of the tour was broken up into two sections beginning in Norfolk, Virginia. The first portion ended six weeks later in Southern California. All the shows were sold out. Michele from the management team joined us, and she recognized that a lot of expectations were put on my shoulders. With Brett out of the band, I had to answer a lot of questions from the press about going to a major label. Michele emphasized that our success spoke for itself and directed the Atlantic Records publicists to build a campaign that ignored the criticisms from the "punk police" and kept the focus on the great success of this tour. I felt that we were well on the way to putting the ugliness of Brett's departure behind us.

Thence began nearly a year and a half of nonstop touring around the world, ending in the summer of 1995. I came home to a nearly moribund marital relationship. Greta announced that there was "someone else," and I went into a panic. I was so busy patching the hole in the ship caused by Brett's departure—rebuilding trust in the fan base and in the professionals and in the bandmates who all were counting on me—to worry about the safety and security of the emotions in my own family. The years when kids are preschoolers are very fragile times in the family. Not so much for the little kids, ironically, but for the parents. The mothers need plenty of support. The fathers need plenty of encouragement. Those basic things were lacking, and I wasn't able to provide my share.

I felt like a failure. The most painful part for me was the possibility that my own children might have to suffer the same bullshit that I remembered

so vividly about my own childhood: having two parents as adversaries, living separate lives, without helping one another establish a common ground
for the family; a university with two campuses, two sets of expectations.
The panic that struck me was serious enough that I sought out, for the first
time in my life, a psychotherapist. Greta agreed to go to marriage counseling with me, which was a dangling carrot of hope, just close enough to get
me out of my funk so that I could continue to function in the band.

I began to write songs about my own struggles but decided to loosely
camouflage them as social diatribes. "A Walk," "Parallel," and "Punk Rock
Song" were all about social ills that could just as easily have described my
feelings of insecurity within the family. "Drunk Sincerity" and "Them and
Us" depicted my disappointment in human relationships. A song called
"The Gray Race" described how the world requires "black and white" decisions, but the human experience is not digital—it thrives in the shaded
realm between polar opposites. So much in life, such as being either in or
out of a relationship or marriage, is framed as an all-or-nothing affair, when
in fact all commitments vacillate from time to time, resembling a bona fide
"gray area" of human emotion. The turning point in my new attitude, after
I had concluded that my marriage was over (despite my continued weak
efforts in marriage counseling), was summarized in "Cease," reflecting an
oddly positive outlook from the recognition that relationships, like life itself, must end eventually.

Through it all, I stayed functionally upbeat around the house. I feigned
interest whenever Ella would say, "Daddy, watch this!" even for the hun-
dredth time. I played ball in the front yard with Graham and took both kids
and their friends for ice cream nearly every day. But inside I knew that I
was just prolonging the inevitable dissolution of the marriage, which would
in turn destroy all the stability that I was working so hard to maintain.

Professionally, I felt responsible to all the fans who had come to expect
great songwriting and engaging ideas in Bad Religion songs. In the absence
of Brett, I couldn't let this next album be less interesting than our previous
ones. It was lonely work, writing without him, and I found myself wishing
for some outside inspiration.

With a marriage on the rocks, Greta and I took the kids on a beach vacation to Montauk, a town at the very east end of Long Island. It was a very private, unannounced getaway. I thought this might resurrect the bond and corral the family, but in reality it was really the last hurrah. There was distance between Mom and Dad, but the kids, being only three and a half and one and a half, were too young to recognize the cold reality.

No time for brooding, our trip was abruptly cut short because Danny and Michele had arranged for me to meet the producer Ric Ocasek in NYC. "Bring your demos," they said. "He'd like to hear what you've been up to."

Ric represented a piece of my childhood that transpired in my Wisconsin neighborhood. Before I was punk, my friends and I would gather round the stereo in Dad's study, with tennis rackets as guitars and letter openers as microphones, and lip-synch the Cars' first two albums. Having no idea I would someday sing into a real microphone, I played the role of Ric and Wryebo played the role of Benjamin Orr. Tommy from next door was the spitting image of Greg Hawkes, and his cousin Dave played a serviceable Elliot Easton. I loved those songs, and they became our summer soundtrack in 1978. We saw the Cars perform that year at the Milwaukee Arena. Now, nearly twenty years later, their songwriter and singer wanted to hear my songs. It was surreal.

Greta and the kids joined me on the visit to Ric's NYC house. Ric had a little boy about the same age as Graham who seemed excited to have a new playmate for the day. Ric's wife Paulina was a supermodel, and she was gracious and sweet and invited Greta and the kids to join her and her little boy for a trip to Central Park while Ric and I stayed back to go over the songs. Even though she was in the presence of fashion royalty, Greta was cool and natural. Her ease in the company of supermodels was honed at the Chart House, where she learned the ropes as a waitress to the stars alongside her friend and coworker Mariska Hargitay, who would go on to become a famous actor. Greta and Mariska bonded over their shared Hungarian ancestry. Paulina had that Eastern European flair too, and today she and Greta looked like two beauties hitting the park with their rug rats.

One of my first orders of business was to let Ric know that if we worked together, I would have to head back to Ithaca once a week for marriage counseling sessions. This was a heavy burden on my creativity, having to preside over the dissolution of my marriage while simultaneously recording the most important album of my career. Ric said this would be no problem, that we would make space for it in our schedule. With his ever-uplifting style of encouragement, he reassured me, "You'll get through it, you're an artist!"

Heading back home we didn't speak much of the future of our failing marriage. Greta and I kept cordial distance from each other, distracted as we were by numerous visitors and house guests. This, combined with the constant visits from the local parents and their kids for playdates, kept the house a festive center of activity for the children. Brian came to visit, having recently moved back to the DC area from Los Angeles. He was excited to drive up Interstate 81 for a road trip and hear some new songs. Before we got to recording, he came in a bit fatigued from the drive. Greta asked him, "Can I get you anything?" He replied, "A Maker's Mark and Coke would be really nice." I didn't even know what that meant; it sounded like some kind of slang to me. I was truly naive about alcoholic drinks and I never paid attention to what people ordered at the bar when we worked at the restaurant. But Greta sometimes took shifts in college as a bar waitress. Imagine my surprise when Greta returned from the kitchen with precisely the drink that Brian ordered. I had no idea that we had hard alcohol in the house! We all had a good laugh. Laughter was the key to my sanity. Everyone who came to visit brought their own kind of mirth and cheer, knowing full well that our marriage was faltering.

No one was more upbeat than my friend David from California. David had lived next door to the Hell Hole in Canoga Park when the band was formed. His mom and dad immediately welcomed us into the neighborhood when we moved to LA. In a huge metropolis where neighbors often don't speak to one another, fate smiled on us as we settled into our new surroundings. David's parents befriended Mom and Chuck immediately after we moved in. David and I became playmates, and I babysat for his little sister, Stephanie. I played all sorts of music from my small record collection and on the piano to entertain David whenever he was bored. When Bad Religion first set up the drum set in Mom's garage, David couldn't contain his curiosity and snuck in after rehearsal to pound the skins on Jay's translucent orange kit.

Though our families were still close, David and I had lost touch with each other for a few years. We rekindled our friendship and I discovered that he had studied sitar, been to India, and was interested in all sorts of music. His worldly experience and sick sense of humor like mine meant that there was no end to comedic pranks and parodies, which kept us constantly amused at life's absurdities. David found something funny about nearly everything, even the most difficult situations that life throws at you.

David visited in the midst of my marital discord. I played him some of my demo recordings. "This one sounds like a David Bowie song on speed," he said. After a minute of laughter, I pounded out the chords to "Drunk Sincerity" on my keyboard, but slowed it down to half-speed and sang it with my best '80s-era Bowie impression. After rolling on the studio carpet laughing for a few minutes, we broke out the microphones and plugged in the electric instruments and made a sixteen-track recording of "Drunk Sincerity," complete with drums, synth, and outlandish electric guitar wails. Although we cherished the recording for our personal amusement, the song was too good to just put back on the shelf. David decided we had to present it to our A&R man at Atlantic Records. I phoned him and said, "Mike! You'll never guess who I ran into at Ric Ocasek's house when I visited. David Bowie!" His interest was piqued. "You also won't believe this. He took a liking to my song 'Drunk Sincerity' and I got him to sing it on my demo!" Now, Mike was elated. "Aaaah. Incredible! Send it to me immediately. This could be huge."

A couple of days later, Mike called me back having heard the recording. I put him on speakerphone so that David could hear the conversation. "David," I whispered. "I think he really believes it!" Since the demo was drenched with plenty of reverb, delay, and other kinds of effects, my Bowie impression sounded believable. Mike said, "I'm going to present this at our next A&R meeting. Can you get back in touch with Bowie if we decide to go forward with making it a single?" Through muffled cries of laughter, we couldn't think of a way to ramp this prank much higher. I said, "Dang it! I didn't ask him his phone number." Mike said, "That's okay, our people can reach out to his people and we will make it happen."

Hanging up the phone, we just burst out in laughter until tears were rolling down our faces. "Can you just imagine? At this moment our demo tape is being presented to a room full of industry execs who are going to go searching for David Bowie's people, ask him about a song he never sang on, at a studio he never stepped foot in!" It was all in good fun. The next time I saw Mike, about a month later in New York City, I asked him about the demo. He just smiled and said, "Asshole."

On another occasion around that time, when Brian visited, he and I concocted a scheme to form some comradery with another band that had their headquarters on a compound near Ithaca. The band was Manowar, a metal band with a "larger than life" stage presence that proclaimed themselves the Kings of Metal. Manowar successfully blended chivalry and medievalism with hard music to create an aesthetic that was unique and which their acolytes took to be "true metal." We found it entertaining, and we wondered if we might be able to forge a friendship by making a visit to their rehearsal compound in Auburn, New York.

My friend Alex, who owns Pyramid Sound Recording Studios in Ithaca, knew where they rehearsed and he got us the address. But Brian pointed out that we couldn't visit empty-handed. We had to bring some sort of gift of friendship. As luck would have it, we were set to head over to England for a press junket. While there, we would appear on a BBC Radio talk show with the singer for Iron Maiden, Bruce Dickinson. Any metal fan would be hard-pressed to have to choose between Iron Maiden and Manowar when deciding who were the kings of true metal. So Brian and I thought, what better gift could we bring Manowar than something appropriately medieval and metal-worthy, from the shores of old England itself? I said, "Brian, let's purchase a sheet of white parchment, and have Bruce Dickinson sign a message of good cheer to our friends in New York, Manowar; a gesture of peace between the two rival factions of true metal." David Bragger, whose favorite band was Iron Maiden, told us that Bruce Dickinson was an avid fencing enthusiast. "Perfect!" Brian said, "Let's ask him to sign a message having something to do with that. It sounds medieval."

After the interview, Bruce very kindly chatted with us about what we planned to do. Brian and I had an elaborate ceremony in mind. "Bruce," I said, "will you sign this ivory parchment with a message of good cheer to our friends across the great water in New York named Manowar?" At that instant, Brian broke out a candle and lit it while I observed the signature, and noted the written message that read: *Dear Manowar, Have an Epee Day!, signed Bruce Dickinson*. We immediately folded the paper into a tiny square and placed it into a golden snuff box that we had purchased at an antique store. The box was sealed with drips of wax from the candle and it was placed inside of my zipped leather jacket pocket.

We returned to New York with the golden snuff box. But one last detail remained. Brian felt that we couldn't show up and present such a special, personalized, symbolic gift without proper dress. Mere heavy metal attire would not do. Brian was intent on something greater. After much deliberation, he concluded that renting a suit of armor would be the perfect gesture to wear as we presented our gift to the Kings of Metal. Only such a formality could make our quest complete.

Unfortunately, there were no rental shops in upstate New York that catered to Knights of the Round Table enthusiasts, and we could devote no more time to our mission of good cheer. And to this day the golden snuff box still sits, unopened, in a glass display box on a shelf in my library.

In the midst of all this mirth, a calamity was brewing in our bustling household. My marriage demanded attention, but it took a back seat to daily conference calls with managers, agents, and label personnel, demo writing, and studio sessions. Being productive and goofing off with friends kept me from having to address my marital woes.

Around this time, Bill Silva, a promoter and manager from San Diego, asked if I could produce one of his new bands, Unwritten Law. In the same melodic vein as Bad Religion, Unwritten Law was at the very cusp of the emerging pop punk sound. Hailing from San Diego, the band's politics were not as interesting to me as their melodic approach and pop-worthy potential. Still, with all that was going on in my life during this late summer of 1995, there was no way I could travel to San Diego to produce them. Luckily, we had a kick-ass studio right here in Ithaca, Pyramid Sound. Pyramid Sound had a Neve console and was the site of some famous recordings through the years including albums by Anthrax, Testament, and Agnostic Front.

Unwritten Law was one of those bands that provoked a lot of punk rockers to ask, "What's punk about this band?" They were a blend of styles. The singer, Scott, had a raspy melodic voice like mine. He grew up skateboarding and listening to second-wave punk bands, but he was always drawn to the melody in the aggressiveness of the music. Same was true of the drummer, Wade. The bass player, John, played with an open finger style using no pick, just like his hero, Steve Harris of Iron Maiden. With influences as diverse as Southern California melodic hardcore, English heavy metal, and early '80s pop punk, such as the Go-Go's, Unwritten Law was an appealing challenge. I thought that with good songwriting this band could prove to be interesting to a new generation of punk rockers. Just as Bad Religion had unwittingly blended influences from 1970s progressive and hard rock into punk, now the bands were starting to blend the genres of the 1980s. I was all for this interesting Oster-izing of musical styles. Thematically, the songs were not deep or political. But catchy and melodic ditties would soon become the norm. Unwritten Law, along with their contemporaries Blink-182 and No Doubt, opened the door to the most expansive period in punk history. Soon, every radio in the nation had punk music on the dial and every television was showing punk music videos to the latchkey schoolkids in every suburb throughout the land. Bad Religion would benefit from this expansion.

Due to the impending recording sessions with Ric Ocasek, there was no way I could produce the Unwritten Law record until later in the fall. Meanwhile, Greta and I would stay together for the sake of the kids for the foreseeable future. But I was going to be away for a while.

I moved in with the band at an apartment building on 50th and 3rd in New York City for the entire recording period, October and November of 1995. Ric's favorite studio was the Electric Lady Studios in Greenwich Village on 8th Street at 6th Avenue. The studio was legendary. Originally built for Jimi Hendrix, it served as the recording space for a long list of classic albums such as *Talking Book* by Stevie Wonder, Kiss's *Dressed to Kill*, and Chic's hit song "Le Freak." Ric was just finishing his production with Weezer (their *Pinkerton* album) as we were moving in.

Our goal was to make a punk album that in 1996 retained the same virtues as our previous records. Making a commercially successful album that earned a lot of money would have been very useful, but we weren't interested in gambling our integrity away. Despite the expensive costs associated with big-name producers, high-tech recording studios, and professional expenses the band incurred, and despite the fact each of us also had middle-class suburban lifestyles, complete with kids, therapists and counselors, and mortgages, we decided it was best to remain committed to our original mission: enlighten our audience with music that made them think.

27F. THAT NEW YORK THING—THE GRAY RACE

Ric and Paulina lived in a five-story urban dream house, a brownstone on 19th Street fit for American royalty. One might rightly think that the Roosevelt family of the nineteenth century could be neighbors in this little-changed neighborhood, each house a page from a textbook on Federal-style architecture. The facades stood erect and were detailed with original stone lintels, expertly repointed with weathered red brick, and featured mullioned windows. The entry door of the Ocasek residence, an iron hinged, one-and-three-quarter-inch slab of oak or hickory, no doubt original, with so many layers of paint that it easily withstood the centuries of urban foulness, was flush with the building's facade. No ostentatious porticos or grand entrance greeted the visitor. In fact, these narrow buildings had rooms that were rather tight. Upon entering, a house assistant led you through a small entrance hallway to the narrow kitchen with handsome wooden cabinetry, modern appliances, stone countertops, and a pleasant, bright-windowed nook in the front where a bench and counter let you enjoy breakfast, lunch, or coffee in domestic privacy as the anonymous public passed by just outside.

Ric was not a kitchen man. He preferred to meet down in the basement where he had built himself a studio for listening to, writing, and recording demos. Populated by his vast collection of analog gear and a twenty-four-channel mixing console, this private space was a songwriter's dream. Though far more developed, it was not unlike what I was trying to do in my more spacious room over the garage at home. All the electronics were in perfect working condition, and all the guitars were strung and in tune thanks to Ric's technical assistant, Heg, who was always present in the house, in the studio, or in the mixing room, quietly soldering a volume pot or performing some other technical duty. It was usually Heg who met me on the ground floor or in the kitchen to escort me down to the master's laboratory.

Ric and I met in his basement studio each day before heading over to Electric Lady for the session work. Even though Brett was out of the band, I was grateful to have a collaborative partner again, albeit a temporary one. Our conversations ranged from specific tweaks to lyrics or instrumentation to more general things like being the leader of a band or the drawbacks of celebrity. On one occasion Ric opened a drawer that was full of well-labeled and organized demo tapes of his own. He pulled out one from the back and popped it in the cassette player. It was his acoustic version of the song "Let's Go." He also played excerpts from another tape labeled "Night Spots" that featured various versions of his poetry recited melodiously over just his electric guitar. The final version of that song on the album *Candy-O*, complete with the brilliant orchestrations and keyboard arrangements of Greg Hawkes, could serve as a lesson in the producer's handbook. The demo and the mastered work sound nothing alike. But the intellectual merits of the lyrics and the feeling that emanates from the lead singer-songwriter come shining through, even in stripped-down form. My demos tended to resemble the finished product, but I craved the scrutiny of a fellow song-writer and in Ric's I put my faith.

Much of my song material surrounded my incipient separation and family dissolution. If punk was supposed to have a theme, then these songs were definitely not conforming to convention. Songs about loss, personal sadness, and helplessness surrounding human relations were the stuff of soft-rock or AOR (album-oriented rock) or country music. There had never been a punk album of love songs, for instance (I always thought of that as an unfortunate thing).

Peddlers of the punk mythos loved to point to songs such as "God Save the Queen" by the Sex Pistols or "California Über Alles" by Dead Kennedys or "London Calling" by the Clash or "I Don't Care" by the Ramones or "Rise Above" by Black Flag as genre-defining examples. In each of them, society is broken, and collectively the punks are going to do something about it. All great songs in their own right, and perfect choices as defining moments in the genre. But the mythmakers are quick to ignore equally influential selections from the early punk songbook. "Ever Fallen in Love" by the Buzzcocks or "Mister You're a Better Man Than I" by Sham 69 or "Adolescent" by the Plugz or "Los Angeles" by X or "Dreaming" by Blondie or "(What's so Funny 'Bout) Peace, Love, and Understanding?" by Elvis Costello—songs that uplift the emotions and offer a guide to optimism despite the personal suffering you may be experiencing as a punk, a citizen, and a human being during your journey through the maze of society. I never shied away from writing about emotional experience, and I felt that punk is short-changed if it's not understood as a broad-spectrum genre, every bit as rich as country music, folk, or conventional rock and roll.

The songs that would go on to form our 1996 album *The Gray Race*, while not purely a collection of emotional tunes, ventured deep into the anguish of human experience brought on by feelings of failure and isolation. "Cease" and "Parallel" depict the intellectual resolution of such anguish, while "Punk Rock Song" brings it to the social collective group experience.

When I showed Ric my lyrics, he would have little to say. This gave me confidence. No red flags. Sometimes, when I wasn't looking, he would jot sarcastic comments in the margins of my song notebooks. His inscriptions read like thought bubbles in a comic strip or allegorical quotations from my conscience: "That damn Ocasek is trying to ruin my song! I will get him in the end." But in reality, there was no acrimony. Disagreements were few and minor through the entirety of the six-week session.

Having a New York driver's license made me feel somewhat at home, though these urban streets were a far cry from my country retreat far upstate. Walking to work, grabbing your meals on the go, never wanting of entertainment or intellectual stimulation, I felt that I was living the life that Dad had championed in his lifelong love and promotion of New York City as the best place in the world.

When we were young, Dad brought Grant, me, and Wryebo here to show us boys what life in the big city was like. In fact, he brought his students here for field trips in those days. For my entire childhood, he made at least two trips a year to the Big Apple. There were no fancy high-priced hotels for the Graffins. The Murray Hill Hotel was our lot. Located around 35th Street and 5th Avenue, this holdover from the 1940s still had rooms with wire-frame beds, bare floors, no TVs, and wash basins right there in the same room where you sleep. If you paid extra you could get rooms that had their own bathroom, but most had shared commodes. Back then, the phenomenon of "airmailing" your trash was still in practice. You could open the window, holler "airmail!" and release the rubbish bag from your outstretched arm hoping that it might hit one of the trash cans below.

Outside, just down the street at a corner restaurant you could get a full breakfast, egg and bacon with toast and coffee or orange juice, for ninety-nine cents. For dinner, it was Myong Dong Chinese restaurant (which was instantly translated to "My dong" by our juvenile sense of humor) right there on 35th Street. Dad showed us everything. We walked all over the city, seeing all the sites for free, standing at the base of the Empire State Building, peering at the twin towers of the World Trade Center from below, cruising in the harbor on the Staten Island Ferry, and getting beckoned by the barkers and propositioned by the pushers at 42nd Street. Dad was proving to us that New York on four dollars a day was actually practicable.

Of course, none of this would be complete without a visit to the New York Public Library, which is as close to a religious monument as any academic could get, and perhaps the best free attraction in the city.

Pinching pennies allowed Dad to save money for the evening's entertainment, which, there was no getting around it, came with an admission price. Dad took us to off-Broadway, avant-garde theaters. These places started out as rebellious enclaves of high culture completely rejecting the trappings of commercial theater. Its patrons and playwrights were essentially predecessors of punk spirit in the realm of literary drama. The theaters, mostly in SoHo, were small gathering places where serious actors cut their teeth on challenging, provocative dialogue. David Mamet, Sam Shepard, and Edward Albee featured their work at some of these unpretentious small spaces. Being able to see shows with lots of swearing on stage and plenty of nudity, all in the name of "high culture," made this one of the main attractions of my memory of "old" New York. Moreover, the good feeling I took away from these special trips to New York made me realize that the counterculture was a stimulating place to be.

Yes, New York was different back then, barely recognizable to many who live there today. They remember it fondly but acknowledge that it's lost a lot of its rough and sleazy luster. "Fuckin' Giuliani" you'll hear a lot of them say, because the former mayor cleaned up the city, made it antiseptic by moving the "undesirable" elements out of Times Square and 42nd Street while simultaneously transforming those areas into commercial tourist traps featuring national chain retail stores and name-brand hotels until nothing was left of New York City's former unique character.

Punk was changing too, and many sentimental types longed for the "old days" when the scene was young. As for Bad Religion, we had no intention of recapturing our former sound or revisiting the aesthetics of the early punk scene. With Brian in the band, and Ric producing, we were sure we could move forward with a new sound that was every bit as exciting and captivating as our previous records.

Around the time of my birthday, November 6, after weeks of recording, we began mixing the album. Just then, however, another blow was delivered to the band. Our manager, Danny, sent out a memo saying that we need to meet up with him and Michele at the studio as soon as possible. What he dropped on us was abrupt and heavy. "Guys, I've been offered a job as a vice president at RCA Records, and I'm leaving immediately." "Huh?" I said to myself. Then privately, "Well, that's okay, we still have Mich . . . " and before I could finish my thought, "And I'm bringing Michele along with me." At that point, I broke down in tears. It's as if I was an infant and someone had just wrenched my bottle away from me. I felt all the burden of my position, and took no comfort from any past success or future optimism. My intellectual activities on hold, my songwriting partner off who-knows-where, my band looking to me for direction, my family in disarray, the kids just wondering when Dad will be back, and now my manager, my quarterback, was bailing out and handing me the ball? Yes, weep indeed, like a baby I did.

I think Ric was present on the sidelines through all of this, and he saw how deeply affected I was. It was a useful and necessary distraction to have those days of mixing the album to take my mind off of where I or the band would turn next. Ric mentioned, "You know, you should talk to my manager, Elliot. He's a good guy." I guess Ric said the same thing to Elliot because within a week an informal meeting happened at the studio. One day at lunch break, Ric casually said, "Oh by the way, my manager is coming by today." That was the day I met Elliot Roberts, and on the same day I asked him if he would be interested in managing Bad Religion. It was all so casual, and he said, "Sure, I'd love the opportunity to manage you guys." There was no negotiating, no quibbling, no conditional statements, no "let me have my lawyer call your lawyer." It was like a new pal agreeing to come along for a ride to the concert.

And pal is just how I'd describe Elliot. Even though it was a brief friendship, he came along at a terribly low point in my career, and his general good cheer, cynical wit, and casual expert style was a shot of optimism that helped me immensely. Soon thereafter, it was time to leave New York City, head back upstate, and see what could be salvaged of the homelife I'd left behind.

27G. ITHACA—NO SUBSTANCE

The fire had gone out in the marriage. Without much progress in our counseling sessions, we came to the conclusion that pursuing individual trajectories was better than trying to meld each other's expectations into a coherent family spirit. Greta didn't want a public life, but I was becoming a public figure. We weren't clever or confident enough to figure out a way to bridge that gap. She wanted a stable salary man, and she found it in someone else who would become her new husband eventually. I was off for a month, home for a month, gone for weeks at a time, then back at the compound for a few. A total seesaw of an arduous but privileged life. A separation was best. The kids would spend as much time at Dad's house as possible. Mom's house was only a couple miles down the road, and that would become their main crib.

After a year of separation, in the state of New York, a couple is considered legally divorced. It's a method of ending the marriage without the burden of a lawsuit. In many states, the wife has to sue the husband for emotional damage, or the husband has to sue the wife for infidelity or some other transgression. We weren't eager to hurt each other in that way, so we decided to take "the good divorce."

But living in a family house with no family is one of the loneliest depths, and psychic tragedies, imaginable for my sentimental heart. Watching them pack their grips, load up the sedan, and drive away brought a paralyzing wave of emotion over me. I felt burdened by the weight of history in what seemed to be emerging as a sad family tradition. The moment that they drove away became etched in my memory, as only a few such indelible marks had been before. The act was a regrettable repeat of the same loss and uncertainty I experienced as a child going through the divorce of my parents. But this time round, I could empathize with the kids while simultaneously dealing with a new suite of emotions as a father myself. Even though the trip down the road to Mom's house was only two miles, I felt as an astronaut would feel as he watched, stranded on the Moon, his mothership head back to Earth. A sense of paternal panic set in, seeing the ones I loved most, the kids, disappearing to become a small dot on the horizon. It was poetic repetition of the same scene that my own father endured when we drove off with our mom to disappear on the western horizon that fateful August afternoon roughly twenty years prior.

Now, it was as if divorce had become normalized in the curriculum for Graffin U. I pondered a dark notion that in order to graduate and become upright citizens of the modern world, Graffin U. prepared all its children by using the methods of divorce as a challenge. Intellectualize it as I might, these tragic ironies didn't quell my sense of failure and utter sadness.

I relished the good fortune in my music career—even though it had its own suite of interpersonal challenges, Bad Religion was still highly successful—but I was tortured by the emerging reality that I seemingly had to choose between professional success and a successful family life. Wasn't there any way to overcome the emotional burdens in Graffin U. besides resorting to divorce? Psychoanalysis was somewhat helpful, but it didn't get to the meat of the experience. I never got the feeling that my therapist could grasp my predicament. This added another layer of unease to my emotional state—wondering if you should trust your psychologist's advice—and it made me generally glum. Worse still, my therapist ended up killing himself. I imagined that my own case gave him so much frustration that it drove him mad! Turned out, HE needed a therapist more than I did. I was only adding to his problems, or so it felt. Of course there were other details surrounding his suicide, and my case played no role in it. But still, I felt like the cynical universe was just watching its plan unfold, laughing at me with a wry smile and shaking its head.

Joint custody, that old familiar dance, was to dictate my schedule from now on. With the house empty for most of the weeks, I entered into song-writing and demo recording for another Bad Religion project. Due to the complexity of our new living arrangements, I asked the band and our sound engineer Ronnie if they'd come to upstate New York to record the album so I wouldn't have to leave. Thanks to their willingness, *No Substance* was made only miles from my house in Ithaca at the studios of Pyramid Sound.

No Substance was an appropriate title, referring as it did to a society (and a punk scene) that had lost its way. With a view toward the festivals in Europe, I wrote songs such as "Raise Your Voice" and "Hear It" to act as big-stage anthems. In America, punk had moved beyond us. Green Day and the Offspring were playing in arenas. They sang songs with shallow topics that were heard on all the top-ten playlists of commercial radio across the entire USA. We named our album *No Substance* as a nod to the current state of the genre and its wave of growing popularity that seemed to wash over and through us, while cresting atop of it were bands who grew up on our influence. We still had enough gas in the tank to command a sizeable following, but in the USA our shows were struggling to fill theaters, as the punk dollar was going to the larger arenas to see the younger bands.

One particularly noteworthy aspect of *No Substance*—and an overt confession of our focus on the European audience at that time—is the inclusion of our friend and musician Campino from Die Toten Hosen as a guest vocalist. To those in the USA focused on the domestic cultural explosion of punk and its suburban lifestyle or mainstream aspects, Campino meant nothing. In fact, few Americans had ever heard of Die Toten Hosen. But in Germany, they were a cultural icon and a national treasure, with millions of album sales, sold-out stadium shows in every town, and ubiquitous media attention. Their advocacy of us as an influential and important band in their genre was momentous.

To give you some flavor of the band, they started out as we did, just a bunch of friends from school playing in dreary punk clubs in 1982. Also like us, they had stints on major labels, and also formed their own label and merchandise company. By 1993, they had already released a number of albums and toured throughout Germany, Austria, and Switzerland, building up a larger and larger following each year with their continual string of catchy punk songs all sung in German. That year, however, they released *Kauf MICH!* (translation: *Buy ME!*) and the record achieved something that no one thought possible, a punk band reaching number one on the German charts. Their tours from that point on were no longer in clubs, theaters, or even concert halls, but, rather, they required stadiums. Their shows routinely brought over fifty thousand fans.

The growing popularity of punk all around the world had not been ignored by the German-speaking world. But like so many other things, from
beer to automobiles to sports to high culture, the Germans have a way of
putting their own high standards and unique stamp of approval on them.
Punk in Germany now was a household word, and that word had something to do with "dead trousers." Everyone loved Die (the) Toten (dead)
Hosen (trousers).

Thanks to our long history of touring in Germany at many of the
same venues that Die Toten Hosen had played, we were a familiar name.
Through our tour manager and now agent, Jens, we had formed significant relationships with many people in the German music industry. After
hearing my demo for "Raise Your Voice," Jens and I began talking about
how fun it would be to do a duet with Campino. After the recording was
finished, "our people" reached out to "their people," and Campino agreed
to a duo with me singing in alternate verses. Sony Music flew him to
New York City, and I met him there for a recording session in early 1998.
Later that year we filmed a video together at the Ambassador Hotel in
Los Angeles.

The song is a rousing stadium anthem with beer-swilling, pogoing, raucous intentions, retaining that wispiest of punk ethics to not be "played
like someone else's board game" and instead raise your voice in opposition.
Die Toten Hosen adopted the song in their repertoire and it became one of
their standards.

Since some of the songs on *No Substance* seemed shallow, and their in-
cision into the question of human existence was not deep, many punk fans
felt as though the album was self-descriptive and disappointing. They had
built us up to be the beacon of guidance and moral compass of the genre.
But with me going through divorce, and without a collaborative producer
or fellow songwriter with whom to work, we struggled to meet their demands. It was an easy record to digest, as the stadium audiences in Europe
testified. But the club-goers in America, so disgruntled at the spectacle of
punk bands they used to love moving to larger and larger stages, wished
that we could reground the genre in the soil of their social discontents.

Yet new fans emerged, many of whom got their start on the pop-punk sounds they heard from their older siblings' music collections or on the car radio cranking out Green Day and the Offspring. Punk had been streaming down these avenues into suburban homes for a few years by this time. While Bad Religion was still being played on the radio, especially KROQ in Southern California, we had failed to keep pace with "hit songs" from other bands. Both of our albums after 1994's *Stranger than Fiction* produced fewer "radio-friendly songs" while other punk bands continued to flood the airwaves with new radio hits. If not for our touring success, and our supportive fans, we might have considered throwing in the towel during this downward trajectory. The writing was on the wall: with so many new faces coming into punk, was there room for an old band with a singer that looked more like a college TA than a stylized punk hero?

We finished *No Substance* in Los Angeles, at the studio of mixing engineer Chris Lord-Alge. Chris had just completed Green Day's huge radio hit "Good Riddance (Time of Your Life)," and he played it for us. This was before it had been released or on the radio, so I was a bit skeptical. Not of Chris's mixing abilities, it sounded incredibly good. But rather that an acoustic version of a song from a punk band would be considered hit worthy. Brett and I had been writing punk songs on our acoustic guitars for years, but we only recorded them as demos and we didn't have the gumption to consider releasing them. Nonetheless, I was pleased with the idea of acoustic songs, stripped-down melodies, and singer-songwriter-style delivery being highlighted. After all, Billy Bragg had been doing this routine for years. Chris's work on *No Substance* was stellar. The song "Shades of Truth" is a mixing marvel but, unfortunately, hits left of the bullseye on lyrical effect. Radio was not interested. Except for the modest success in Europe with the song "Raise Your Voice" (the duet with Campino), the album was invisible to the mainstream. Its few highlights included "Hear It" and "Sowing the Seeds of Utopia," which became fan favorites and nightly fixtures in our live sets.

Returning to upstate New York from the mixing sessions, I came back to a large empty house. The kids' rooms were still as messy as when I'd left for California two weeks prior. There were, however, no kids to be seen. They were at their mom's house, two miles away, settling in to new routines, under new rules from a soon-to-be stepfather, no longer under my guidance. The thought that another man might have more influence over your children than you have is maddening: that your own influence over your children might have nothing to do with how they turn out. Logic saved me. I had to accept that married or not, there would always be outside influences on your kids. They will have friends, acquaintances, and heroes, many of whom will be completely hidden from you, their father. Since you can't preside over their entire lives, nor predict their outcomes, it becomes imperative to live your own life, to be true to your own "calling." These were the same logical shreds of wisdom that drew me into punk as a teenager and now they served as a rejuvenating logic that would lift me out of my funk and sustain my motivation for bigger and better things.

Now, with the house empty, I started to jot down some of my most emotional outpourings, and I wrote songs that I never thought would see the light of day. Our new A&R guy from Atlantic, John, was interested in some of the solo work I had been writing. I told him that the songs came from the depths of my despair, and it sounded more like Todd Rundgren than Bad Religion, and that it probably should be kept private. Nonetheless, I shared some of the songs, and John thought that it would make for an interesting solo project.

For weeks I worked in my home studio and piano room, writing and recording. I set up drums that Bobby had left at my house after using them on the *No Substance* recording sessions. I decided to create a project *à la Todd Rundgren*, by playing all the instruments myself, singing all the background voices, and mixing and producing it alone (this is, after all, the familiar process I used for all my Bad Religion demos). Ronnie was there to help me with some of the audio engineering. The result was a solo album, released a day after my birthday in 1997, called *American Lesion*. Filled with songs of sorrow and somber hopefulness, loneliness, and despair, it is an autobiographical footprint of my life in the year that my family changed forever. *American Lesion* was a satisfying summary, a tale of the life I had lived, or wanted to live, up to that point in time. Devoid of academic rigor, punk angst, and combative politics, it had a small audience. But it had wide potential appeal due to its subject matter: the emotional landscape shared by all human beings.

Even though it represents the bottom of my personal life, it was the beginning of a rebuilding. The huge edifice of family, academia, and band had crumbled at the base, but it had not completely toppled. The countless cracks in the masonry had to be repaired. I felt that as long as I could write and sing music, and as long as there was an audience to hear it, then I was up to the task.

28

REBUILDING

28A. THE NEW AMERICA

One afternoon, in February 1998, I was taking a drive up to a furniture store in Syracuse to purchase a new Stickley bookshelf for my growing library. I turned on the radio to check in with the "latest sounds" on Syracuse's own modern rock station. I heard what seemed to be a new NOFX song. "Wow!" I thought to myself, "Finally NOFX is on commercial radio." I thought this was good that the edgier element of punk was being popularized, since most of the punk on the radio was the softer, more emotional kind. Fat Mike's voice sounded a bit smoother and had matured a bit, but I thought to myself, "Maybe that's just the effect of FM radio on his voice. It sounds great!" The song had familiar SoCal elements to it, not unlike our own "American Jesus." A single-note guitar line was the hook in the intros and between the verses. But the subject matter, something about "growing up," seemed thematically unusual for them. "I guess that's what Mike had to do to get played on the radio," I said to myself, assuming that NOFX had chosen a sappy sentimental subject (breaking up with a girlfriend) in order to reach a wider audience.

I listened to the entire song, giving it the once-over, and found that it had no melody, but like so many NOFX songs, a memorable guitar riff and refrain: "I guess this is growing up." Then the DJ came on and said, "Hey, that was Blink-182 with 'Dammit.'" Huh? "So that's how this thing is going now?" I thought to myself. "Knockoffs of NOFX are getting the national spotlight now?" And that's just the way it was! I wasn't upset or disturbed, I found it astonishing. It was telling that the new audience was so much younger than me that they didn't care about musical origins—they just loved it. And that was a hopeful, rejuvenating sign that our music still was significant.

Blink-182 came to embrace their own unique sound and charted their own path in music eventually. But at the time, 1998, they reached heights with their song that must have surprised even them. "Dammit" was a top-five hit on stations all across the country. This meant something important to me. A band we influenced deeply (NOFX) formed a sound template, mimicked by another band (Blink-182), that was now appropriate for massive airplay all over the country! It turned out, as more light was shed on Blink-182, that they themselves cited Bad Religion as heavily influential and important. And one day, in the near future, they would prove it.

Punk's infusion into every suburban enclave across America was apparent anywhere you looked. The malls had record stores that showcased punk albums in huge window displays. The national chain retailer Hot Topic sold T-shirts with punk band logos, jewelry, and accessories such as chain wallets and spiked wrist cuffs to round out any suburban kid's weekend wardrobe. I went on record claiming that punk had become democratized. Around this time I began writing new songs for what I saw as a new American landscape.

The kids shopping at my local Hot Topic in upstate New York struck me as ironic, purchasing clothing and accessories with their parents' credit cards, depicting a curious longing for something grittier than their coddled suburban existence provided. I wasn't critical of them. I, too, grew up in suburbs. I understood that longing. Still, they made for interesting subject matter and it dawned on me that these kids romanticized, and probably sympathized with, punks on the street living in the concrete jungles of the big cities.

I wrote a song called "A Streetkid Named Desire" that came from these observations, and that song formed the beginning of a project that would result in the album *The New America*. Even though our newest release *No Substance* hadn't even hit the stores yet (it came out in May 1998), I was already writing new material for what would be our final album on Atlantic Records and Sony Music.

Meanwhile, there were new touring opportunities on the horizon. Our friend named Kevin, who we knew as a stage manager at Fender's Ballroom—that bastion of chaos, slam-dancing, fighting, and anger during the dark days of punk back in the mid-1980s—began experimenting with different kinds of concert promotions. In 1995 he devised a traveling punk rock festival that showcased bands on multiple stages simultaneously throughout the day. It began as an experiment of sorts, a concert called Board in the South Bay, with the best punk bands of Southern California taking the stage alongside professional skateboarders competing on ramps alongside the musical performances. Held at California State University in Dominguez Hills in 1995, it featured Bad Religion as headliner along with professional skateboarders and a slew of other bands. One of the sponsors of the show was Goldenvoice, our old friends who were fast becoming the most successful promoters in the nation. But another sponsor was simply called Warp, publishers of a fanzine that covered "skate, snow, surf, sound, and sass," all hallmarks of the budding "extreme" sports scene of Southern California. The success of the all-day-long outdoor event was astronomical, with more than ten thousand people in attendance.

We didn't know it at the time, but percolating inside of Kevin's head was the idea to take a Warped Tour festival across the country and make it every American punk kid's summer highlight. And that's just what happened. The tour was a series of all-day events full of music and skateboarding. As many as thirty or forty bands traveled together on tour buses that pulled into huge parking lots every day, usually at an unused stadium or arena.

The tour hit every major metropolitan area in the country. Travel was so extensive—a different city every day—that there was little downtime. Load in and set up every morning began at sunrise. Tear down and load out each evening occurred at sunset. Then it was on to the next city, often requiring six hours or more of overnight driving.

We had heard from others in our circles that the tour was going forward and growing in size over the summers of 1996 and 1997. Still, we weren't really interested in playing because the Warped Tour overlapped with some of the most important festivals in Europe, and these were our focus at the time. But in 1998, Kevin posed a question to his partner Darryl, an agent at CAA (Creative Artists Agency): "Can you think of a way to expand the Warped Tour into Europe?" Darryl knew immediately after hearing Kevin's idea that there was only one punk band with enough stature on both sides of the Atlantic to fit the bill: Bad Religion.

Our standing in Europe had grown significantly thanks in part to our association with Die Toten Hosen. But our pal Jens was equally indispensable. He could negotiate with the top German promoters and advocate for us in his native tongue. Jens, Kevin, and Darryl all helped to put together a tour proposal for Bad Religion to headline the Warped Tour in Europe as well as in the USA. This would preclude us from playing some of the European festivals that year, but the proposed tour would put us in front of a lot more American punk fans—at outdoor festival grounds instead of in theaters and nightclubs.

The only way we could receive a formal offer was through an agent. Our agent for the USA at the time was more of an assigned "middleman" who received offers for Bad Religion, a guy named John Branigan at the William Morris Agency. John was cool, but coming from an old-school rock background, not really our peer. Desiring a more collegial relationship, we asked Darryl if he might be able to add us to his CAA roster. Darryl understood the band, its origins, and our individual quirks. He also had a good notion of where we could be headed. He agreed to act as our agent.

We promptly accepted the offer from the Warped Tour. Simultaneously, we parted ways with our London-based agency in Europe. We weren't as popular in England as we were on the European continent, and the Anglocentric chauvinism of British agent culture was not conducive to Bad Religion's global focus. We decided to go where we were loved the most, Germany. Jens had an office in Hannover. From that point on, Bad Religion's European touring headquarters would be in Germany, and our most important business activities there would be conducted in *Muttersprache* (mother tongue).

We were headed out on a world tour but one hitched to a wagon-train festival along with thirty other bands, most of them getting national exposure for the first time. Kevin's attitude was that every band should be treated equally. This is a nice and proper punk attitude to adopt. But for a band like ours that was used to certain creature comforts, having completed numerous world tours in established venues, it was a bit of a step backward. We knew it was going to be rough when the only beverage on tap in the artist area was a communal eighty-gallon drum of Kool-Aid being prepared by stage hands using their naked arms as mixing stirs. Needless to say, it was a "fend for yourself" affair when it came to nutrition in the early days of the Warped Tour.

We brought along our own barbecue grill, and each day we had our own roadies go to the nearest grocery store to buy more than enough food to feed our band, crew, and any fans who might wander by. Our pal (and future tour manager) Rick cooked the food and ran the hospitality tent that welcomed all visitors with a huge crossbuster logo.

Nightly barbecues were community affairs. A feeling of comradery and new collegiality was emerging at these gatherings. A new archetypal character was emerging right before our eyes: Southern California's new breed of ruffian—the extreme sports personality who somehow avoided jail time in the '80s only to find that his sport of choice (skating, surfing, BMX bike riding, or motocross) was now a multimillion-dollar industry. The cookouts were always characterized by colorful guys and gals who drank too much, and the constant availability of recreational drugs. It was a nomadic music subculture reminiscent of the 1960s only now updated with elaborate tattoos, faster music, and different narcotics.

Few and far between were the sensitive musicians, the closeted intellectuals, the readers and thinkers. These enlightened types, like the drug-addled partyers, can be insufferable too, but their scarcity was definitely noticeable. So, without much interest in the social milieu, and in order to preserve my singing voice, I decided to leave the festival site as often as possible. I began driving myself and staying in motels. Long hours of driving served me well. The meditative hum of the wheels and engine, often in complete radio silence, was a perfect accompaniment to deep thoughts.

The European leg of the tour had more structure, better facilities, and better production than the American leg. The Warped Tour's business model would have to be tweaked significantly, especially because Die Toten Hosen was chosen as the headliner in Germany and their fans were used to seeing them in stadiums. All the bands benefited from playing on the stage with Die Toten Hosen. None more so than us. We sang "Raise Your Voice" with Campino, and many of their fifty thousand fans sang along with us. Playing huge stadiums, night after night, was a stretch for the Warped Tour. For one thing, these were nocturnal affairs in Europe, but the Warped Tour's American tradition was daylight shows. Skating and surfing, snowboarding and BMX riding were daylight activities, after all, and the bands were merely the soundtrack. Excellent European catering, VIP accommodations backstage, and overall inflated production budgets meant that the Warped Tour was far less profitable in Europe than in the USA. After only two years, Kevin and his partners decided that the Warped Tour would avoid Europe from that point on.

The most curious thing began to dawn on me during this tour. Even though our latest album, No Substance, was seen as a commercial step in the wrong direction, having no songs that were considered radio "hits," and selling fewer copies than our previous album, this didn't translate into reduced enthusiasm or smaller turnouts at the concerts. In fact, our touring business had never been stronger. We were being swept up in the wave of popularity that bands like Green Day and the Offspring—and now Blink-182—created with their hit songs on commercial radio. Even though many of the new punk fans had never heard our songs, word of mouth spread far and wide. Most punk rockers had at least heard of us.

Our own "hit songs" came from earlier in the decade, but they were well known by enough punk fans to fuel a feeling that they were witnessing something authentic: perhaps the seeds of inspiration that ignited their own favorite bands. In this respect, I recognized that the band had a life of its own. We already had what can best be described as a "legacy." It didn't really matter that our latest album was not as commercially successful as our last one. So long as the audience showed this much enthusiasm, the promoters would continue to view us as an important addition to any punk festival. Furthermore, thanks to the newer bands and their widespread commercial appeal, there would always be a guaranteed punk audience ready to take notice whenever Bad Religion toured or promoted a new record. The legacy became more important to me as opposed to worrying about whether I was "punk" enough to relate to these new audiences.

A legacy in music depends on its dissemination, not just its style but its substance as well. The ideas in punk music are as important as its sound. At this point, the ideas were a bit lacking in punk, but the sound was spreading fast. I figured that if someone wanted to put punk on the radio, that would be an incredible boost to the popularity of the idiom, as an art form or even as a cultural hallmark. Although the style and substance of punk might ebb and flow, becoming popular is not a death knell, but rather a challenge and an opportunity for a songwriter. The challenge comes in trying to identify what makes a song punk—or a person a punk, for that matter. But the opportunity is that more human beings might be receptive to the good things in the music. Breaking down social stigmas and opening the way for newer bands just nourishes the richness of the genre.

Still, there was the question of whether Bad Religion had the same ingredients for greatness that we had a decade prior when we released *Suffer*. After all, I didn't want to become a "heritage" act, just playing songs off our early records to make people sentimental for the good old days. Operating on a "need to know" basis, I assumed that our A&R department at Atlantic

Records and Sony Music were still eager for new material. On this assump-
tion, I continued to write songs for yet another major label release.

Skeptical as I was, I asked our lawyer, Eric, if there was any reason to
assume that our recording fund might be reduced since the last record
"performed" so badly on the charts. He replied that "they are more eager
than ever for a new album. The fund is higher than ever before." In fact,
because of the way Eric structured our major label deal, like many sports
contracts where a team has to decide if they want to trade a veteran quarterback or keep him at a higher salary, Atlantic was faced with the option
of either dropping us from their label or paying the highest advance we
ever received for the next record. Because they couldn't fathom the bad
press that might come from dropping Bad Religion at a time when punk
was among the most commercially successful music on the radio, they
opted to pay us. We had virtually unlimited funds to record the next album, *The New America*.

Having already written a slew of new songs for the band, I reached out
to Brett, who had been completely out of touch with me for a few years. As
luck would have it, he had some business meetings in New York City and
agreed to meet up with me at his hotel. I drove down from Ithaca, and when
we got together it was like old times. That's the thing with old friends: if
your relationship is strong there's no skip in the beat between meetings,
no matter the elapsed time separating them. We joked as usual and didn't
discuss business, except for the business of songwriting. Brett said he had
been working on some cool riffs and had a cassette with him, but he was
in no way interested in rejoining the band or touring. He wasn't even very
confident about his songwriting abilities since he had been out of practice
for many years.

His hotel room had a stereo and a cassette player so he popped in the
tape and mouthed along some placeholder ideas for lead vocals, and I dug
what I was hearing. The song was decent, but mostly I just enjoyed the collaboration and the restoration of a line of communication with my old pal.
We agreed to develop the song further, and the meeting adjourned with
hugs and "see ya's."

There was another reason for me to be in the Big Apple. Michele had left her job at RCA and was interested in management again. She was set to open an office on 21st Street and asked me to come check it out. It was a great opportunity for me to share the exciting news about writing with Brett, but also I was getting ahead of myself in thinking that she might want to work with Bad Religion again. There were some nitty-gritty details that needed sorting out.

For starters, the guys didn't really think we needed a manager. We had hired Elliot on Ric Ocasek's recommendation, but he didn't fit the bill in terms of the DIY democracy that we had sort of become. Elliot really favored me as the creative element of the band, and he was one of the biggest advocates of getting Brett to write with me again. But I was always putting things up for a vote, when in reality bands operate best as a friendly dictatorship. Elliot said, "Greg, YOU are the leader of this band. But right now, you're being a bad leader." The guys chuckled at that because they not only agreed with his second statement, they also questioned his first. I took it in stride and decided to learn from the master whatever I could, but left it up to the guys to decide if he really was best for the band.

Elliot had so many connections and knew so many people, but most of them were not able to bring Bad Religion any kind of success that we hadn't already achieved on our own. For instance, Elliot was friends with Lorne Michaels. Originally we thought, "Great! Elliot calls Lorne, and BOOM! we're the musical guest on *Saturday Night Live*." But that never materialized. Lorne Michaels had better things to worry about besides a punk band with a controversial logo that might offend all the late-night sponsors and break the FCC rules with their equally offensive lyrics. In all the decades of the show, only a small handful of punk rockers had made the cut, and only one from the SoCal scene, and that was Fear, the hand-selected choice of John Belushi almost two decades prior.

Elliot knew how to build reputations. It was his forte. But Bad Religion's reputation had already been built. I asked Danny Goldberg, who had signed us to Atlantic when he served as president there, what he thought about having Elliot as a manager. He said, "Elliot is smart, and he is a very important person in the music industry." But even Danny Goldberg couldn't really see how Elliot could bring us more status than we had already achieved. Although I wanted to work with him, and I relished his wisdom, I had to concur with the other guys that there wasn't much that he could do for us. In place of Elliot, we went back to a more DIY management style with Michele handling our day-to-day administration.

Michele's first task was a crazy one. I confided in Michele that I needed a collaborator-producer for our next album. "Can you get in touch with Todd Rundgren?" I asked her, half joking. She went to work immediately.

Michele knew all the people at Atlantic Records, and she sat in on countless marketing meetings and strategy sessions regarding Bad Religion over the years. When she told the A&R people about my idea to have Todd produce the record, they thought, why not? He was a big name, and Bad Religion could benefit from such an association. They liked the effect that Ric Ocasek had on us, so it was worth a shot. In reality, Ric had had a number of big hit records with bands such as Weezer, and Todd was considered a studio wizard but not very commercially successful as of late.

I didn't care about any of that stuff. I trusted Todd, even though I had never met him. I didn't listen to any of the rumors about how difficult he was to work with, nor any of those things that creative people get accused of by less creative types all the time. I was just motivated to write good songs, and I thought that maybe the guy whose music inspired me all my life could help me produce them.

At this point, less than six months after my marriage dissolved, with the house emptied of family members for much of the week, and band business showing little sign of slowing down, my mom, ever the wise administrator, was nearing her retirement. She had been working almost two decades as a human resources director at a large firm called Unisys, in the Washington, DC, area. Close enough for visits on long weekends and holidays, me and the kids made frequent car journeys to see her, and she spent plenty of time coming up to Ithaca to see the grandkids whenever her busy schedule would permit it. On one of these visits, she advised me, in her ever-casual way, while discussing the everyday dirt, disguising strong advice—as she was so good at—in the form of wise, caring opinion, by saying, "Honey, you're going to need to get a personal assistant." Before this I had never dreamed of such a thing, but as usual, she was very astute. She could see, as she had been a witness all along, from the first rehearsal in her garage to our latest dramas with Brett leaving, sporadic management, and being passed over on the latest radio hit parade—she kept tabs on all of it—that the band was in need of better administration. She also knew intuitively that I was not the sort of soul who was up for the administrative tasks. I was a creative type whose productivity supported a boatload of other people. She understood better than I did that if I was stifled by the day-to-day administrative tasks, the creative enterprise might fail. Since she ranked as possibly the biggest fan of Bad Religion in the world, she did not want that to happen. But closer to home, she also knew that I was happiest when someone else was tending to the desk details so that I could feel free to pursue creativity.

I wasted no time in taking out classified ads in all the weekly newspapers in Ithaca, Elmira, Syracuse, and Rochester. The homemade ad read something like this in the Jobs for Hire section: "Wanted: personal assistant for music industry person. Must have typing skills and excellent organizational abilities." I didn't really expect to get many responses because, after all, this wasn't Hollywood, where there was an entire guild of people looking for personal assistant jobs to work for celebrities.

I was surprised to receive over fifty calls that week, and an equal number of emails, all seemingly enthusiastic about being a personal assistant, without even knowing who I was. I had former event planners, former graduate students, former grocery workers, a real estate agent, and a car salesperson, among the many people who responded to the ad. I only met with two or three of them in person, but the one who stood out the most seemed most qualified from the start. Her name was Treva, and she had no idea who I was or what band I played in. That was just fine with me. Treva had been a children's special needs coach for the last five years after she graduated from college. I thought, "Hmm. Virtually all of the people around me in the band and music industry could be qualified as children with special needs; she might be perfect!" Indeed she was. Smart, diligent, and witty, Treva fit right in among the cadre of people who made Bad Religion their daily business. I hired her after our first meeting, and she showed up promptly at my doorstep the next morning at 9 a.m.

There's no real job description manual for personal assistant, so we had to wing it. In general, it was going to be a learn-as-you-go adventure, and it didn't come with any guarantees. She seemed up for it, so we agreed on a pay scale and she began her daily work in my home office by answering phones, organizing my calendar, distracting the kids when they were there, and doing any household chores that were necessary. Since nothing went forward in Bad Religion without me, Treva was on the phone every day with Michele in New York City.

Without a songwriting partner, and with the expectation that the next album would have the highest recording budget we'd ever received, I took it upon myself to work extra hard at songwriting. With Treva as an assistant, and Michele handling the management, I didn't have to worry about band business or my calendar or domestic chores. It seemed that I was spending more and more time in the studio writing and experimenting with elaborate song ideas. The writing and demo process for what would become *The New America* was a solitary act. Nonetheless, it was time to meet the producer.

Michele and Treva had been in touch with Todd, but I still had never spoken to him. We had label support, because John, our A&R man at Atlantic, gave the go-ahead to approve Todd's exorbitant producer fee. Todd cost a lot of money, but we could afford it with the huge advance we were to receive. Treva informed me that I could hand deliver my latest round of demos to Todd himself because he was playing a concert in Cleveland in a few days. I rode my BMW motorcycle to Cleveland, where I met John on the night of the concert.

The concert was well attended but not packed. It was similar to so many other shows I've seen where legendary performers play various selections from their huge song catalog without much marketing or promotion surrounding their tours. The true fans, of which there are many, come out of the woodwork to see it, but the concerts have a subdued, casual vibe to them, like checking in with an old friend.

After the show we went backstage and found Todd and his band all hanging out. It was June of 1999, and in only three months we were slated to be in the studio at his compound in Hawaii working together. I delivered the latest round of demos to him, and he said, "I will give these a listen and call you in a couple weeks." At that, I made my exit. It was a blast to meet Todd, but now I had to steel myself for criticism because I knew that my demos left a lot to be desired. The next time I heard from Todd it would be as my producer, so I couldn't feel too attached to anything I had written.

Todd called me a few weeks later and said the demos all sounded cool, but we might have to refine some of the lyrics a bit. He mentioned that it sounded like Bad Religion was moving into our "rubber soul" period. I had no idea what he meant by this, so I asked him to elaborate. "Well," he said, "*Rubber Soul* was the album when people began to see the Beatles as serious songwriters. These are serious songs you've given me, so they need to be refined a bit and then the songwriting quality will shine through." I wasn't sure that Todd was aware of how many good songs Brett and I had written over the years. But none of that mattered. He didn't have to know our history in order to produce this album. Punk was evolving. The original genre had dissipated. The styles were all over the place. But the one thing that I could do in the absence of Brett was write good songs, and I felt confident that Todd understood how to help me achieve that goal.

We announced after the Warped world tour ended that we would take our time to prepare the next album.

Summer had passed. The kids were headed back to school. The north wind coming down off of the Canadian Shield and over the Great Lakes told us that soon the leaves would be turning blaze orange and blood red for their annual autumnal chromatic transformation. But instead of sticking around to see it, I was off to Hawaii where I'd meet the guys for our recording sessions with Todd. Treva had arranged for me to rent a house for six weeks in the little village of Hanalei, on the island of Kauai, only steps from the beach and close to Todd's house. It was large enough, with a nice kitchen and two bedrooms. Treva traveled with the kids and they all spent some time with me, riding boogie boards and sightseeing. Michele came and made it an official business trip, so she and Treva could chat about the next year's touring schedule with Jens, who also made the trek. Even my mom came out to the island to spend some time with the grandkids. I was happy to have everyone there because they could entertain each other and leave me to work with Todd.

I wouldn't say that we had the most rigorous working schedule, but it was consistent. Todd set the tone early on. "Let's get started around eleven or noon or so," he would say. By five or six o'clock, our day of "work" was over and we'd hit the beach or go get fresh fish at the nearby market. Todd didn't actually have a studio per se. He was an early adopter of making records on computer, and he had a Mac G3 desktop computer combined with Pro Tools software that could be set up anywhere as a studio workstation. He decided that we should record the drums and bass in a "live room," and we would overdub the guitars later. To accomplish this, he rented an old barn from one of his friends down the road from Hanalei. The barn was constructed of beautiful tropical wood and had a damp, earthy feel to it. Bobby set up his drums in a little corner that seemed like it once served as a feeding stall for an animal, but it was surrounded by carved totems with some kind of aboriginal designs. Todd mic'ed the drums himself, did all the engineering, using basic tools and rock 'n' roll know-how. The technical specs were simple: Shure SM57s for the drums and guitars, and a Telefunken (Neumann) U87 for the vocals. This probably doesn't mean much to most readers, but it means a lot to anyone who has listened to Todd's productions. These are the microphones responsible for his most successful work, some of which are the largest-selling rock albums of all time. Patti Smith's *Wave*, Grand Funk Railroad's *We're an American Band* and *Shinin' On*, Badfinger's *Straight Up* or Meat Loaf's *Bat Out of Hell*, the Band's *Stage Fright* or XTC's *Skylarking*. In addition to all the Utopia and Todd Rundgren albums that he engineered and produced, these works all have a signature sound. Much of that comes from Todd's preferences for "57s and 87s," which produce clear voices and unbiased instrumental accompaniment. Todd's recording style captures a band's rock-worthy prowess without a lot of makeup, studio relish, or signal processing. Even though his work ethic was very leisurely and his studio homemade, he masterfully captured Bad Religion for our first-ever fully digital recording, which proved itself to be a great sounding piece of work.

The band members thought Todd himself was "a piece of work." Jay and Brian particularly didn't like his casual attitude toward them (they were used to getting more respect from producers, not realizing that Todd was neither keen to, nor cared little about, their status in the punk scene, nor mine for that matter). One day, they complained to me that Todd would routinely ride his bike to the grocery store to buy beer, and drink two six-packs a day. Although I doubted its validity, I couldn't understand how to read this criticism. The guys in my band had a love affair with all kinds of substances, including alcohol, but for some reason they expected a higher standard from their producer.

I was less judgmental. I worked closely with Todd, and all I cared about was his attention to the details of our recording sessions. As with my own bandmates, I employed a consistent work ethic: so long as anyone involved in the creative endeavor continued to add valuable ideas, skills, and techniques to the project, I could overlook their drug or alcohol consumption. But if they became impaired and it depleted or hampered the outcome of our mutual endeavor, then we had a problem. It never came to that, or anything close to it, during the weeks we spent in Hawaii. All in all, with the family visits, the lax workdays, the creative conversations with Todd, and the tropical paradise location as a constant backdrop, I saw the experience as a great one.

Fun or not, the label was not happy with the digital files that Todd sent them. They immediately called me when I got back to Ithaca and asked me to come down to the city to discuss some options. They played me Todd's mixes and they weren't very good. Todd wasn't used to mixing this kind of fast-paced hyperdriven rock music and it showed. There is a skill to mixing punk music that differs from the techniques of mixing slower, more dynamic rock 'n' roll. While it's true that Todd produced and mixed one of the first punk records ever made, the self-titled debut of the New York Dolls, punk had come a long way since its release in 1973. The tempos now were much faster and, in Bad Religion, the lyrical attack is tightly syncopated with the snare drum instead of lilting around the accompaniment as is heard on early punk records. Our decision was to have another person mix the album.

In keeping with "big names" as collaborators, the A&R department approved the selection of Bob Clearmountain as mixer. Bob's legendary reputation stems from his work recording Bruce Springsteen and, before that, with Nile Rodgers engineering for the band Chic. Bob had a studio at his house on the Westside of Los Angeles, and we spent a week together doing some overdubs with Brian on guitar, some vocal patches, and some sound effects sprinkled in on a couple songs. Bob wasn't a punk mixer either, but he saw the project as a unique challenge and he ended up doing a great job on the album.

In an interesting way, *The New America* can be seen as a kind of benchmark, or bellwether, not only for our own chronology but for understanding the historical trajectory of the genre at large. While I might argue that the use of a renowned producer and mixer who refined their crafts on classic albums from the 1970s was a creative move, there are critics who might see it as an example of how far astray from its original DIY ethic punk had become by May 2000 (the month that *The New America* was released). With bloated budgets from major labels, commercial marketing, and corporate teams of personnel overseeing each punk album, the music was bound to suffer, or so the critics might contend. The critics were disgusted with the commercialization of the genre. The "punk police," those stalwarts of the "scene" who thought they represented the central core of true believers, held tightly to the tenet that punk loses its power if too many people find it appealing. They were still reeling from the incredible popularity of punk. Just as we did with *Into the Unknown* back in 1983 when we released an album that pissed off the punk rock fan base, we were poised to do it again in 2000 with *The New America*. But now we had coconspirators: the multiplatinum-selling bands like Green Day, the Offspring, and that year, Blink-182, all of which were way more popular and commercial than we were.

Being somewhere under the radar, many older punk fans expected us to recenter the genre and recapture its essence like we did with *Suffer* in 1987. But this album wasn't going to fit that bill. Instead, *The New America* was an ironic commentary on the current punk genre itself. We were heartened by the legions of new punk rockers who kept showing up at our concerts. They were attracted to our reputation, which was starting to be seen as legendary by the newer bands that cited us as their influence.

No band was bigger at the time than Blink-182. Their album *Enema of the State* came out in 1999 and contained three radio hits that resonated with the youthful suburban punk fans, skateboarders, and concertgoers who took their style cues from MTV and Hot Topic. By the spring of 2000, they were poised to embark on one of the highest grossing concert tours of the year. Blink-182's audience loved music but by and large did not care for the messy, grungy accoutrements of the punk lifestyle. In other words, they liked a slick, clean, glossy version of guitar-driven, fast rock 'n' roll, and Blink-182, with their catchy songs, well-produced albums, and shimmering stage productions, delivered the goods in spades. They ushered in a huge wave of fans and introduced them to the friendliest kind of punk imaginable, which was comedic, jovial, upbeat, and energized by the now-timeless sound of galloping SoCal drum beats behind snarly vocals with catchy melodies. Most of this wave of newcomers to the genre were totally unaware of any Bad Religion songs. Now three album cycles removed from any airplay on MTV or commercial radio, we were in danger of falling to that ever lurking status in the music biz, insignificance.

28B. BLINK

It's always such a fine line between extinction and population explosion. One disruption in an ecosystem can cause irreversible decline in a species, while one keystone species, if healthy and thriving, can sustain an entire ecosystem. There were some ingredients missing in the ecology of Bad Religion's at this time. Bringing back Brett for one song on *The New America* started to restore that shortcoming. But also, our original fans were aging out of the punk scene. Many of them were busy with nine-to-five jobs, raising families, and quite simply not interested in going to concerts anymore. Without MTV playing our videos, without commercial radio, and with the local punk scenes morphing into more commercialized, mall-centric, and regional megagatherings—concert halls and amphitheaters now took the place of the local punk venue—Bad Religion was lagging behind the other bands who were capitalizing on these newer ecosystems of fans. There was no way to reach them without a hit song on the radio or a clever MTV video, and there was no way to recapture the original fan base who had retreated to their domestic affairs and middle-aged lifestyles. It felt like we were in some kind of time warp, and Jay and I had numerous discussions about the future of the band because, at that time, we were not sure what to do about the situation that we were in.

We were admired by many bands. Our fellow noncommercial punk bands such as NOFX and Pennywise cited us as influential, and they were busy at this time reestablishing the hardcore punk fan base. Meanwhile, commercial bands like the Offspring and Green Day also had acknowledged their debt to Bad Religion as they continued to ride the wave of popularity that they ushered in a half decade prior. The new face of pop punk was Blink-182, and they did their best to make every new punk fan aware of Bad Religion. Furthermore, Rage Against the Machine knew that Bad Religion played an important role in the modern landscape of music, and their members, Zack, Tom, and Brad, all were self-acknowledged fans of ours. And their legion of followers took notice. So there we were, with all these new bases of fans that had heard our name, maybe even thought that we might be noteworthy, yet we had no way to reach them with our new album because commercial radio and MTV had, by that time, turned away from Bad Religion. Luckily, an opportunity came along at just the right moment. Blink-182 invited us to be the "special guests" on their 2000 North American tour. Adding to the good fortune, it was slated to begin right around the time that *The New America* was hitting the shelves in stores, so the marketing department at Atlantic was thrilled.

It was the dawn of a new era, but the end of one too. Just after the tour commenced, Michele informed us that she was moving on from managing the band and moving back to LA to work with Rage Against the Machine at GAS Entertainment. Although we were sad to see her go, we were swept up in the massive blitz of publicity and rigorous travel schedule of the tour. We were essentially on autopilot, so her absence didn't feel so acute as it would have during off-tour periods when little else was going on.

The new era was a bit more cryptic, but definitely coming into view. The Blink-182 tour brought us face-to-face with the mainstream youth of America. We were hoping that they'd contain some musically curious, discerning, music fans too, but in general we could say that the tour attracted everyone who was sympathetic to punk rock across the entire suburban landscape of North America. If this was, in fact, punk, it sure had morphed into a friendly, unchallenging style of music. Many of Blink's songs, even though they were well-crafted tunes, were about superficial topics such as breaking up with or meeting girls and being in relationships. Even though they busted out a big hit song about a teenage suicide, which was a heavy topic, most of their set was jovial and lighthearted. And their banter on stage was self-acknowledged juvenility. Maybe this new crop of punk fans weren't interested in songs with deeper meaning. Would this group recognize our sound as authentic and take our approach to the genre seriously?

Even though the audiences were less-than-enthused when we took the stage—many fans couldn't care less about the "opening" bands—we nonetheless put on our usual impressive stage show. With our legendary soundman Ronnie at the helm of our live performance, no fan of music could watch with dispassionate nonchalance. We sounded incredible in those amphitheaters and big stages, and we made a lasting impression on many of the Blink-182 fans. This was only confirmed in later years, as countless people have come up to us and said: "I first saw you with Blink back in Y2K!" Hence, we were paving the way for our next step, even though we didn't know it at the time, and we didn't even know what the next step would be.

When the tour for *The New America* ended, we were exhausted and unsure of our future. Bobby decided to retire, hanging up his drumsticks at the end of the South American leg, in March of 2001. He must have been planning his retirement for a while, because I could see that his shoulder was bothering him during much of the last few concerts. Indeed he had developed a serious joint injury, only made worse by nightly wear and tear from being on tour. At the end of the last show, which was in Brazil, he simply walked around the backstage dressing room shaking everyone's hands, thanking everyone for his adventures in the band. "Well, Greg," he said, sticking out his right hand, "It's been great, but I'm done. That was my last show." "Huh?" I said, "You mean for this tour, right?" "No," he quickly cut me off. "I'm hanging it up."

In the bustle of backstage aftershow activity I didn't really process what Bobby had told me, but on the way back to the USA, on the flight home, it felt like a great loss. Not only was a great drummer leaving the band, but a fun friend who consistently lightened the room with his clever wit and comedic attitude. His retirement added another question mark to what the future would hold for the band.

We were now out of our contracts with Atlantic Records and Sony Music, essentially "free agents," having delivered the required four albums. But I questioned what kind of album I was capable of writing anymore without Brett involved. I wasn't even sure that I wanted to write any more Bad Religion songs.

Upon arriving back home in early spring of 2001, the future seemed open-ended. No album contracts to fulfill, no world tours planned, I was happy to be back in the domestic fold with the kids, but I was also unsure of what tomorrow might bring. Never one to wallow in uncertainty, I seized upon the moment to challenge myself in the never-ending quest that had been put on the shelf for the last six years: enlightenment.

———

28C. ENLIGHTENMENT

Back in Ithaca, my friend and writer Megan wanted me to meet one of her academic advisers at Cornell named Will Provine. "Do you know him?" she asked. "I know of him, of course—he's famous. But I never met him," I replied. Like many punk fans' relationship with Bad Religion at the time, I had heard OF him, but I didn't know any of his songs. Will was one of those professors who all the students lined up for in order to take his class on evolution. Like his Cornell colleague Carl Sagan, Provine had a captivating style and was able to make difficult topics not only intelligible for introductory students but also fun. Unlike many professors in the natural sciences who project a "do-not-challenge-me-child-or-I-will-crush-you" persona, Will had a welcoming, warm, respectful style and always wanted to hear what students had on their mind.

This style, in addition to his encyclopedic knowledge on history of science and evolution, made him a favorite speaker at conferences and a cherished opponent in debates, even in situations where he knew his audience would not embrace his position on the topic at hand. Provine was one of the only evolutionists in the country who was embraced and even championed by the evangelicals because of his willingness to appear at religious conferences and public debates. Without belittling his opponents, he respectfully and mercilessly argued the incompatible facts of evolution. Never to back down from his famous quote, "Evangelicals make a lot of sense, so long as you check your brain at the church-house door," Will nonetheless agreed with his opponents on one crucial point: if you study evolution, the logic inevitably leads to atheism. There is no intellectually honest middle ground, according to Will Provine. This is why the evangelicals loved him. He was the one scientist in the country who could publicly admit that science, particularly evolution, is fundamentally incompatible with conventional religion. All the other scientists and politicians liked to dance around the difficult question of whether we should teach kids evolution if it leads them to reject all the tenets of Christianity. Ask a hundred teachers of science and they will all give you a wishy-washy answer about the compatibility of religion and science. But ask Will Provine or an evangelical and you will get the same answer: there is NO compatibility between evolution and religion. Religion depends on an intelligent designer and caring deity. Evolution rejects both and ultimately leads to atheism.

Given this reputation, and his important published work on evolution, I was eager to meet Will, who Megan had called and asked to lunch with us one day. Will knew about Bad Religion (mostly because his college-aged sons had listened to our music), and since he was on the faculty of my department, he knew that I was presently "on leave" from my PhD work. At lunch I explained how I had been too busy with touring and family to continue my academic studies. My project was heavily based on fieldwork out West and expensive laboratory analysis on campus. But Will said something that really resonated. "All of my students finish their PhDs without those logistical concerns. Their tools are books, which can be read any time, and the writing can be done anywhere." Then he went on: "I think you could do a wonderful dissertation in the field of evolution and religion. It's now an official topic in the Library of Congress." "Really?" I was intrigued. "I've spent my adult life studying evolution, and I'm in a band called Bad Religion." He replied, "So, it seems you're as well qualified to pursue the issue as any graduate student I could imagine." I thought about it as the lunch chatter continued, and as we were wrapping up the meeting I asked bluntly, "Would you be willing to sponsor me for such a dissertation?" And he said, "Yes, on one condition. You have to dissolve your old advisory committee. I don't want to cause any friction in the department with colleagues. Then you may form a new committee that I will chair, and then we will be on our way." Handshakes with Will, hugs with Megan, our lunch had come to an end. I left feeling rejuvenated.

Having already completed my coursework, teaching, and hours in the laboratory and field, the only thing lacking in my PhD requirement was a dissertation. With Will as my sponsor, and with unlimited access to his world-class evolution library, I was confident that I could come up with an interesting topic to write about. Will was a strong advocate of history. He used history of science, particularly genetics, to illustrate the areas of concern that require more research. He always said the best way to understand a scientific problem is to know the original questions that investigators were trying to solve, and then ask the current crop of investigators to elaborate on their findings. "Interviews and polls of scientists are a lasting testimonial contribution to any field," he told me. This influenced my decision to write a dissertation on the scientific incompatibility of evolution and religion, the two intellectual forces that seemed so provocative to me and about which so many Bad Religion songs had been written.

It wasn't but two weeks later that Jay called me and said that he and Brett talked on the phone, and it seemed like Brett was open to having Bad Religion return to Epitaph. "Hmmm," I thought, "that would only make sense if Brett thought we had another record in us." Soon thereafter, Brett called me, and it was like old times. He just started right in talking about a new song that he had written and how fun it would be to do another album. I could tell that Brett was rejuvenated. Maybe all those years without writing a song had finally welled up inside him and he had a newfound inspiration, just what the doctor ordered for productive songwriting. I, on the other hand, was kind of in the middle of shifting gears. Having just committed to a pile of academic objectives, I hadn't put songwriting on my agenda for the foreseeable future.

Still, the pull of enthusiasm from Brett, coupled with the joy I get when we collaborate on albums together, made my spirits soar. I felt uplifted by the possibilities. Brett said, "I think we could write a new record and put it out on Epitaph. We could produce it just like back before we signed to Atlantic." It all made sense to me, but I expressed a worry because I wasn't sure if Brett knew that Bad Religion was drummerless. "I heard Bobby quit," he said. "But that just means we have to find someone new. Can you come out here for some auditions?" And just like that, the band had a new objective, and the old songwriting team was back together.

Jay, meanwhile, was doing a lot of thinking about our touring. Even with the declining record sales, our fan base, upon whom we could always depend as a foundation for touring, was solid and even showed growth worldwide. With Jens handling our affairs in Europe and Darryl overseeing our touring in the USA and the rest of the world, there was no reason that we needed a manager. Instead, Jay took on a more active approach to our touring affairs and Brett brought with him the managerial functions of an entire record label with offices in Europe and LA. Being the boss at Epitaph meant that any calls for Bad Religion could be routed to Epitaph and handled by their publicity and marketing department. All business for the band therefore was securely and adroitly handled by a team of professionals, many of whom had been working with us for years. Brett and I would continue, like in the old days, to create songs and be responsible for making new albums.

There were still two big questions looming: (1) Could we write a good record? and (2) Could we find a new drummer? We had to address these in reverse order. First off, we wasted no time in finding a replacement for Bobby. We held auditions, and it took only a couple of beats into his repertoire to know that we had found our new drummer. His name was Brooks Wackerman. Brett said, "Brooks is such a great drummer that it means there are no constraints on the kinds of punk beats we can put into our new album." His driving style and perfect meter, coupled with elaborate fills and technically perfect execution, were a vital part of the band's sound upon our return to Epitaph. It's just what we were looking for to make our homecoming seem rejuvenated and fresh. Instead of a sad shadow of our former selves returning from our foray into commercial major-label land, we sounded like a resurrection. As if a lost wise man in the wilderness suddenly came out of the woods with a new technology to share his wisdom. It was the same old Bad Religion, but with Brooks our sound took a step forward.

Brett's return to the band, and the band's return to Epitaph, was a celebration. But more than that, it bolstered an intellectual drive in both of us that helped solidify our legacy as a band that could keep up with the times and still provide the mental grist that defines our legacy.

We laid important groundwork by touring with Blink-182. Having been seen by over a quarter of a million punk fans in amphitheaters that year, we were poised to give the world a new album that they could sink their teeth into. But instead of trying to win over an audience that was clearly interested in a more pedestrian form of punk, we decided to make an album worthy of our nascent form; to inspire and provoke thoughtful listeners, regardless of their backgrounds or biases. Such was the motivation that set me and Brett back on our course as a songwriting team.

For most of 2001, Brett had been writing songs. When I went to visit him, he played me a demo of one his best songs in years. "It's called 'Sorrow,'" he said. "Brett, this is a hit!" I said. Then I shared a demo of one of my songs that was inspired by the research I had been doing for my dissertation project. "Here's one called 'Materialist.'" This song emphasized some of the difficulties in trying to make evolution compatible with religion. One of the lines in the song states: "The process of belief is an elixir when you're weak. I must admit at times I indulge it on the sneak. But generally my outlook's not so bleak. I'm materialist!" Brett said, "That's a cool idea for an album title." After we had concluded the recording sessions later that year we all agreed to call the album *The Process of Belief*.

Released in early 2002, the album *The Process of Belief* was a great success. Two factors helped it achieve its notoriety. First of all, there was a ton of publicity around Brett rejoining the band and us returning to Epitaph Records as a homecoming for the founders of the label. But equally important was that the song "Sorrow" had been picked up by KROQ—still the most important modern-rock radio station in the country—and they played it on heavy rotation for three months before the album's release date. Finally, with this song, Bad Religion had found the listeners that were lacking for the last several years. Now, we were poised to fire on all cylinders. We had the professional representation we needed to succeed in touring, and with Brett's reinvigoration and motivation to make records again, we had his capable label personnel at our disposal to promote them and help us continue the shaping of our legacy.

29
PARADOX AND LEGACY

The band entered a busy but tranquil period of productive equilibrium. It provided me with clarity of mind and a rejuvenated feeling of motivation to complete my doctorate.

It was August of 2003. Jodi, my smart friend from high school (the one who helped me apply for an NEH grant), had gone on to be an entertainment lawyer by that time. She was friends with Wryebo's sister Katy, who, unbeknownst to me, met Jodi shortly after Katy graduated law school at Marquette University in Milwaukee. Katy also went on to become an entertainment lawyer. By 2003, Jodi had developed cancer, and after her chemotherapy she needed somewhere peaceful to recuperate. I welcomed her to come stay with me in Ithaca. It was far from the madding crowd of Manhattan (where she was currently practicing) and I was busy in quiet reflection most of the day as I wrote my dissertation. I made meals, tended the kids three nights a week, but other than that, the house was as calm as

Eden, surrounded on all sides by green lawns and forest. She welcomed my invitation and moved into the spacious guest bedroom.

Some days, we didn't see much of each other, and she spent many days resting and not wanting company. But on other days, she had more energy and was curious to look over and help edit my dissertation. She spent most of the month of August with me slowly getting stronger and back to normal. She met my adviser Will, and they had a special bond. Will too had been through chemo, battling a brain tumor, but they didn't dwell on their ailments. Rather than that, Will just said, "Jodi, Greg is so lucky that you're here to act as a reader. It sure must be motivating for him." He was right. I felt motivated to write because I knew that I had an intelligent wordsmith in Jodi, and she would be first to see my drafts. Her comments were always helpful. But most of all, I felt rewarded by her daily improvement in health. I was on target to finish my dissertation right on time.

But the day before I turned it in an unbelievable occurrence took place. The eastern USA had one of its largest electric blackouts in its history. Fifty million people without power for thirty hours because a tree had fallen on an electric line somewhere near Cleveland. The grid went dark, and there were no estimates of when power would be restored. Imagine my panic of having to print a 250-page manuscript with no electricity and an imminent filing deadline. If I missed it, my PhD would be delayed by at least a semester. Jodi, whose experience with legal documents and deadlines was greater than mine, stayed calm and collected. Although cities for hundreds of miles were without power, Jodi had a hunch. She made a phone call on our landline and found the one place that had its own generator. Kinkos! Somehow, even though all the businesses around town had to close down, Kinkos stayed open. I was able to print my dissertation and deliver it the next day, even though the university was still mostly without power. I earned my PhD, with Jodi being the first person to congratulate me.

It's strange how certain individuals can be so significant in your life's events, having direct contact with everything and everyone you hold dear, and yet at the same time be physically distant even to the point that you don't spend much time together. Day to day, Jodi played only an insignificant role in my life. One could say she wasn't that important to me. But on the timeline of important chapters in my life's events, she seemed to be there at every important turn. Jodi was at Oki-Dog when I was hanging out with street punks, and she was there encouraging me to write an NEH grant when I was a budding intellectual at high school. She knew my childhood friends, my punk friends, my bandmates, and my academic adviser. She even was there at the finish line for my highest academic achievement, my PhD. And yet, through all of this, over the decades, we spent only fleeting periods of time in contact with one another.

The last of these influential episodes took place in the spring of 2004, a year after her Ithaca visit, and it may have been the most significant meeting of all because it changed the course of Graffin U. forever.

I was off tour and up for a trip to the Big Apple, so Jodi invited me to come for a visit at the Manhattan office building of her legal firm. Taking a train to Union Square, I emerged from the subway on a bright sunny day and entered a ten-story building on 18th Street. I took the elevator to her floor and was greeted by a lovely young woman, one of her coworkers, who let me know that Jodi was in a meeting. "Okay, great. So that means I'll just have to talk to you until she's done," I said. "I'm Greg, what's your name?" "My name's Allison," she said. Then I asked my usual "getting to know you" first question. "So, where did you go college?" "Marquette," she said. "Marquette?!!" I exclaimed. "You're a Milwaukee person?" I told her that I was too and that my friend Katy, who is friends with Jodi, got her law degree at Marquette too. The chitchat went on and on, and soon it was established that both of our families had deep roots in the Badger State.

Allison and I started seeing a lot of each other, and pretty soon she was joining me on my world tours. I remembered stories that Ric Ocasek told me about his courting relationship with Paulina, traveling the world together when the Cars were on tour. I copied his playbook, because I wanted to take Allison on tour everywhere we went, splurge on all the finest things, and let her know that I wanted her to be with me every step of the way. For the first time in my life, I had reached the point where I finally felt that I could provide the essential ingredients to build a lasting relationship.

A true romantic might say that Allison and I were "meant to be." But I prefer to believe that we found each other at a time when we were equally equipped to give what it takes for a mutually beneficial loving relationship. If it was preordained, then the deities sure did have a cruel side effect in mind when they concocted their scenario.

Tragically, Jodi died shortly after Allison and I were married. The cancer would not abate. She had moved back to LA and left this earth just a couple miles from where I first saw her at Oki-Dog in 1981, amid a sea of punk rockers, looking so out of place in her green BMW. How could I have known at that moment the significance that this person was going play in my life story? Only the most self-centered person could envision that her untimely death somehow played into a preordained plan.

By 2004, Bad Religion was firing on all cylinders and we became nearly a self-sustaining institution with an able and caring team of professionals on board, working alongside us and administering the increasingly complex business details. Like clockwork we went on summer tours in Europe and regional tours in the USA every spring and fall. Brett made it clear that he would continue to be in the band as a co-writer and co-producer and co-whatever we needed him to be, but in order to continue his day job as Epitaph label chief, he would not go on tour. Nonetheless, we completed fifteen additional world tours over as many years, introducing the fans to five additional new albums, each one more successful than the one before.

After receiving my PhD I began to teach evolution, first at UCLA then at Cornell. While maintaining a heavy touring schedule, my semesters on campus were escapes back into the familiar fold of ivory tower intellectuals. Through it all punk morphed once again into a hypertrophied caricature of itself, until one couldn't discern any distinction between it and American society at large. Meanwhile, Bad Religion grew more viable and relevant than ever. Punk had lost its uniqueness somewhere along the way, and yet it still had something to say. We found ourselves at the nexus of this unlikely circumstance.

The contradictions of punk were there from the outset, but we were too immature and inexperienced to call attention to them. "I've got no values," as the Black Flag song goes. This in itself is actually a value statement doomed for immediate rejection. But the fate of that statement was not the dustbin of history. Rather, it is still to this day a rally cry for every kid who decides to shave their head or grow their crown into an elaborate-colored mohawk. Leave it to the later years to deal with the incongruity of the statement's logic.

In Bad Religion we didn't wade into such murky waters. We never claimed to be the high priests of punk values. It's safe to say that none of us knew what punk was, even back when we were so sure that we were it. Today, speaking for myself rather than for the rest of them, I'm even less sure. I somehow have stood the test of time to emerge as one of the spokespeople or figureheads of punk rock. But like Admiral Stockdale, who was Ross Perot's running mate in 1992, back when Bill Clinton won his first presidential term, sometimes I look out onto a crowd of punk rockers and ask rhetorically, "Who am I? And what am I doing here?"

From my childhood rompings on the porch in Racine with Wryebo and André "Peg Leg" to my attendance at two of the legendary LA police riots of the early punk scene (Baces Hall and the Hideaway), some events just seemed like random connections to the main line of my life's chronology. Others are more significant, like meeting a guy with blue hair who introduced me to my future bandmates, or an out-of-place girl in a BMW who would go on to introduce me to my wife twenty years in the future. We pick and choose the events and people that are most significant to the stories that we want to tell about ourselves. The creation of identity depends on this process of ascribing meaning to past events. How we envision ourselves dictates the story we tell.

But what about the stories that other people tell about us? That is called legacy.

In trying to wrap my head around the significance of the band in the popular imagination, and our unusual longevity, I like to think of it in terms of a paradigm shift. Paradigms are opinions and "norms" of practice within the sciences. For instance, a central paradigm of evolution is that species change through time. It used to be thought that this process was gradual and continuous, meaning that a species slowly transformed into something different over long periods of time. Around the middle of the twentieth century, as more biologists began to study rates of evolution in various species, a huge amount of data accumulated to suggest that some species' lineages showed very little change over time. Furthermore, a lot of animal lineages show incredibly rapid bursts of drastic change—short periods of time showing extreme anatomical changes. These phenomena created a stir among evolutionary biologists, and the field began to debate the long-held paradigm of gradualism (constant, gradual change in species). In the 1970s, Stephen Jay Gould and his associates coined a term (punctuated equilibrium) to describe an alternative tempo of evolution: very long periods without any change (aka stasis) followed by short, periodic bursts of rapid change.

It wasn't immediately embraced by the evolutionary biology community. Punctuated equilibrium was debated fiercely. But one thing was certain: no biologist went back to the old paradigm of slow, gradual change for all species. The paradigm in the field had shifted away from that. Now, all evolutionists readily accept that rates of change are not constant in all species. Some show gradualism, but many, perhaps most, show punctuated bursts followed by long periods of stasis.

The point of all this is to illustrate how perceptions within a field of study are not fixed in stone. Even though evolution has been the bedrock of biology for over a hundred years, the ideas that are acceptable and valid within the field today are different than those of the past. No one debates the fact of evolution within the field, but how it is studied (the practice, gathering the data), and how the data is interpreted (the style of reporting, the built-in assumptions), is different today than it was fifty years ago. Hence the "culture" of the field has changed; there has been a "paradigm shift."

This same idea can be applied to punk rock. The punk community used to have certain "norms," such as mohawks, bondage straps, and spiked collars. They signified allegiance to a way of life that could only mean one thing: "I'm a punk rocker." Even though these things are still acceptable accoutrements of a punk wardrobe, other fashionable items have emerged that would never have been appropriate in the past.

One day in 2021, Allison and I went out to dinner at a pub near our house. We brought along Stanley, our son who serves as the latest addition to Graffin U., and though he's only a young tike, he loves pub food. We wandered in to the Watkins Glen marina, a small but picturesque hot spot for tourists and locals alike. It was the first time in over a year that we could go out to dinner because of the COVID-19 restrictions on public places. Restaurants in New York had finally opened their doors to customers now that the pandemic seemed to be ending. It seemed like the whole town came out to enjoy the lovely May weather and mingle with the early season holiday travelers who had gathered on the boardwalk next to the restaurant. As is common in large groups of vacationers, all kinds of fashions, shapes, sizes, and temperaments were on display. But generally, the mood was upbeat and happy.

One of the happiest people I saw was a wavy-haired blonde woman, perhaps in her early thirties, casually styled in cutoff denim shorts and a brightly colored T-shirt, passing by our table heading to the bar on the other side of the dining room. I noticed something on her shirt that gave me a start. "Allison, that woman is wearing a Misfits T-shirt!" Normally, this wouldn't be such a big deal. On numerous occasions we've seen punk T-shirts, even Bad Religion shirts, on vacationers near our house. But this one stopped me in my tracks because it had a peculiarity about it: *it was tie-dyed.*

Now, I'm not sure that Glenn Danzig, the singer of Misfits and the king of black horror fashion in punk and metal, was consulted in the manufacture of this particular mass-market T-shirt, but I don't think he would find congruence in his iconic band's logo blended with the archetypical colors and pattern of the hippie movement (tie-dye). Joking aside, that T-shirt was an obvious, blatant piece of evidence that much has changed with respect to the paradigm of punk. What was once a cherished, sacred logo to many fans, a true calling card of punk affiliation, is now blazoned on a background that shows allegiance to the Woodstock generation from decades prior. The woman wearing it probably couldn't have cared less about what tie-dye represented, or what the band represented, for that matter. She simply wanted to show the world that she loved the band, and she probably liked the way the colorful shirt looked too.

This is not altogether unexpected. And it's not a bad thing per se. It's not unusual these days to find music fans who aren't affiliated with any particular scene, they just love going to concerts and festivals. It's not at all weird to hear someone say they like the Grateful Dead AND the Misfits. Maybe this T-shirt appeals to people like that. Whatever the case, it also says something important about punk. There HAS been a paradigm shift, one that has been going on for quite some time.

In the early punk scene, anyone wearing any kind of hippie fashion would be confronted (possibly violently) and, shall we say, encouraged to take it off. The adherence to hippie fashion and hippie values were seen as the antithesis of the punk "movement." Tie-dye was anathema, as were feathers and bells, headbands, and leather frills running down the seams on suede jacket arms. Furthermore, peace signs were almost nowhere to be found. Peace was the rallying cry for a different generation. Punks wanted to be unique, and therefore they distanced themselves from their predecessors. Symbols and logos depicting "Peace and Love" became replaced by "Destroy and Anarchy."

But what emerged later as punk, what became the democratizing force of punk, what seeped into every household in America—the land of endless technology and consumerism—were the commercially relevant accoutrements that could be marketed and peddled to the endless cravings of young kids, the neat little things to wear and the lifestyles that embraced them, such as "extreme" sports like skateboarding, snowboarding, motocross, and surfing. Soon after followed the technological boom of computer gaming that simulated not only these lifestyle sports but invented new ones for a rapt generation of couch potatoes who likewise considered themselves punk.

What incredible fortune! For without this democratizing movement of our genre, Bad Religion would have been a little footnote in the story of twentieth-century music. But instead we became a relevant force for the twenty-first century. If only remembered as the band that contributed a handful of songs to the world's most popular computer games (*Tony Hawk's Pro Skater 2, Crazy Taxi, Guitar Hero, Forza*), our legacy would be enviable. But it's grown to be more than that now.

Along comes Bad Religion, and without any desire to rewrite the genre's rulebook we crept our way beneath the mainstream and offered something more precious than gold records: a particular ethical position, and a commitment to a seemingly endangered ancient value system called enlightenment. Enlightenment values, the challenge to closed-mindedness, are what we've sung about all along. How paradoxical indeed that such an important ingredient for society and civilization should come from a punk band whose genre, now popularized by consumerism, formerly was committed to destruction, anarchy, and nihilism. Destruction may still prevail as a punk archetype, but in our case, the only thing being destroyed is ignorance, falsehood, and superstition.

So, it seems then, we come face-to-face with perhaps the most intractable paradox of all: punk as a positive force in society.* If the paradigm that Bad Religion established is believable, then there is no other conclusion. Like the self-correcting framework of scientific investigation, our

---

* Note that "positive force" was conceived as a "movement" within the punk community in the 1980s and '90s. The "positive force" activist group was started by the punk band 7 Seconds from Reno, Nevada, and included many other, mostly East Coast, bands. They tried to start a "movement" among themselves that included certain prescriptive behaviors, such as "straight edge" (rejecting alcohol and drug use) and living according to a set of "humane values." But this movement didn't really spread into any sort of general acceptance in the rapidly expanding punk rock world. And why would it? Most people want to be entertained rather than be told what to do. They want music, not prescriptive lists of appropriate behavior. Punk is, after all, a form of entertainment. It's not social engineering. If punk fans wanted to be told how to live, how to think, what is "appropriate behavior," they could go to church or start a cult religion, precisely the things against which Bad Religion stood all along.

musical catalog—steeped in big-picture questions such as challenge to authoritarianism, self-empowerment, and promotion of enlightenment values—seems dedicated to the betterment of the human condition. What an odd thing to dedicate one's life to. One might as well talk to the wind. Wouldn't it have been better to be a carpenter or machinist like my Graffin ancestors? Or perhaps carried on the tradition of my great-grandpa Zerr as a Bible scholar and minister? But no! These all carried with them a closed-mindedness, a reluctance to change. My life experience taught me that change is inevitable, so you better be able to accept some of life's unpleasant, harsh realities and use your intelligence to adapt and live to learn another day. Punk has been a fine journey so far, even though it is constantly beset by naysayers, detractors, petty thieves, and prejudiced fundamentalists. It persists despite these ugly human adornments of civilized society. My antidote? Pushing on in spite of these obstacles, championing the spirit of enlightenment values, and sharing knowledge rather than doctrine. Such practices have turned out to be perhaps the most punk thing that anyone can accomplish.

EPILOGUE

I drove my car out to California, escaping yet another drab April in upstate New York. I'm sitting at an intersection at Wilshire and Merv Griffin Way, just a block from Santa Monica Boulevard, that corridor of sin and adventure that led us east and astray into Hollywood so many years ago "back in the day." Departing from the famous Beverly Hilton hotel where I'd spent the last four nights sleeping, I emerge from the hotel's parking lot. Traffic in all directions is halted while a lone pedestrian makes her way casually across the busy intersection. As the traffic piles up behind me, I notice a long line of slowing cars in the oncoming traffic. Leading the charge is the unmistakable faded green Toyota truck of none other than my pal, and bass player, Jay. Since the lights seemed in no hurry to turn green, I pushed the Call button on my steering wheel to use the voice recognition function. "Call Jay Bentley," I say with my hoarse morning voice. Within a second the computer returns a successful connection, "calling Jay Bentley."

He picks up and says, "I'm right outside your hotel, can you see me from your room's balcony or something?" "No," I say, "look at ground level in the cross traffic!" "Haha, great! Let's caravan!"

We were on our way to Hollywood, only a few miles down the road, to film a fortieth anniversary concert for online streaming at the famous Roxy nightclub. Waiting there was a cadre of professionals, camera operators, a film editor, our crack team of technicians, all quarterbacked by Rick, our tour manager and the show's producer. The concert was going to be a four-hour, multiple-episode special, featuring songs from each decade of the band's existence. Many selections were rarities or "deep cuts" that appeared on past records but never were played on stage before.

Forty years earlier, you might have found Jay and me stopped at that very same intersection in a truck of the same color, with Jay behind the wheel, heading in the same direction and to the same destination to see a punk show at the Roxy or its next-door nightclub neighbor, the Whisky a Go Go. A momentary flush of nostalgia overcomes me during the phone call. "Jay, imagine if, forty years ago, I said that in four decades you would be at this same spot, right here at this intersection, during a global pandemic, following me in my car with New York plates heading to the Roxy to celebrate seventeen studio albums of songs in a concert that would be seen all over the world." "Unbelievable, isn't it?" "Yeah," I said, "about as unbelievable as our chances of meeting at this intersection today!"

As I savored the moment of serendipity, my emotional brain took over, evoking memories and associations too complex for math, and I realized that there's no way to adequately catalog the long chain of improbable events that brought me to that moment. Selective memory is what everyone uses to write their own story. Savoring the moment is one thing, but understanding how you got there can be a lifelong pursuit. Such is my lot as a student of human nature. The moment prompted deep reflection that I put on hold until after the concert.

Back at home, I finally read the book that had been staring down at us from Dad's bookshelf since 1971, *The Armies of the Night* by Norman Mailer. The book shows that, by 1968, Mailer had already pretty much summed up the anti-authoritarian stance of the American youth "movement." In essence, Mailer's description shows that the New Left was in fact a criticism of the Old Left, which had served as an accomplice with the Right to create the evils of "authority." In its simplest form, labor served the needs of the industrialist. The New Left sought to end this in their hippie "revolution," which, as Mailer pointed out, was ambiguous in its predicted outcome. The marches on the Pentagon in 1967 were concrete acts with ambiguous aims. They had no end game, not knowing what storming the building to turn in their draft cards would accomplish. But this action typified the anti-authority spirit that was the central trait of the New Left in the 1960s.*

Hence, the so-called authority hadn't changed much by the time punk came along. Scranny from Wasted Youth and Jim Lindberg from Penny-wise, twenty years apart, both implored us to "fuck authority," but they were essentially singing the song of the 1960s. The kids that Mailer was describing saw authority as the "manifest of evil . . . who had covered the land with those suburbs." Those were the same suburbs we railed against on *Suffer* that ended up housing the legions of fans who would go on to im-mortalize punk rock as a viable musical form. Novel as our approach may have been, it nonetheless exemplifies a continuum rather than a revolution in the spirit of a movement that far predates us (and in fact predates the hippies too). There is nothing new under the sun, as stated in Ecclesiastes. So one might as well know thyself.

As I continued reading, it was like cracking a code. The secret words were written plainly in this book. It was as if Dad telepathically projected them to us as a guide for good living. The moral compass of the Graffin creed. Mailer mentions the clue of his title on page 157 in a quotation taken from Fitzgerald, presumably: "That long dark night of the soul when it is always three o'clock in the morning"—meaning, RESPON-SIBILITY. Here, specifically, the responsibility to do good work as a writer and a teacher. "As the power of communication grew larger, so the responsibility to educate a nation lapped at the feet." Even though Dad never spoke in such prescriptive terms, and the excerpt was out of context to some degree, the words jumped off the page at me. It is as if the "spirit" of our household (the restrictions and tolerances that guided our behav-ior) determined the industry of its inhabitants.

Being responsible for my work, my songs, my ideas, was infused by the spirit of Graffin U. from the get-go. The campus is larger now, with the original building and its small library still occupied by Dad in Racine, Wis-consin. You can find some of my handiwork, from when I was a toddler,

---

* How ironic that now it could be seen as the central tenet of the New Right. Right?

still proudly displayed on the walls of my bedroom there, unmoved from when they were hung originally in the 1970s and '80s. The latest expansion project is in upstate New York: a forty-acre campus with a two-story domicile constructed with newfangled, "green-certified" building materials. Allison is its administrator, and our newest pupil, Stanley, is the latest to endure the curriculum.

Sadly, the San Fernando Valley campus was gutted in 2018. Mom passed away after a courageous fight with CLL (chronic lymphocytic leukemia). For the last two years of her life, she kept her suffering and daily struggles private. Even though I was on tour through much of it, I felt her slow decline acutely. I could only watch helplessly from afar. We family members and friends were there by her side nonetheless, as she took her last breaths.

Mom's death brought reconstructions of her life: tales from archived photos, saved scraps of notes, documents, and attic artifacts. Mom followed the dictates of her own conscience when she donated her garage to our band and unobtrusively encouraged me all along the way that something good was always on the horizon so long as Bad Religion was active. Her own private pleasure in our success went beyond maternal love. Her encouragement was tinged with anti-religious, pro-enlightenment values, the ingredients in her lifelong rebellion against the closed-minded society from whence she sprung in rural Indiana.

The profound sadness that enveloped me during the long goodbye of my mom made the departure and ousting of my bandmate and pal, Greg Hetson, feel less acute. But it was a loss too. Greg deserved better from me, but I couldn't be there for him when his tenure in Bad Religion was revoked. How this came to be is a tale for another time, and it's best to let him tell it someday. But like so many events, it too seemed random and unpredictable.

Jay and I reminisced about a remarkable fact: punk has been the backdrop to our lives for over forty years. "What remarkable resilience, this punk thing!" I exclaimed. Instead of trying to fit in, I instead forged a constant meander between academics (intellectual fuel) and entertainment (my pedagogical tool). Remaining true to Graffin U. was my focus over the years, rather than worrying about whether my actions comported with some outdated notion of what was punk.

This simple conclusion satisfied me as I took the stage to perform the concert at the Roxy. But later that night, after the show, alone in my car I returned to a mental exercise: the inextricable tangle of culture and human behavior. They emerged simultaneously rather than one creating the other. The ancient cave paintings of prehistoric humans were the product of an imagination that could only have been predated by other art. Likewise, punk didn't create punk rockers; it was the other way round. To take this view requires one to identify the "ur" punk. Who was it? When did he/she/they/it emerge? Trying to find its source will be an endless puzzle. My story can add texture and context, perhaps. But, so far as I can tell, there's no definitive origin of punk's source. Happily, I can also conclude that there's no evidence in sight to signal its extinction.

ACKNOWLEDGMENTS

The author wishes to thank the following individuals for their involvement in this project:

Matthew Elblonk, agent at the DeFiore & Company literary agency

Ben Schafer, editor at Hachette Books

Mike van Mantgem, copyeditor

Fred Francis, project editor at Hachette Books

Christina White, Mutiny PR

All the friends, family members, and colleagues past and present who helped to shape the events depicted on these pages.